IMAGES
of America

WICOMICO COUNTY

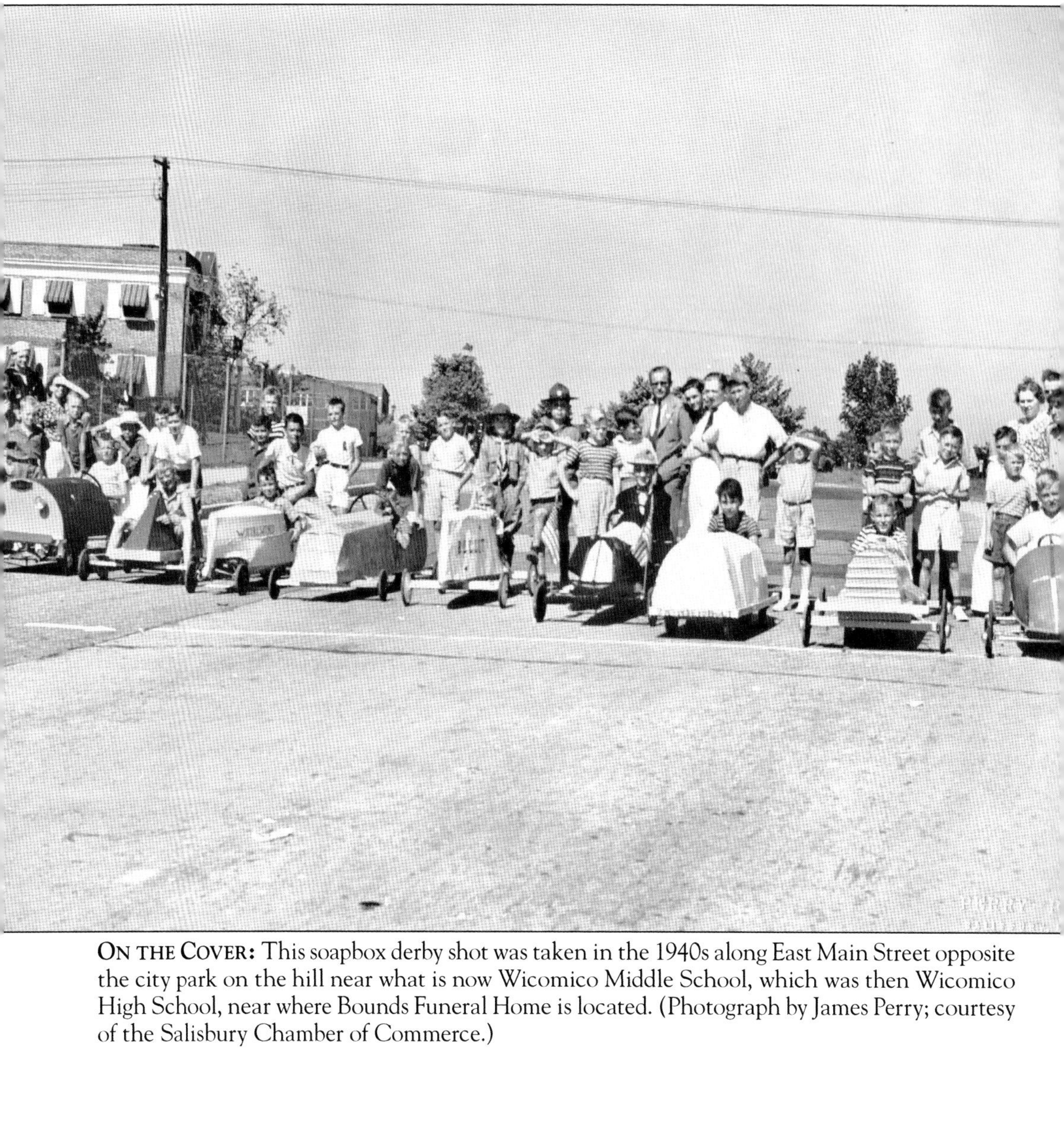

On the Cover: This soapbox derby shot was taken in the 1940s along East Main Street opposite the city park on the hill near what is now Wicomico Middle School, which was then Wicomico High School, near where Bounds Funeral Home is located. (Photograph by James Perry; courtesy of the Salisbury Chamber of Commerce.)

IMAGES
of America

WICOMICO COUNTY

Gianni DeVincent-Hayes, Ph.D.,
and Andy Nunez

ARCADIA
PUBLISHING

ISBN 978-0-7385-5321-4

Published by Arcadia Publishing
Charleston SC, Chicago IL, Portsmouth NH, San Francisco CA

Printed in the United States of America

Library of Congress Catalog Card Number: 2007932893

For all general information contact Arcadia Publishing at:
Telephone 843-853-2070
Fax 843-853-0044
E-mail sales@arcadiapublishing.com
For customer service and orders:
Toll-Free 1-888-313-2665

Visit us on the Internet at www.arcadiapublishing.com

To my long-suffering family: I love you all. Thanks for your patience and for forgiving me for the times I could not be with you while completing this project.
—Andy (husband and dad)

To my loving husband, Jimmy, for appreciating why I couldn't spend more time with you while doing this book and for your patience and unending assistance. I thank my wonderful daughters, Brynne and Marta, too, for understanding why I could not be with you while working on deadline.
—Gianni (wife and mom)

Contents

ACKNOWLEDGMENTS

We wish to thank the many people, companies, and institutions that have helped us put this book together. We cannot possibly name everyone, so if we have overlooked thanking you here, please understand our heartfelt gratitude. In particular, we would like to express special appreciation to: Brad Bellacicco and staff of the Salisbury Chamber of Commerce for the loan of their print collection, their books, and other helpful materials, as well as their time and input; George Chevallier, noted historian and postcard collector, for his endless hours helping us; Brice Stump for his assistance; Sylvia Bradley for her generous time and sharing of photographs; Palmer Gillis for his kindness in allowing us to work with his extensive photographs; Donna Richardson, community relations director of Peninsula Regional Medical Center, for sharing her hospital archives with us; Susan Purnell of Kuhn's Fine Jewelry for access to her archives; Robert Culver for providing us with historical background material and for sharing his yearbook; and the many others who allowed us use of their photographs (Betty Webster, Charles M. Truitt, Walter Sullivan, Hilda Fowler, John E. Jacob, James Jackson, Jessica Anderson, James Perry, the late Orlando Wooten, Walter Sullivan, the late Ruth Heam Parsons, John Holloway, the late Thomas Irvin, reproductions by the Wicomico County Historical Society, Dr. Laurence Claggett, Maryland Transportation Authority, Chesapeake Bay Bridge-Tunnel Authority, et al.)

And a special thanks to our spouses and our children for all their assistance and patience.

INTRODUCTION

Wicomico County is both unique and exceptional. Its uniqueness comes from its strategic location on the Eastern Shore of Maryland, where it's about 30 miles east of the Atlantic Ocean and 30 miles to the Chesapeake Bay to the west. This positioning also puts it no farther than a few hours from such major metropolises as Philadelphia to the north, Baltimore and D.C. to the west, and Norfolk to the south.

It's exceptional in that it is the most active county on the Eastern Shore in growth and in service. The county serves a metropolitan core of over 400,000 people. Its hospital, Peninsula Regional Medical Center, is rated in the top five nationally, and its zoological park is right about there in ratings as one of the nation's top 10 small zoos. Its educational institutions, retail centers, and electronic and hospitality industries provide vital services, as do its legal, recreational, and religious offerings. Culture abounds, with celebratory festivals, galas, symphonies, live performances, museums such as world-renowned Ward Wildfowl Museum, author readings, and much more.

Salisbury is the hub of the Eastern Shore and the seat of the county. Its landscape of old homes to new ones, bungalows to mansions, family stores to big-box retail outlets, flat ground to protected wetlands, along with its slew of attorneys, medical personnel, professors, and everyday people who love walking and shopping on the downtown plaza, or hitting the north corridor for all its major stores, give the area much diversity and flavor.

Everywhere one looks, there is construction. This once-sleepy county with its extensive farmlands and the good-ole-boy network, where residents knew each other as well as they knew their own families, has changed. Condominiums are now shooting up along the beloved Wicomico River—the heartbeat of the county—and new businesses open their doors daily. No longer can longtime residents go somewhere and instantly recognize an old friend or neighbor, as too many new faces overshadow the familiar ones. Business transactions that were once done with a handshake now require sessions in front of one of the many attorneys in the county. Expansion is everywhere, and perhaps none is more remarkable than the doubling of the already 300-bed hospital. New heart and cancer centers are going up, the highest technological and state-of-the-art equipment is being moved in, and newly built garages are complimenting the spreading hospital. Wor-Wic College and Salisbury University are pumping out well-taught students to fill professional jobs on the shore. Salisbury University has grown from a few thousand students to well over 7,000, and it is one of the four largest employers in the county after the hospital. The other two are Perdue Poultry and the county government.

The county always seems to recover from major hurricane damages, rare blizzards, tumbling bridges, and devastating fires, of which it experienced three major ones—1860, 1886, and 1944—not counting significant smaller ones. Perhaps this resilience is due to the residents' love of their area and desire to make things right when they're looking wrong.

Residents enjoy fun as much as they take seriously the work they perform. Besides trotting a few miles to the beaches (Ocean City, Assateague, Rehoboth, or Dewey), they enjoy the Community Players or the symphonies, the special celebrity shows at the civic center, and the carnivals and festivals, as well as applauding the many local artists' works in literature, painting, sculpting, and all the many other art forms that thrive here.

Natives call this area "The Good Life" because of all that it offers and the many subtle things not readily noticed by newcomers who are outnumbering those born here. There is always the debate between the "born heres" and the "come heres" as to whom is more important or more entitled or more annoying, but always the residents come together and make the county better every day. The debate, though meant to be light, is at times tantamount to the roughness of the Union and Confederate armies when they met on this soil some 120 years ago.

The year 2007 saw the installation of the county's first executive director, who now essentially runs the government, along with county council. This was a historic election, as it paralleled the change in thinking of residents and reflected the growing sophistication of the people. Wicomico County's official formation began in 1867 with a referendum to its County Constitutional Convention, which won in the election instead of polarizing sides or politicians, as much of that goes on today.

Throughout this book, you'll see the makings of a county into a metropolis. You'll understand how the people banded together to save their churches or their schools, how education was always revered and treated with respect and gratitude, and how medical care went from a small house serving as a clinic to a multi-level, highly complex hospital. You'll feel the heartbeat of the people who made it all happen, you'll smile at some of the unorthodox acts caught in a snippet of a flash, you'll see faces who went to school with you, and most of all you'll reminisce about the good old days.

Come, open the page, and walk down memory lane with us.

One

SWEEPING VIEWS

Most people don't have the opportunity to pay for a small plane to fly over an area, but thankfully some photographers have done that for us. The following pages give oddments of what Wicomico County looked like years ago. Most striking is how much it has grown over time, yet this is just a taste of the growth to come. Wicomico County embraces the city of Salisbury, which is the seat of activity not only for the county but for the entire shore, as this is where the major universities are, and where a nation-wide class-A hospital offers state-of-the-art care coupled with an ongoing expansion that doubles it size. Wicomico provides not only educational and medical care but also big-time shopping with big-box stores and mom-and-pop boutiques. A top-10 zoo is here, as are the many eateries and lodging, along with attractions and festivals that give no excuse for being bored. Salisbury operates the second-largest airport and second-largest water port in the state. Legal services galore are in this busy county, with their numbers almost equaling the amount of physicians. Perdue Farms, Pepsi, shipbuilding, a 360-plus-bed hospital, colleges, a multitude of professionals, many waterways, new condos, a bustling downtown, abundant antique stores, high-tech electronic industries, and movers and shakers all pepper the county map. For many, though, Wicomico County is not only the heart and soul of all of the Eastern Shore, but it's also just a hop, skip, and a jump away from the beautiful Chesapeake Bay to the west and the popular Ocean City, Maryland, resort to the east. It's termed the "Crossroads of the Delmarva" because nearly everything on the shore intersects with this county where big metropolitan areas are only a few hours away.

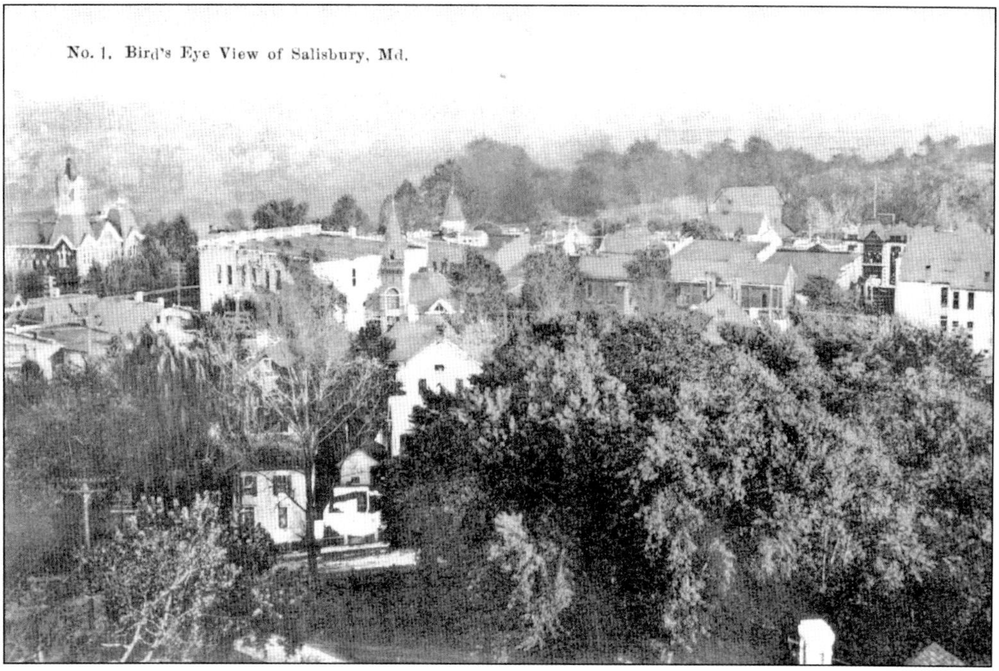

AERIAL WITHOUT AN AIRPLANE. This *c.* 1905 photograph appears to be an aerial shot, but in reality, the photographer had climbed to the top of the standpipe of the John B. Parsons home and took this amazing panorama of Salisbury. In this view, the courthouse is visible to the left of the picture. (Courtesy of George Chevallier.)

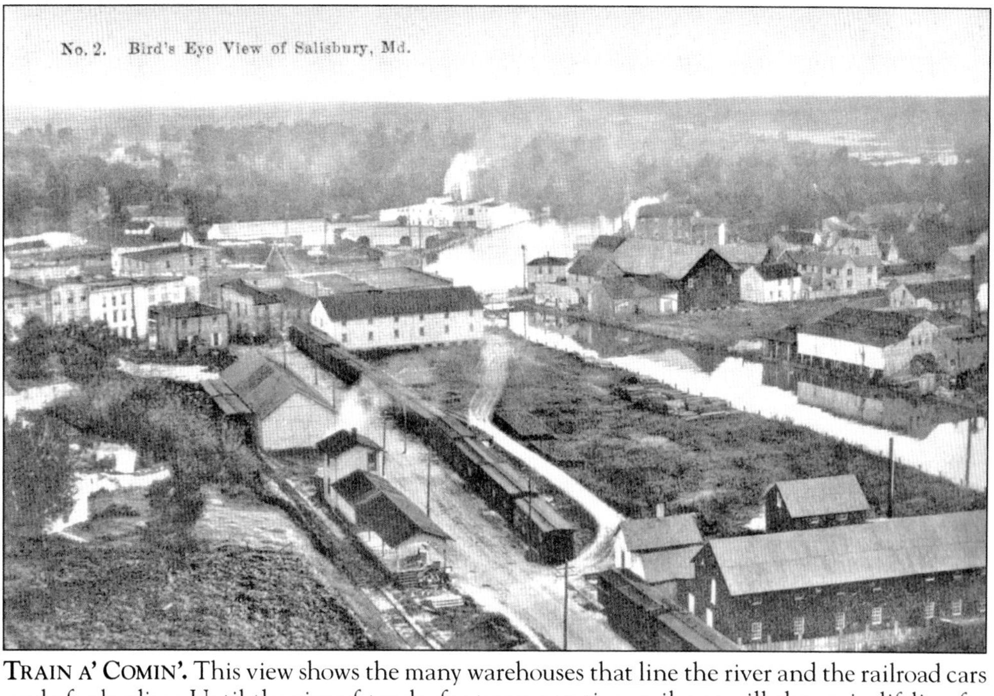

TRAIN A' COMIN'. This view shows the many warehouses that line the river and the railroad cars ready for loading. Until the rise of trucks for transportation, rail was still the main lifeline for industry and travel. How different the area looks today. (Courtesy of George Chevallier.)

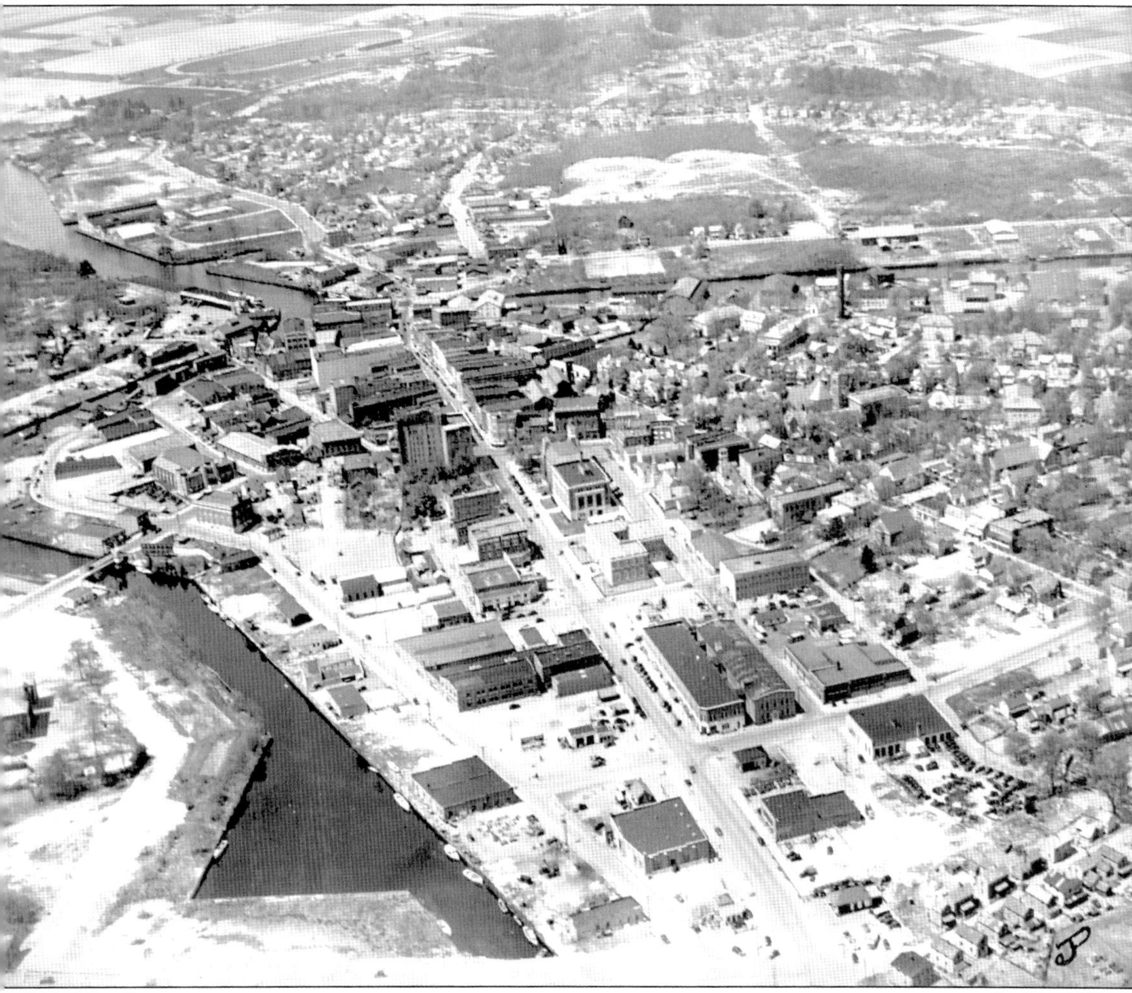

REAL BIRD'S-EYE VIEW. Taken in the mid-1900s, this aerial shot of Salisbury still shows the relatively small-town look of what would soon mushroom into a modern city. Industry still dominated the riverfront, but that was soon to change. (Photograph by James Perry; Courtesy of Salisbury Chamber of Commerce.)

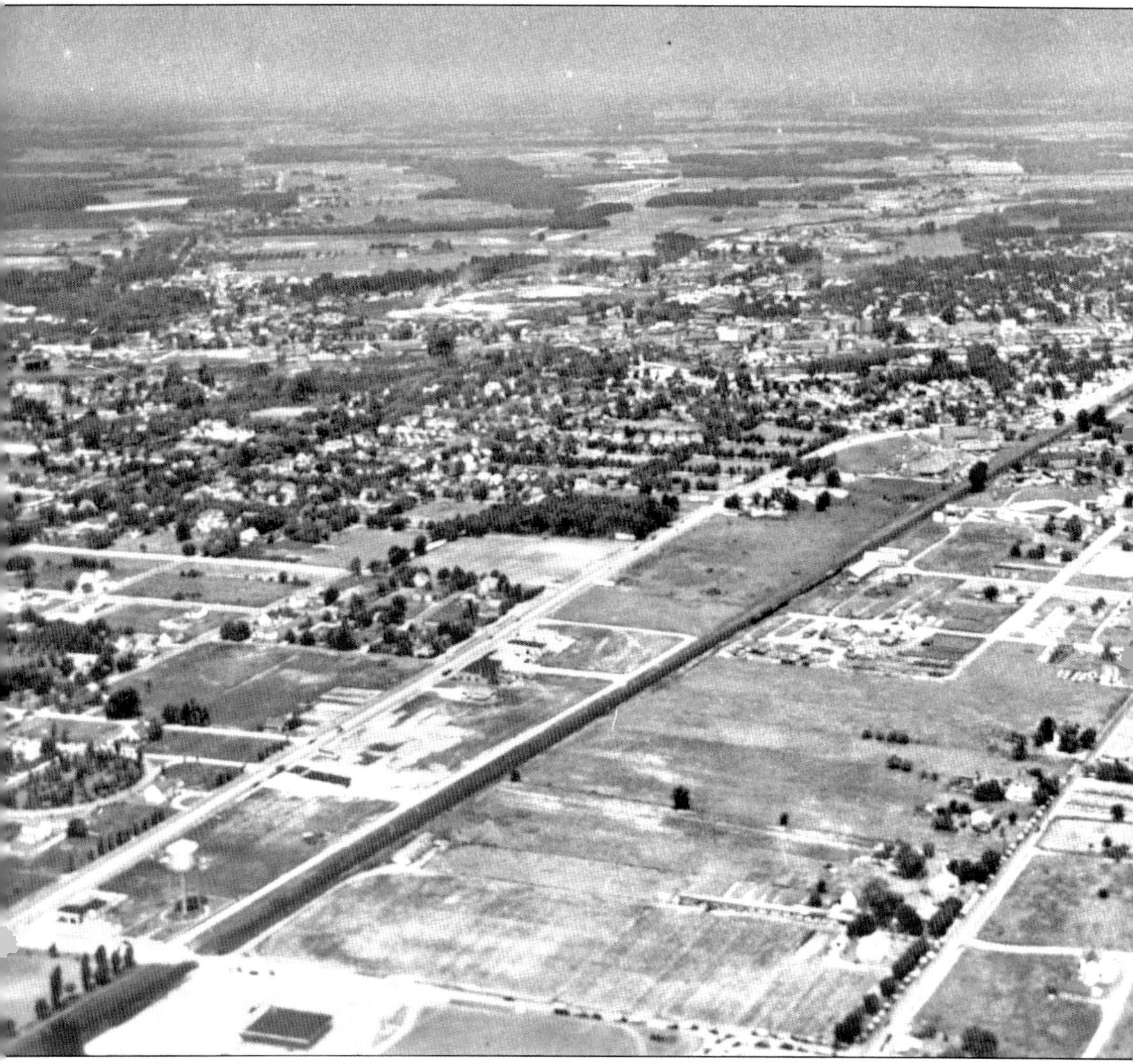

All Roads Lead to Salisbury. This image, *c.* 1910, shows unpopulated Salisbury. The water tower at the bottom left benchmarks the location of this aerial. The dirt road beside the tower is College Avenue. Perpendicular to it is Route 13 winding up north, as seen by the S curve. Today College Avenue and Route 13 are filled with businesses and the bustling activities of shoppers and motorists. (Courtesy of Salisbury Chamber of Commerce.)

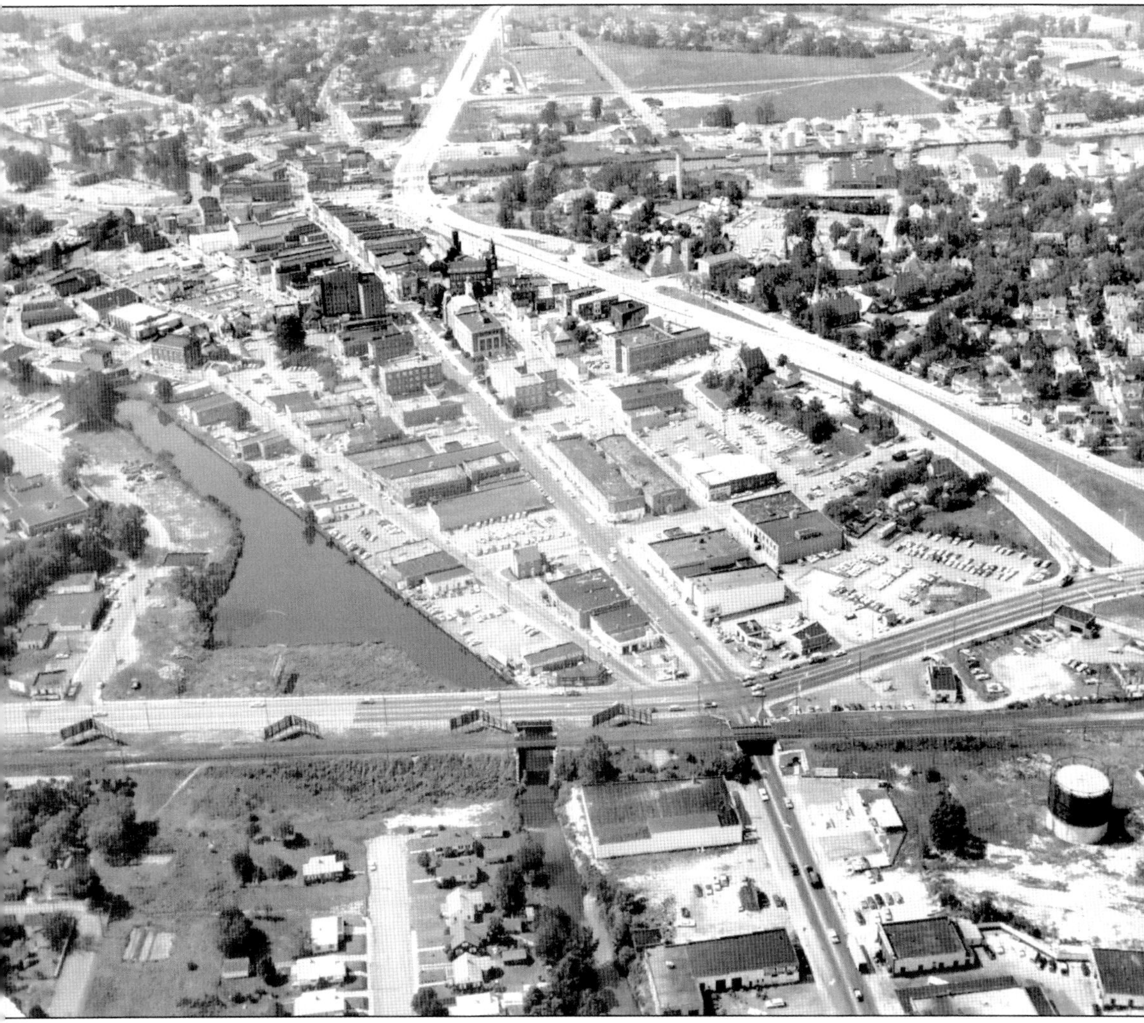

CROSSROADS OF DELMARVA. This later aerial view shows the massive roadwork that cut the city in fourths. Route 13 and Route 50 were upgraded and expanded, the latter wiping out a large section of the African American neighborhoods and obliterating an unmarked graveyard. With faster roads, the county was poised to grow. It did. (Courtesy of Salisbury Chamber of Commerce.)

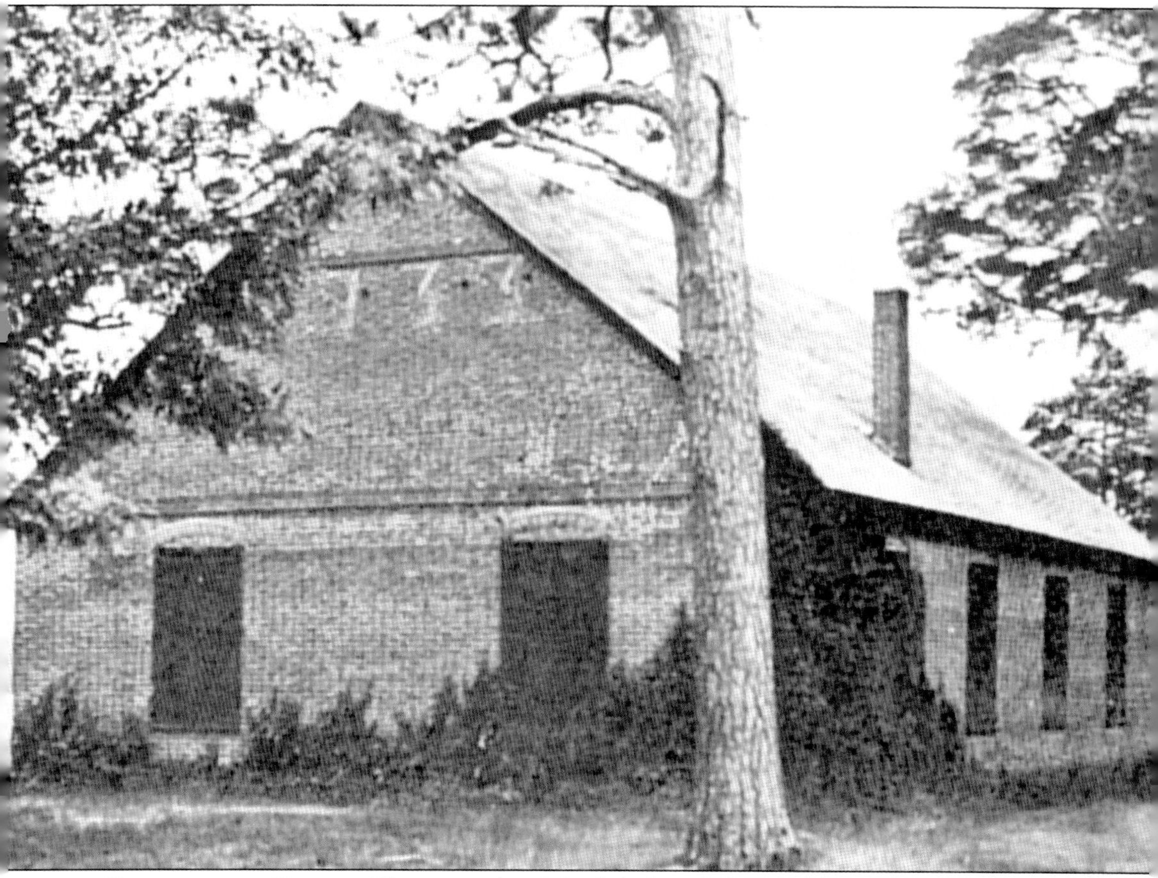

STARTED WITH PRAYER. This was a church built before 1733, as emblazoned on the brick. It fell to neglect until about 1928, when the congregation beat it into shape. Some of the disrepair can be seen in this photograph. An annual service was held on the last Sunday in August. (*Salisbury: Heart of the Maryland's Eastern Shore.*)

Two

CRADLE TO GRAVE

Birth, health, worship, and death constitute life's journey. This chapter clearly shows that. The first European settlers in what became Wicomico County were English and brought the Anglican church of England with them. Not long afterward came the Presbyterians, and they lay claim to the first church building in the county in 1683 in Rockawalkin; it has moved several times but remains at its final location on Church Street in Salisbury. The Anglicans, or Episcopalians as they became known after the Revolutionary War, established a series of "chapels of ease" in what became Stepney Parish, starting in 1711. Two well-known examples of this growth still stand, Green Hill Church and Spring Hill Church, both on the western end of the county. The religious tolerance established by the colony's founders allowed worshipers of all stripes to live in peace in the region, and a steady stream of denominations came and flourished in the county—Methodists, Baptists, Catholics, and Quakers. As centuries passed, fires devastated many wooden structures, and good-hearted folk became benefactors and patrons of the beautiful stone structures that dot the city today. Besides those mentioned above, the explosion of various Christian groups in more recent times has put in motion the construction of larger and larger churches, some holding as many as 2,500.

Meanwhile, other faiths have taken hold in the county, as seen in their synagogues, mosques, and Hindu temples. Diversity after the Civil War has seen the prospering of many churches for the African American community, and the county boasts the first gospel radio station established by an African American denomination.

With a budding population composed of young professionals, baby boomers, and retirees, a variety of medical care is needed. The Peninsula Regional Medical Center is rated as one of the top five nationally, particularly in specialties such as heart and cancer care. It is currently doubling its size after many years of additions. Walk back into history through the following pages and see how important religion and health were to the very people who made the county the sprouting region it is today.

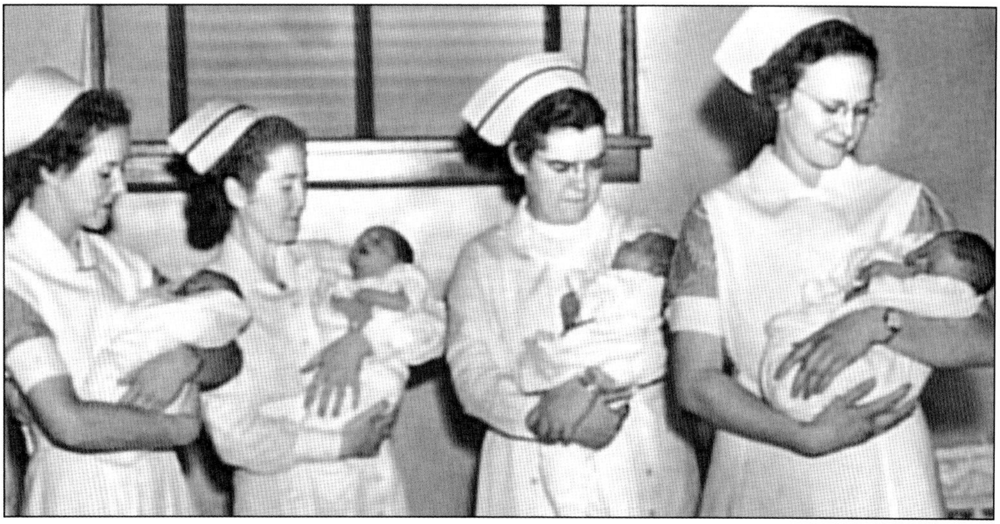

FROM CRADLE. In this old 1939 hospital photograph at then Peninsula General, nurses adoringly hold newborns. Since its inception, the hospital has progressed with numerous additions. Cute infants remind one of birth, followed by death, and medical care in between, as well as prayers of hope—as this chapter shows throughout this progression—and the importance of church in our lives. (*A Heritage of Caring: Peninsula Regional Medical Center 1897–1997.*)

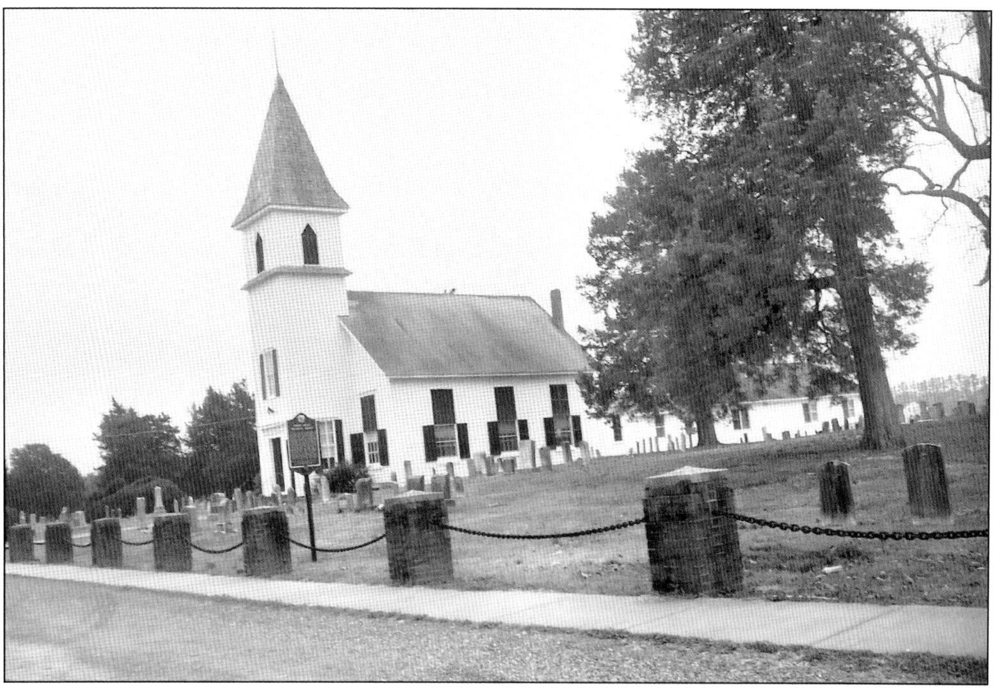

METHODISM PREVAILS AT FIRST. Reigning in serene stateliness above its large cemetery, Asbury United Methodist Church in the tiny ex-mill town of Allen near the Somerset County line has been around since the 1829. The steeple was added in 1883. The church still retains its upstairs gallery, where slaves were allowed to sit. On the National Register of Historic Places, this church is a prime example of the many fine country churches that dot the Wicomico landscape. (Photograph by Andy Nunez.)

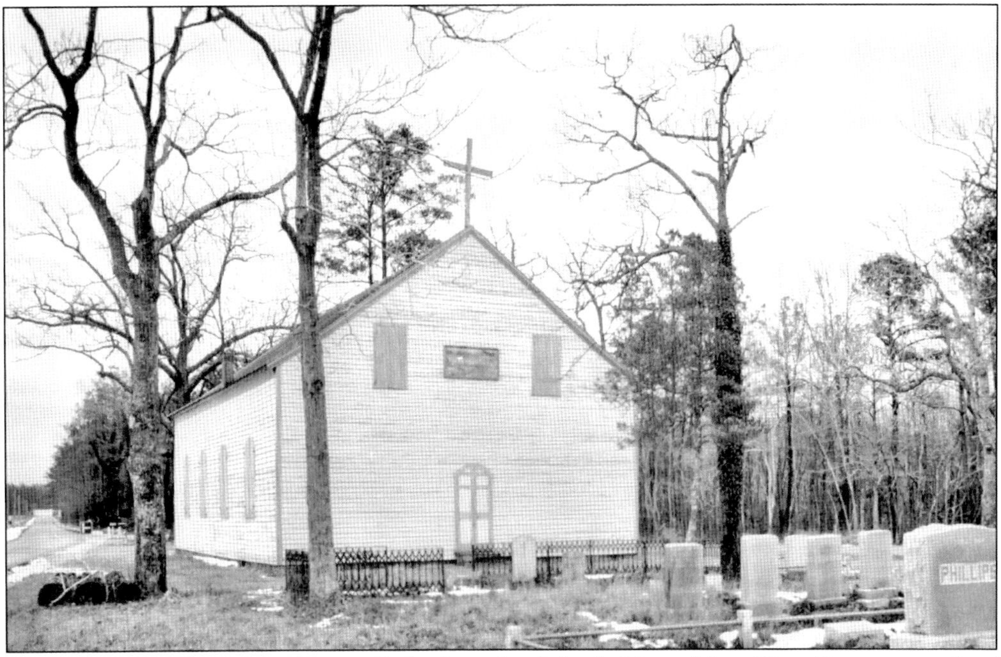

FAITH SPRINGS ETERNAL. Originally built on land deeded from Mary King Hampton, wife of a deceased pastor and known as "the King who became a Queen" for her wealth, this Anglican chapel of ease is the second to stand there. The present structure was built in 1773 and had become an Episcopal church. (Courtesy of Salisbury Chamber of Commerce.)

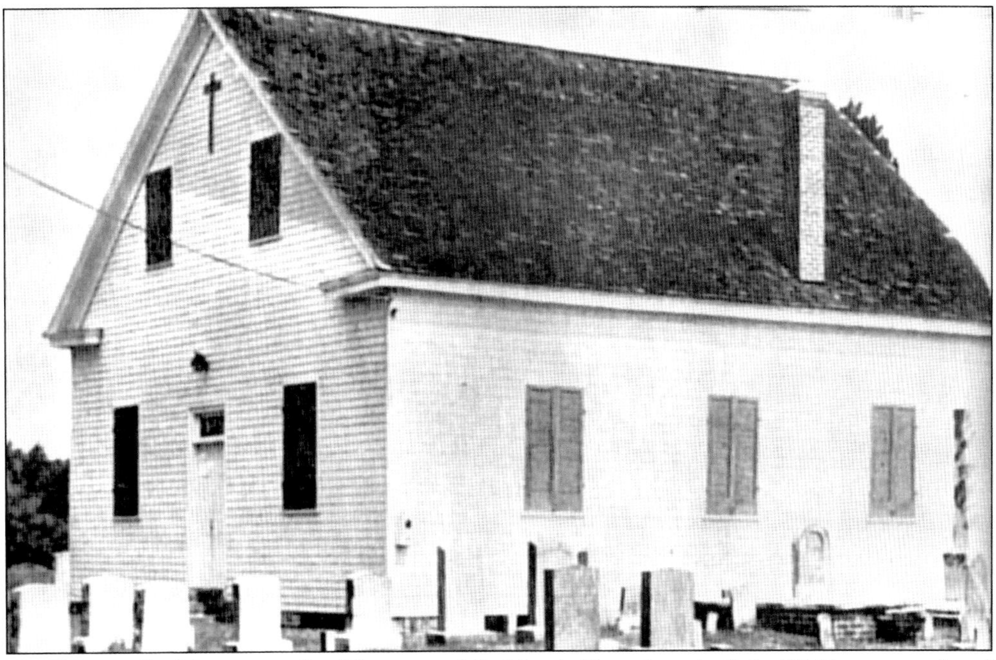

THE SAINTS GO MARCHING IN. The original St. Mary's Chapel was built in 1834 but was replaced in 1845. From about 1912 through 1916, extensive remodeling was done, such as replacing the walls and ceiling, and later two chimneys were built on each side of the church. The cemetery has been in use since its origination. (Courtesy of the Betty Webster Collection.)

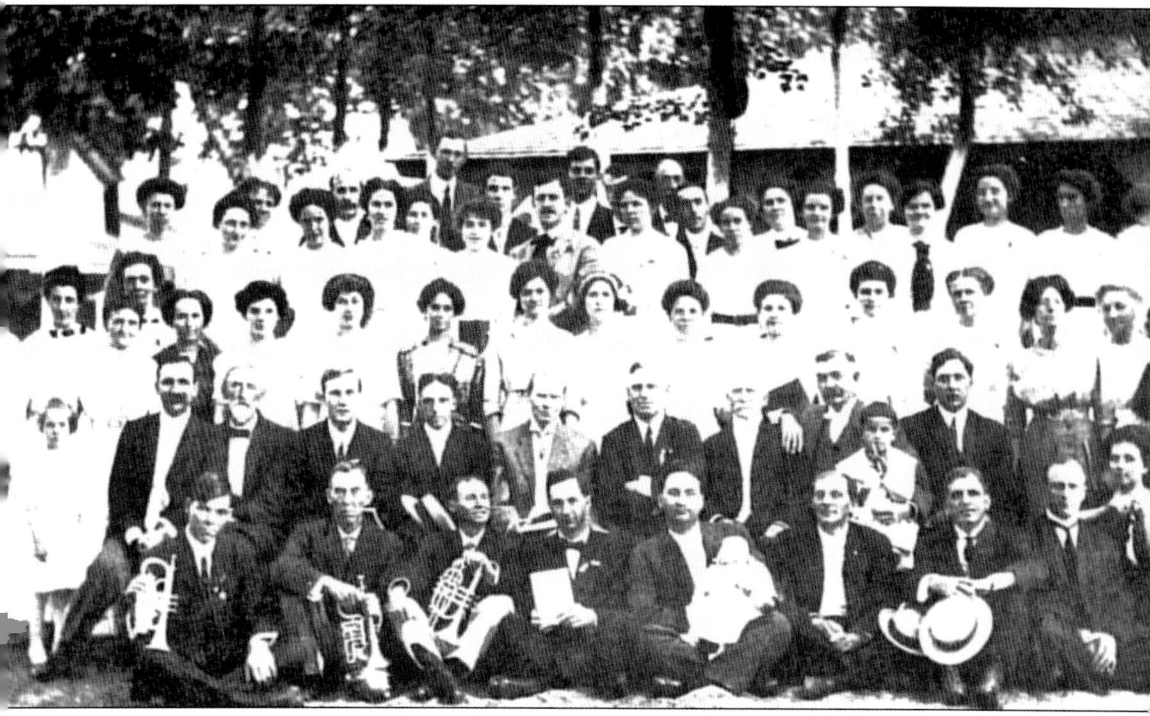

MUSIC AT HEBRON CAMP MEETING. Church camp meetings were common in the early 1900s, as in this image featuring a Salisbury group assembling for a religious retreat in the town of Hebron. Notice the black-and-white dress motif and the musical instruments flashed by the men in the first row. The main structure is to the right of the picture, but the tents are to the left. Tent entrances would roll up in the morning to start the day. (Courtesy of the John E. Jacob Collection.)

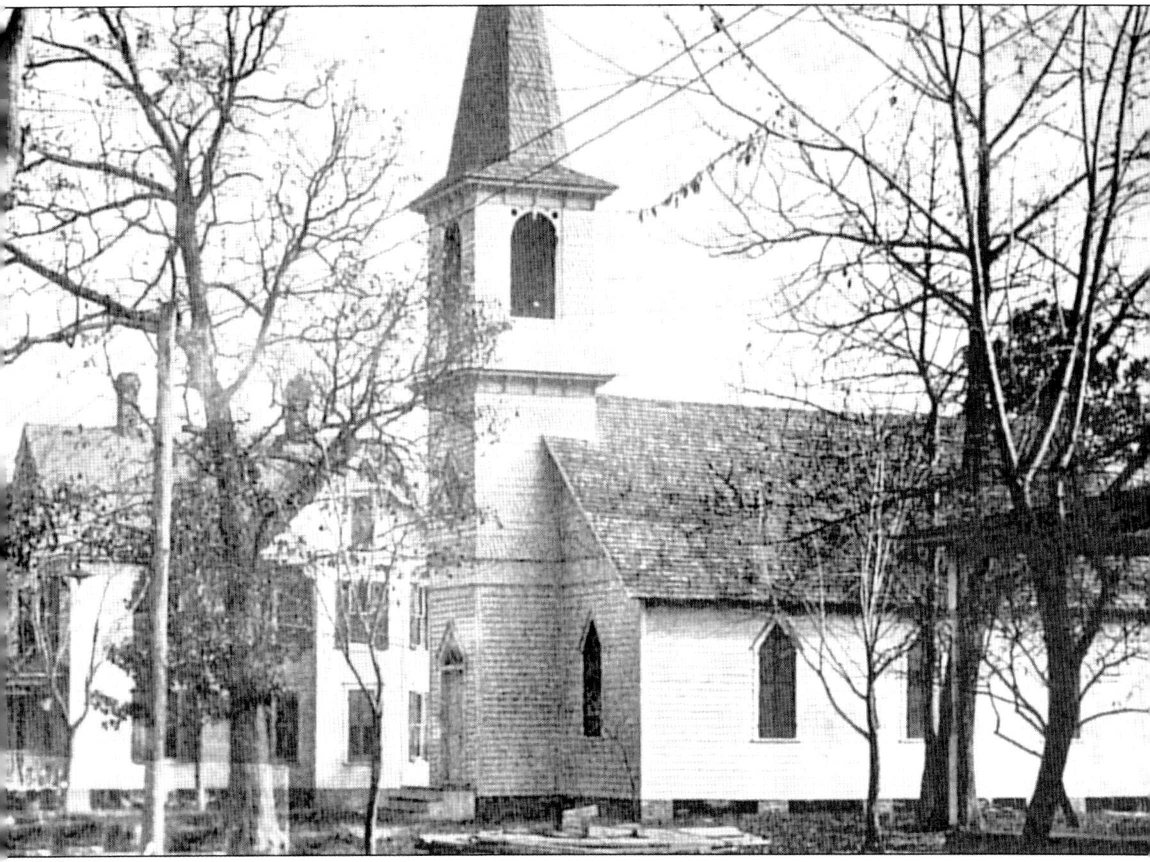

SALLY NELSON'S CHURCH. In 1892, Sally Nelson donated land for this memorial church that was originally called the Nelson Memorial Church, though now it is a private residence. It was relocated in 1916, and a brick structure was erected. An addition was built in the mid-1900s. (Courtesy of James Jackson.)

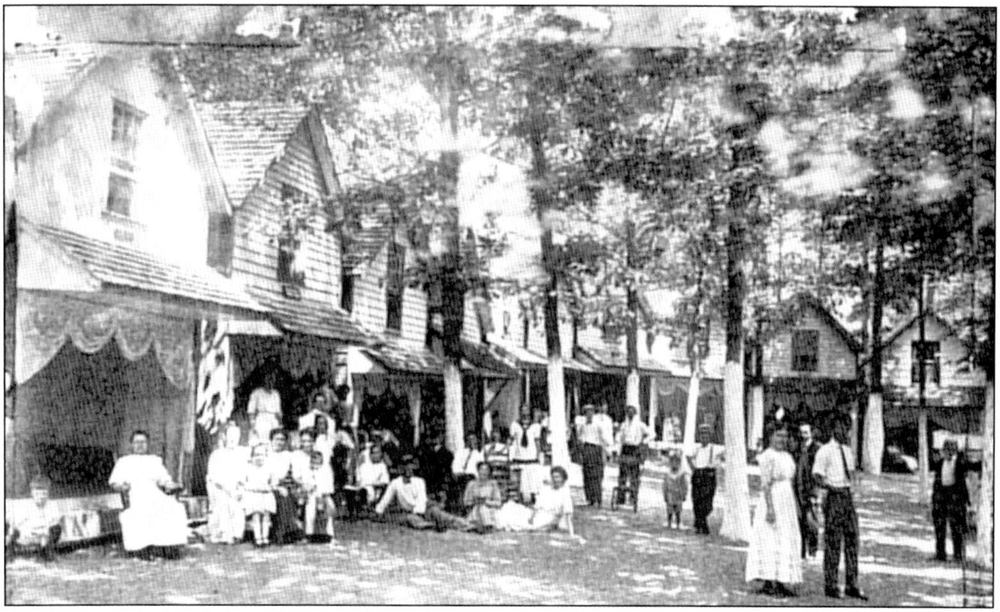

Camp Town Meeting. This was the Parsonsburg Camp sponsored by the Jerusalem Methodist Church. There were solid structures and tents, as can be seen in this c. 1908 image. The promenade was where campers met up with each other and chatted, especially with those of the opposite sex. The hellfire-and-brimstone preachers shouted their sermons across the promenade because there were no amplifiers. (Courtesy of the John E. Jacob Collection.)

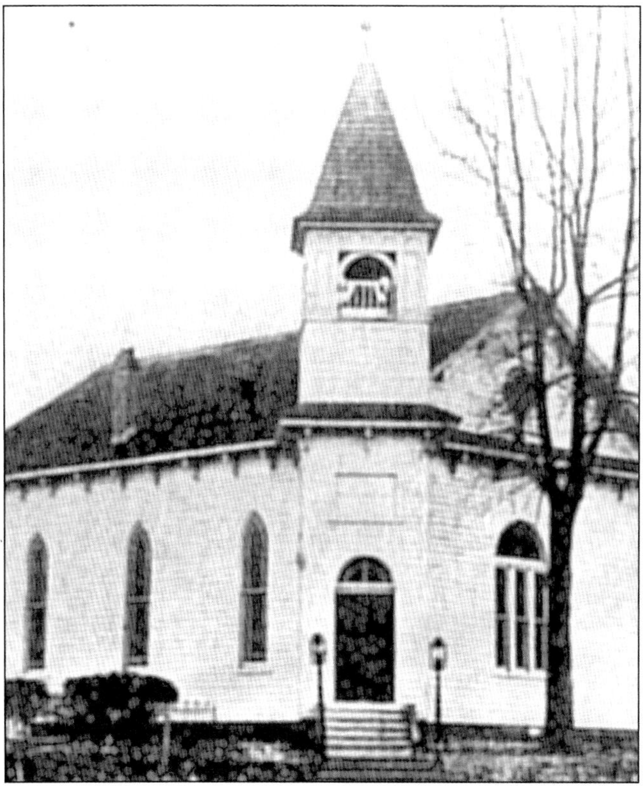

Jerusalem Methodist Church. In the Hilda Fowler collection, this photograph spotlights a church established in 1839 by George K. Perdue based on a dream of a pine tree he had. He started the church with a few whacks at the tree, and then, one by one, neighbors came around and pitched in, so its construction was truly a neighborly project. The original church was torn down in 1875 to construct a new one. (Courtesy of the John E. Jacob Collection.)

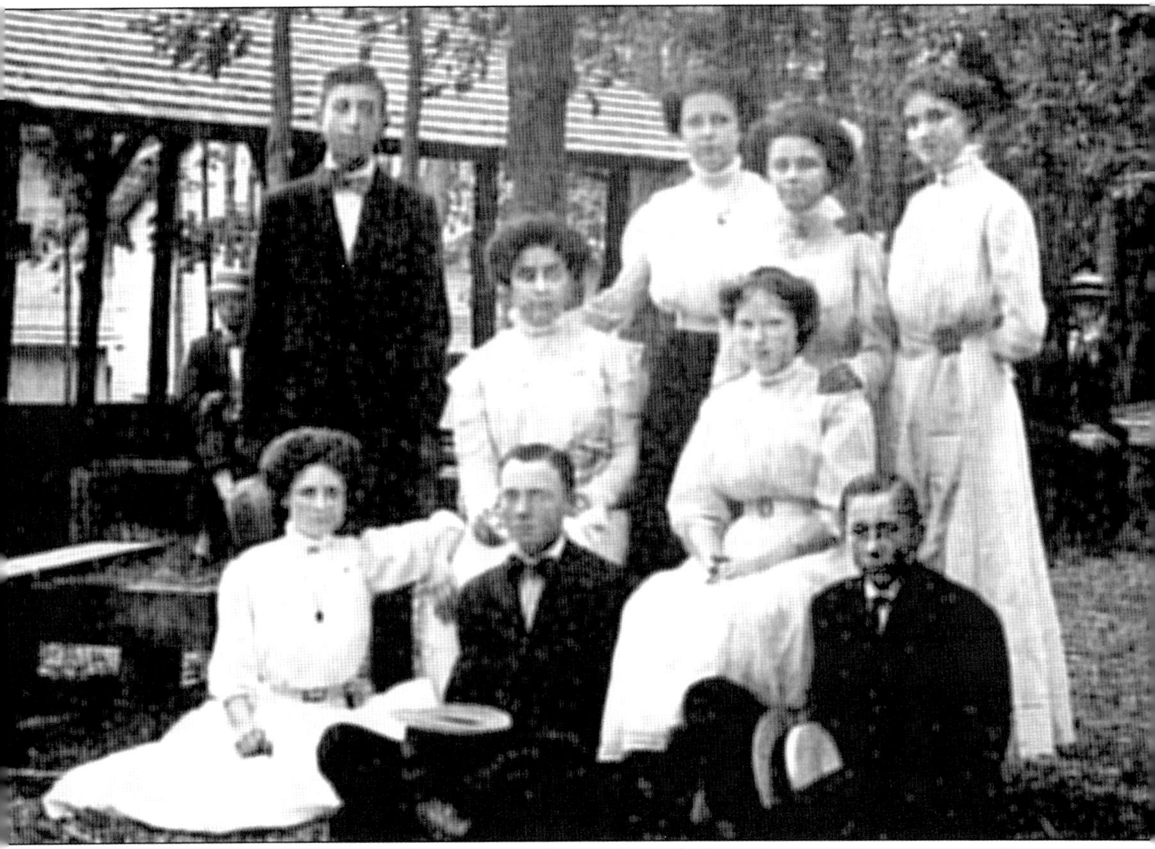

Retreating to Siloam Camp. The attire and hairstyles tell about the era. This image was likely taken around 1900. Notice the bow ties and hats and the tight buns the women wore. Though sponsored by the Methodist church, most everyone saw the retreat as a summer social event. (Courtesy of the John E. Jacob Collection.)

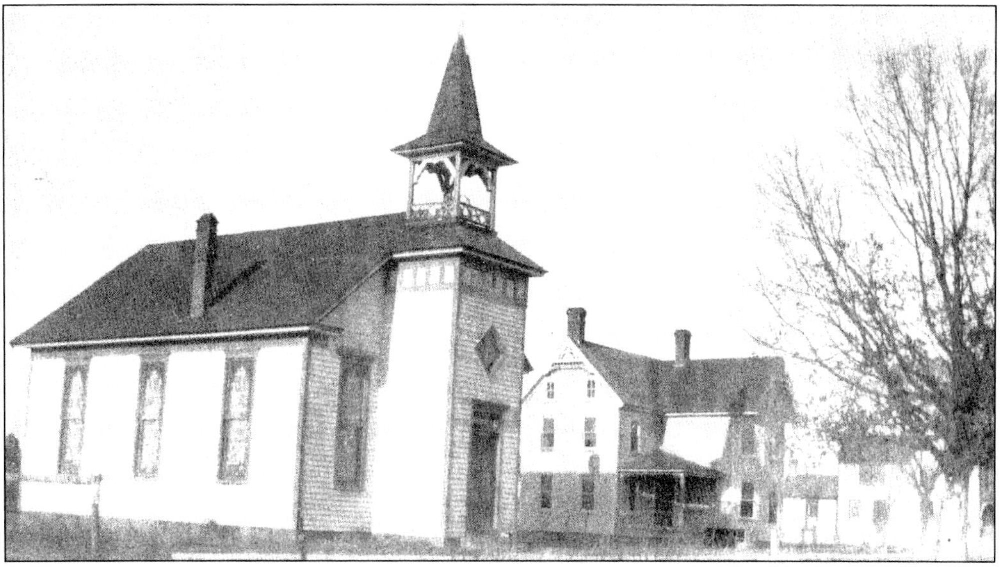

PITTSVILLE PARSONAGE. This 1920 card for Grace Methodist Protestant Church speaks to the journey of the congregation. It managed to remain separate from mergers of Protestant and Methodist churches only to lose its autonomy when Ayers Methodist Episcopal Church, established in 1840, and Grace Methodist Protestant Church combined. In 1990, the building sold for $5,000 to Full Gospel Church; the money was used for its Methodist Protestant parsonage. (Courtesy of James Jackson.)

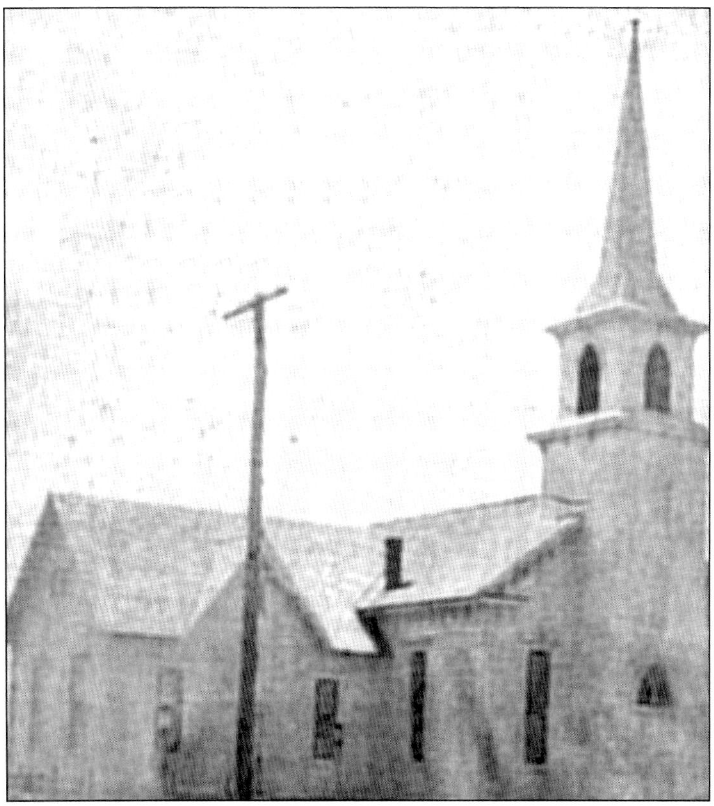

SHARPTOWN'S ASBURY CHURCH. In 1832, a Methodist Episcopal church was built too far away for Sharptown residents to travel. Years later, a new church, Asbury United Methodist Church, was constructed on Main Street. But wanting a Methodist Protestant church, residents held services in Sharptown homes until they erected Harmony Methodist Protestant Church in 1845. Eventually parishioners built a new church on the corner of Railway Street and Church Street. (Courtesy of the John E. Jacob Collection.)

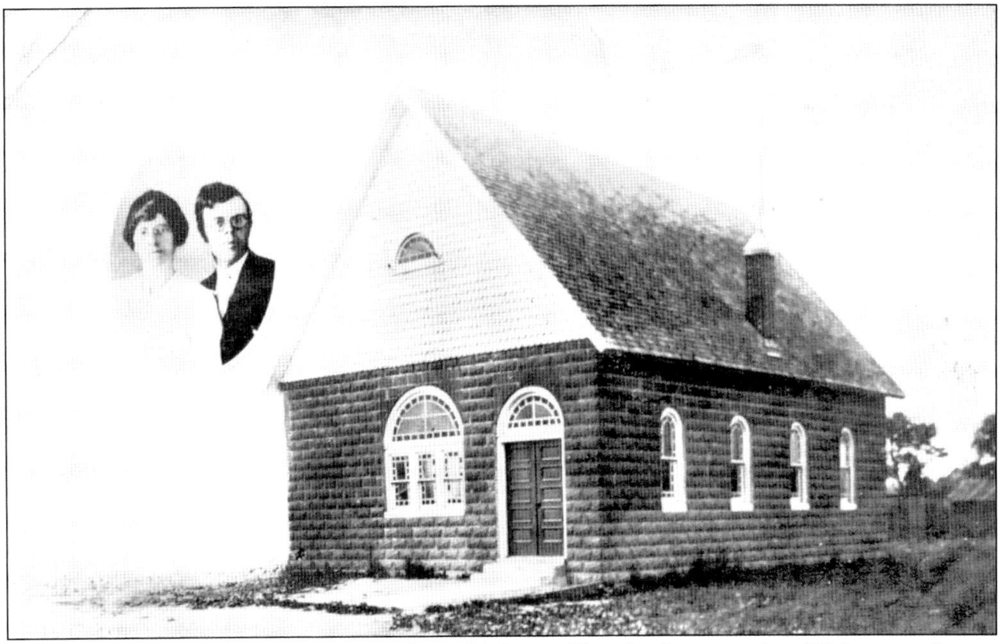

PILGRIM'S PROGRESS IN SALISBURY. Pilgrim Holiness Church, shown in this 1904 postcard, gave way in later years to the Salvation Army. The Salvation Army's thrift store stands on the original location. (Courtesy of George Chevallier.)

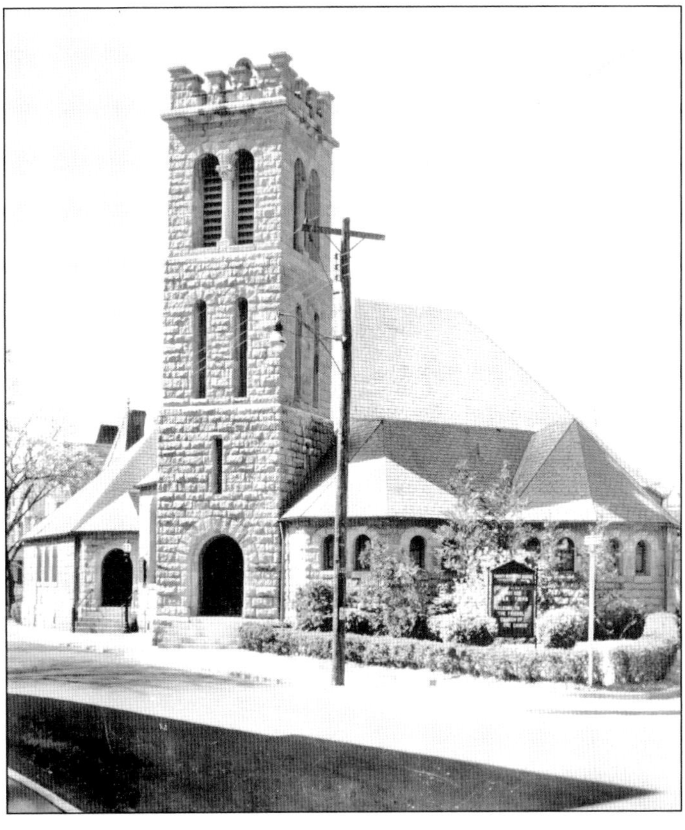

LADY TRINITY. Trinity United Methodist Church on North Division Street in Salisbury was founded in 1866 as a result of divided loyalties that smoldered in the wake of the Civil War. Destroyed twice by fire, the present structure was completed in 1905 thanks to the generosity of Gov. Elihu and Annie Rider Jackson, residents of Salisbury. The interior was ravaged by fire in 1940 but was carefully restored with the addition of a Skinner organ. Still going strong, the congregation now boasts over 1,000 members. (Courtesy of Salisbury Chamber of Commerce.)

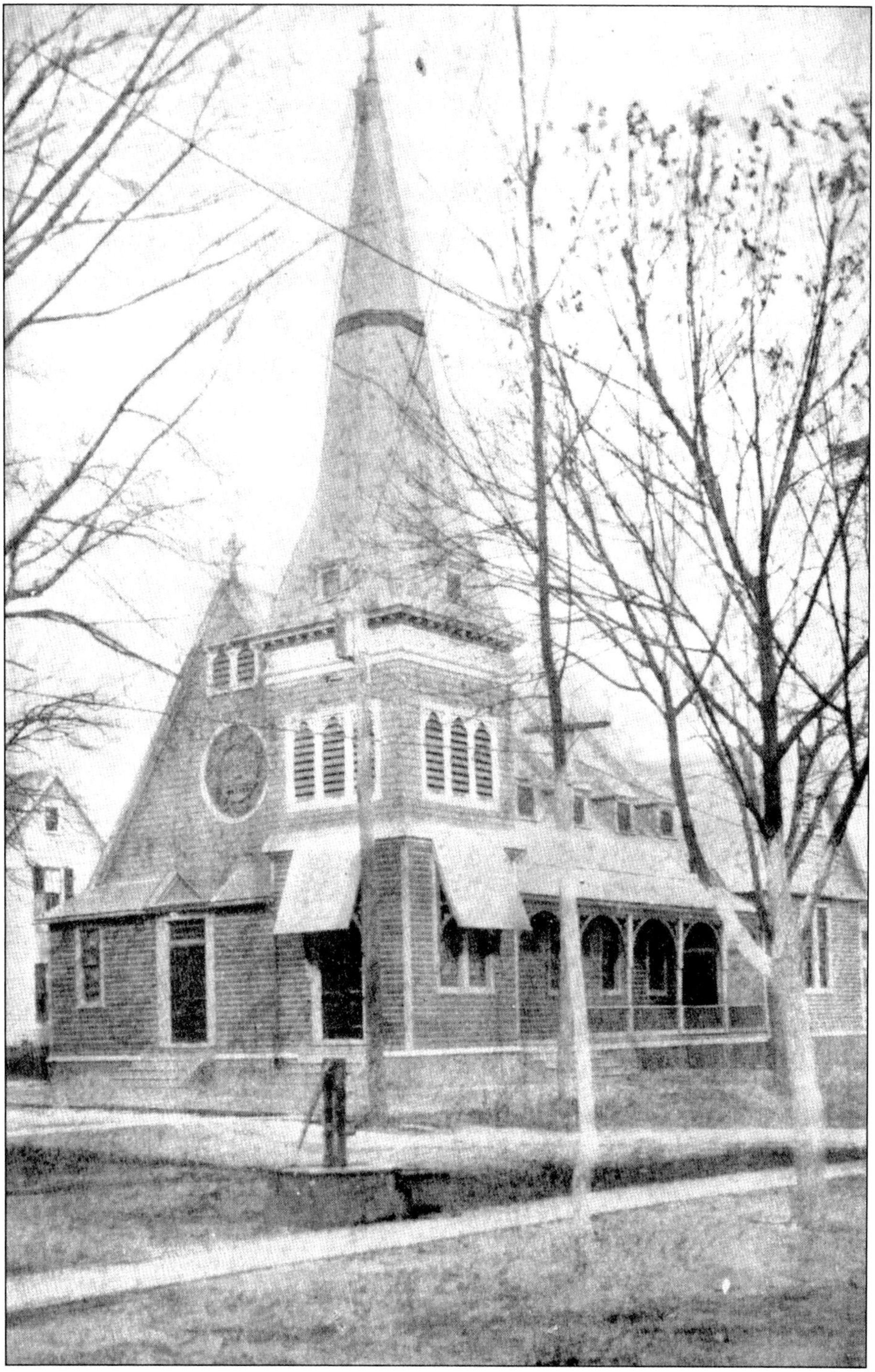

Catholicism in the County. This 1910 shot of the original St. Francis de Sales Catholic Church is at its first location at the corner of Bond and Calvert Streets. It formerly housed Trinity Methodist Church. The congregation moved to its present Riverside Drive site in 1964. Bond Street was buried under revitalization projects. (Courtesy of George Chevallier.)

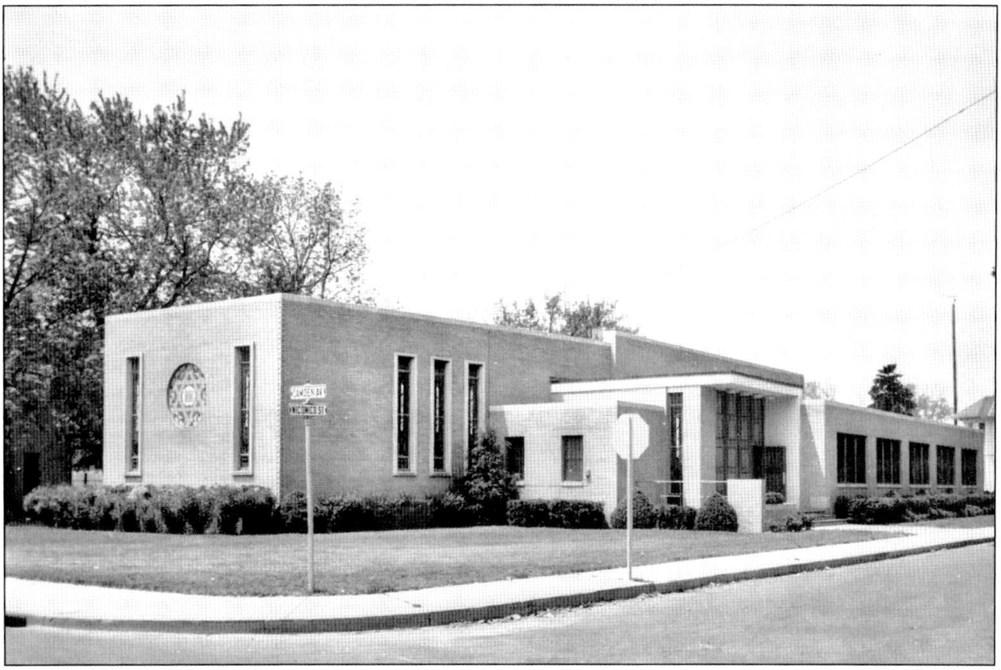

MANY FAITHS ABOUND IN THE COUNTY. Beth Israel Synagogue was founded over 70 years ago. The present building was constructed in 1951 on Camden Avenue in Salisbury, is the worship center for over 110 membership units, and is an anchor of the Jewish faith in the county. (Photograph by James Perry; courtesy of Salisbury Chamber of Commerce.)

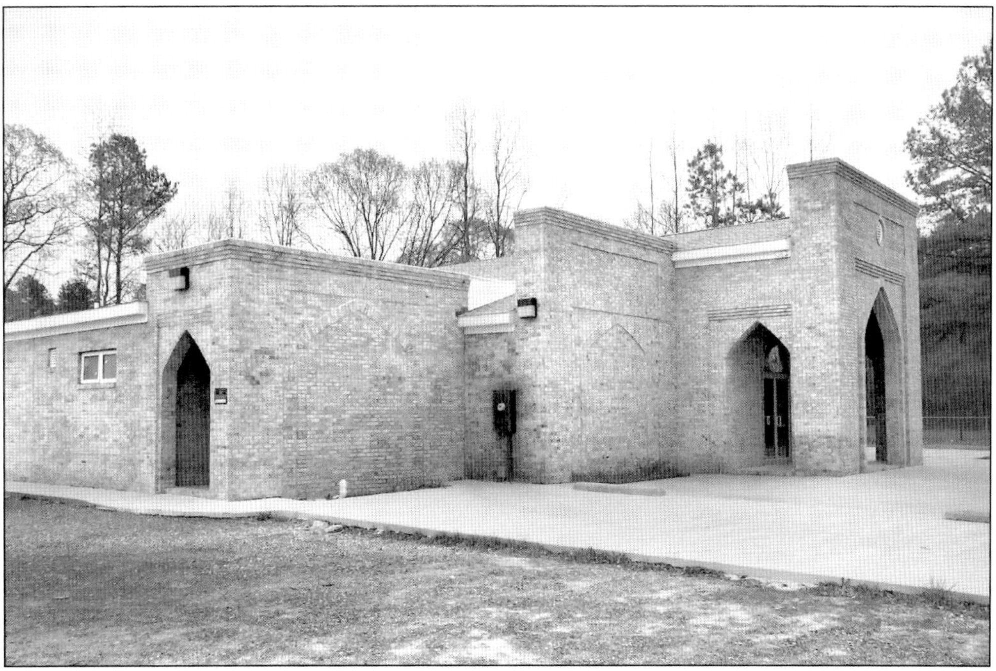

ANSWERS TO THE CALL OF PRAYERS. The Islamic Society of Delmarva was established in 1996 to meet the needs of a growing Muslim population in the area. It now has over 140 members who meet in their center on Jersey Road. (Photograph by Andy Nunez.)

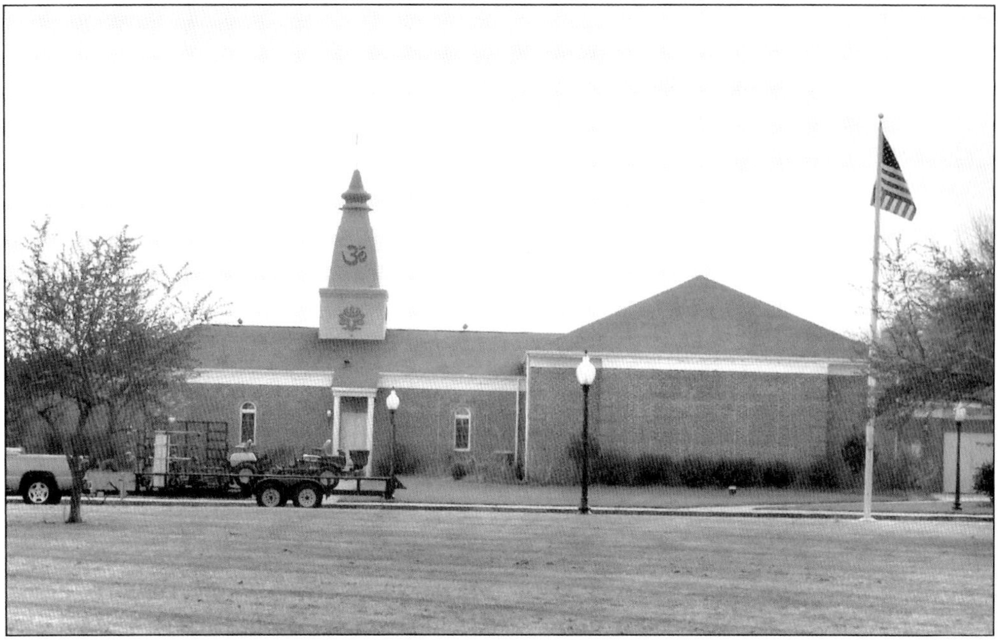

EAST MEETS WEST ON THE EAST SIDE. The Hindu Temple of the Eastern Shore was constructed on Parker Road east of Salisbury to serve the burgeoning Hindu population of the area. It holds cultural events related to the religion and lifestyle of India and serves as a center of worship. (Photograph by Andy Nunez.)

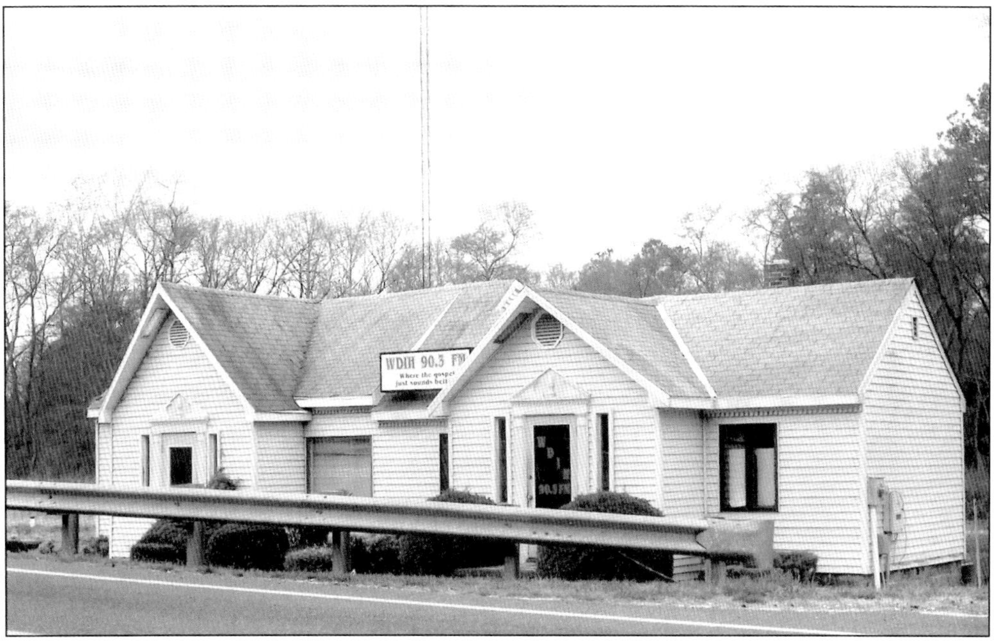

SENDING OUT THE MESSAGE. Bishop George Copeland recently expanded his United Faith Churches of Deliverance to encompass the airwaves, founding the first African American gospel radio station in the county on June 13, 1990. WDIH 90.3 FM serves the community with outreach, contemporary gospel music, and the best in syndicated gospel programs. Bishop Copeland is planning to further expand his facilities on Jersey Road. (Photograph by Andy Nunez.)

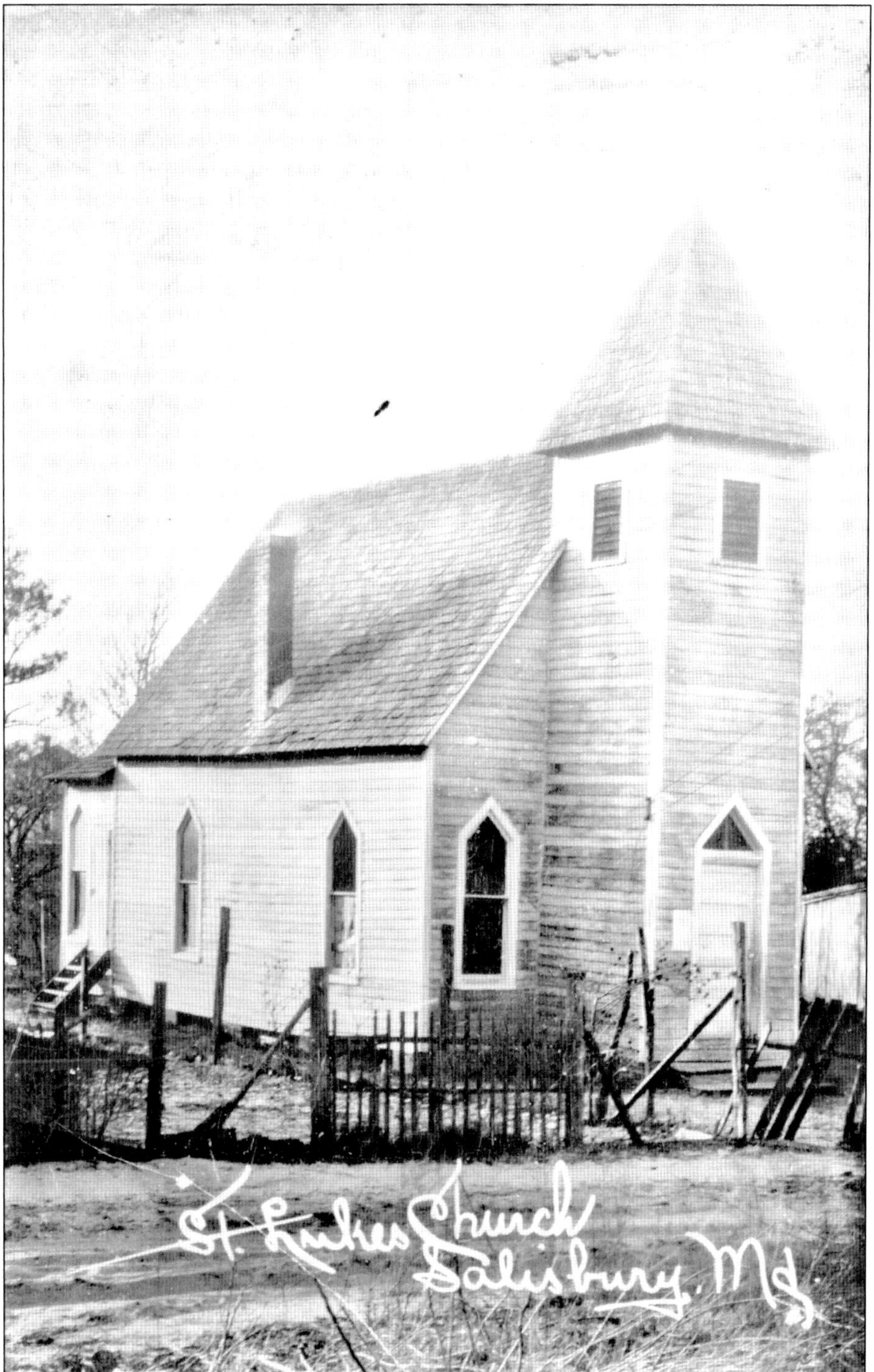

SOUTHEAST METHODISM. St. Luke's Methodist Church is pictured in this early 1900s photograph. The building on St. Luke's Road near Fruitland still stands but has fallen into disuse. (Courtesy of George Chevallier.)

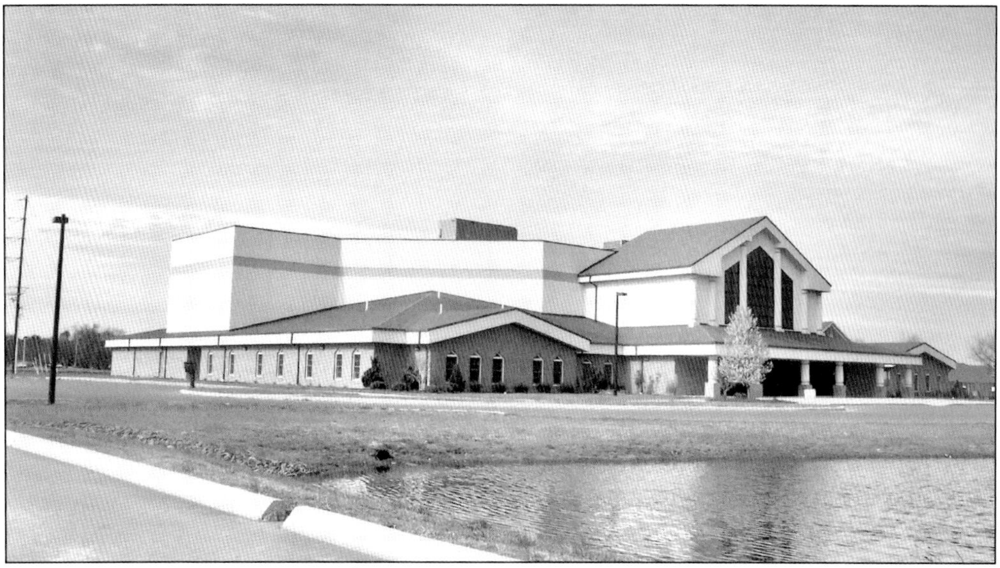

Rise of the Mega Church. Thirty years ago, Emmanuel Wesleyan Church had a mere 90 members. Under the leadership of Rev. Tom Bunting, membership soared in the 1990s, and even the 500-seat facility built in 1982 under Reverend Bunting's predecessor was inadequate. The congregation embarked on what some deemed a foolish mission, to build a church to serve the entire community. A new 2,500-seat facility was dedicated in 2002. Other congregations are following suit. (Photograph by Andy Nunez.)

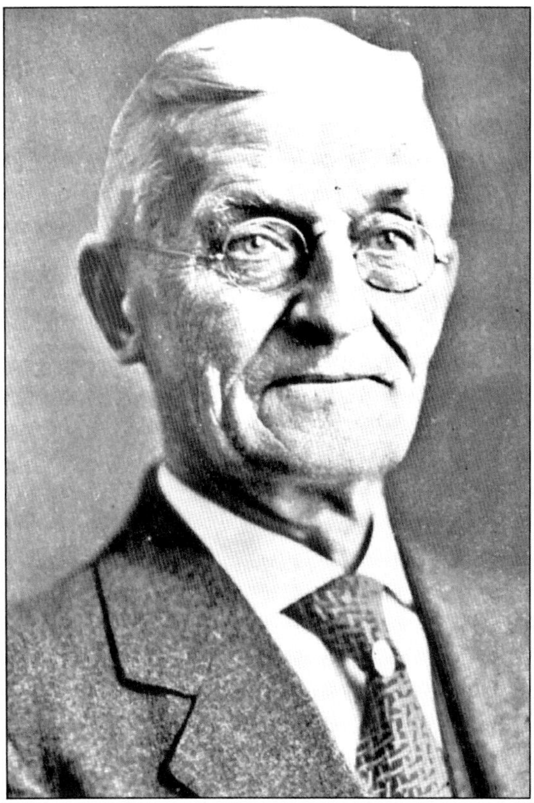

Chief of Staff. Born in South Carolina in 1871, Dr. James MacFadden Dick was the first surgeon at Peninsula General Hospital (today Peninsula Regional Medical Center) and remained chief of staff for 37 years. He became Dr. George Todd's assistant when Todd's call went out for one. Dr. Todd was the founder of the hospital. Today there are over 300 active staff members at Peninsula Regional Medical Center. (*A Heritage of Caring: Peninsula Regional Medical Center 1897–1997.*)

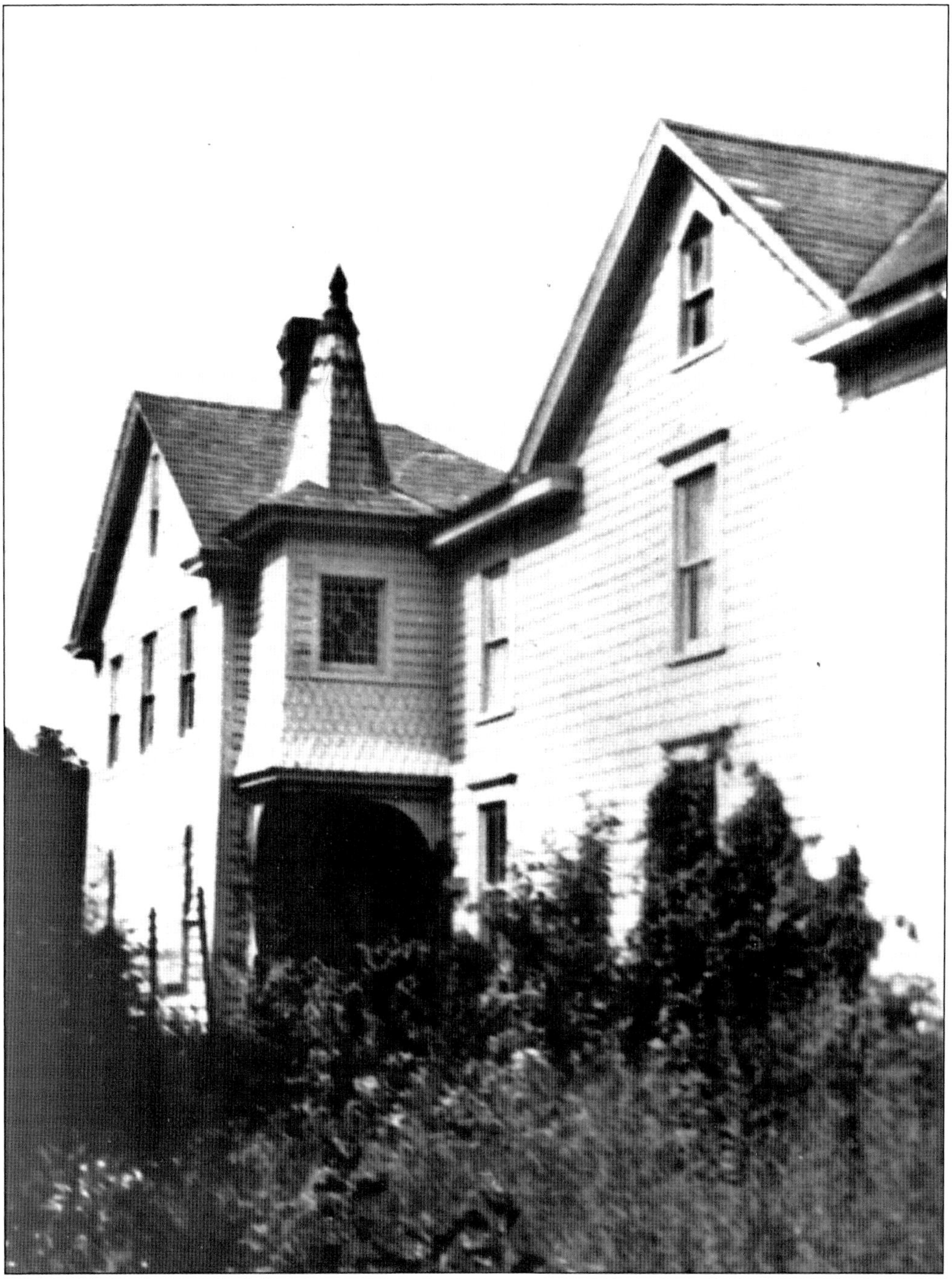

OLD PENINSULA REGIONAL MEDICAL CENTER'S BEGINNINGS. Peninsula Regional Medical Center is the mainstay of wellness in Wicomico and surrounding areas. In its 110-year history, it has grown from one building in 1897, as shown here, with a few hundred patients, to a major medical complex comprised of 366 acute- and 30 subacute-care beds with state-of-the-art specialties in cancer, heart, and orthopedics. (*A Heritage of Caring: Peninsula Regional Medical Center 1897–1997.*)

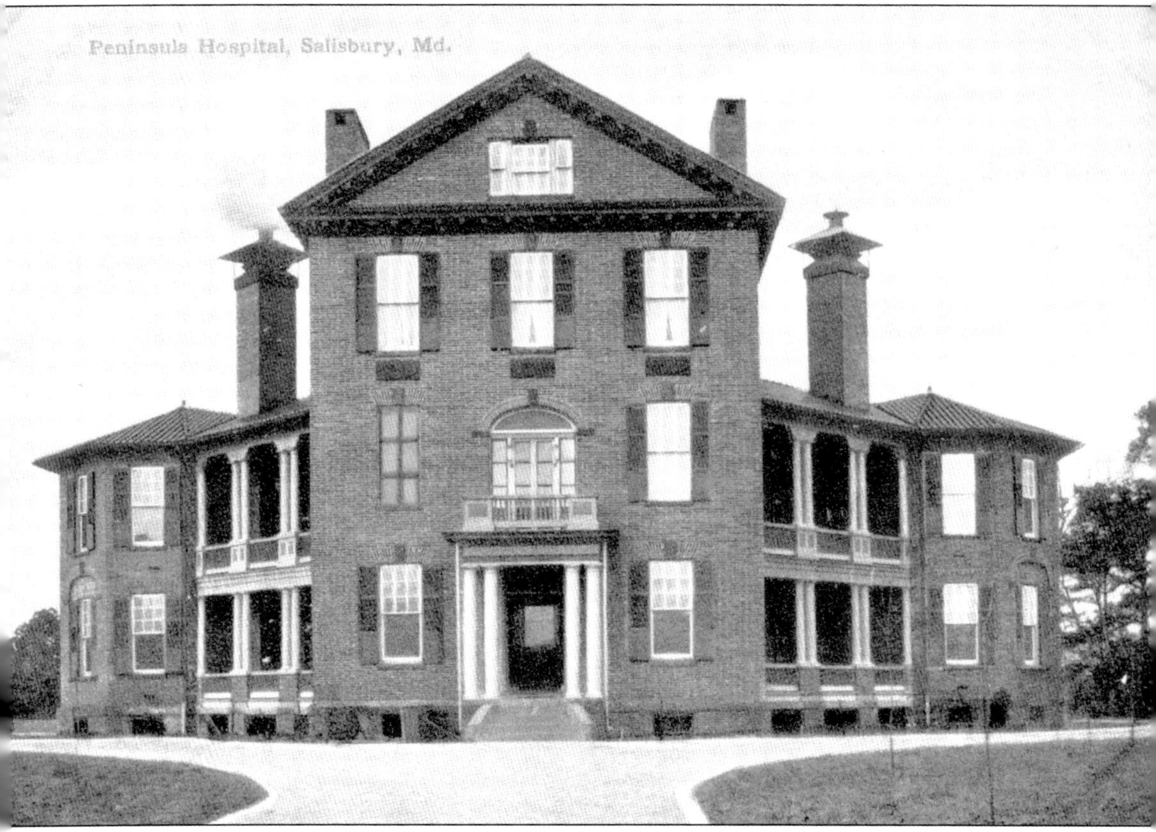

GROWING PAINS. This 1907 postcard shows the original Peninsula General Hospital—now Peninsula Regional Medical Center—which opened in 1904. Dr. George H. Todd was its first superintendent, and Dr. James McFadden Dick was its first surgeon. The original building was razed in 1978, and the new facility has been rated one of the top 100 hospitals in the country. (Courtesy of George Chevallier.)

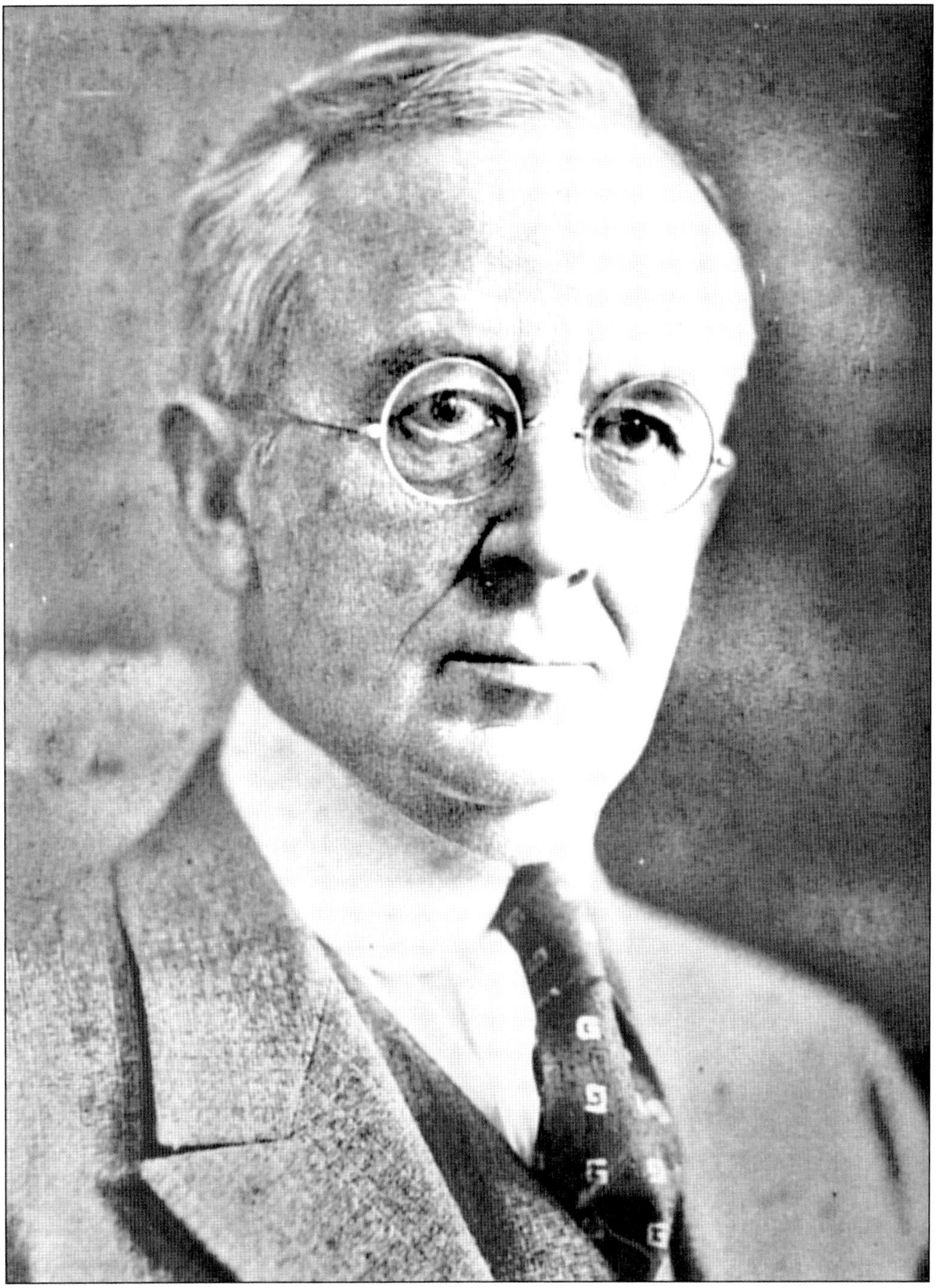

HEART OF THE HOSPITAL. George W. Todd, M.D., was the founder of Peninsula General Hospital (now Peninsula Regional Medical Center) and was born in 1860 on a farm in Delmar, Delaware. He was the third physician in his family, and the tradition has continued until today. (*A Heritage of Caring: Peninsula Regional Medical Center 1897–1997.*)

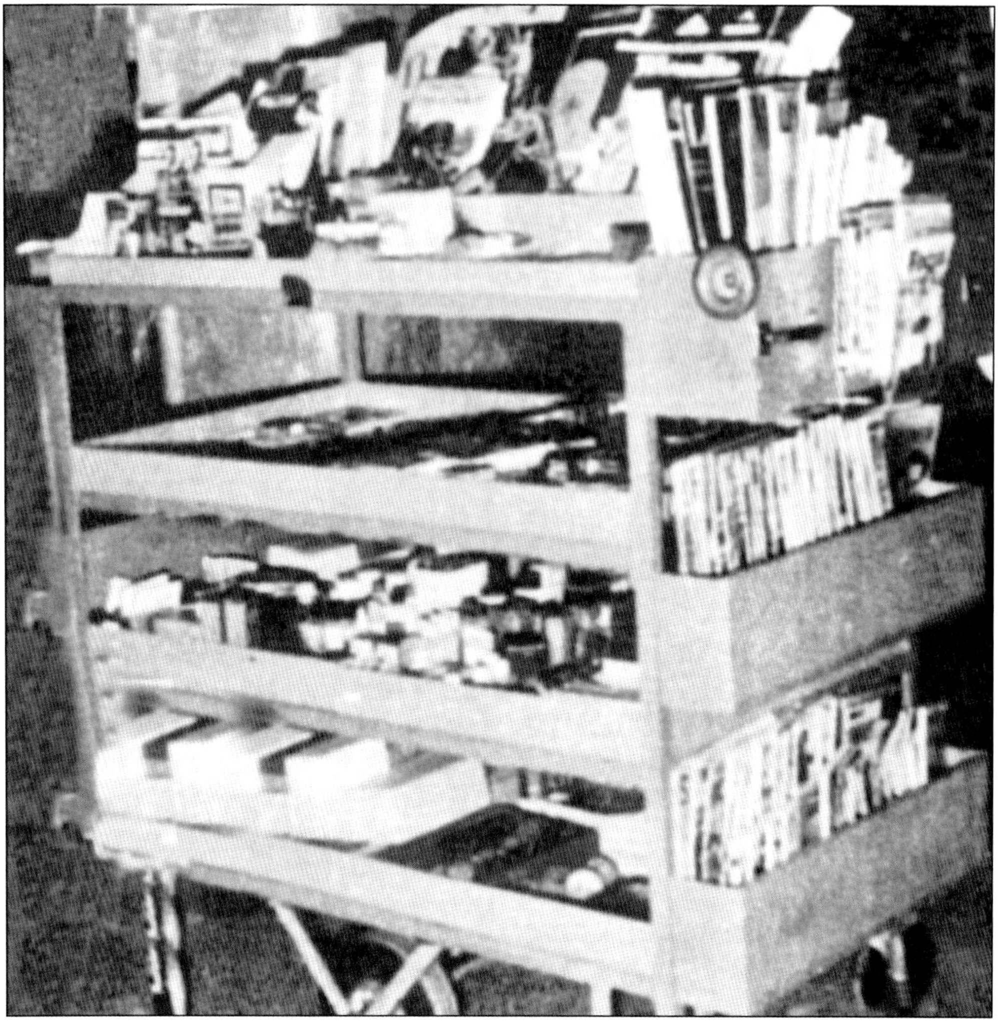

MAGAZINE ANYONE? The Junior Board Auxiliary of Peninsula Regional Medical Center started with a cart that went from floor to floor. It's been in existence about 85 years and now has an active membership of about 200 volunteers who not only work the restaurant/gift shop but also do such loving tasks as knit hats for newborns and chemotherapy patients. (*A Heritage of Caring: Peninsula Regional Medical Center 1897–1997.*)

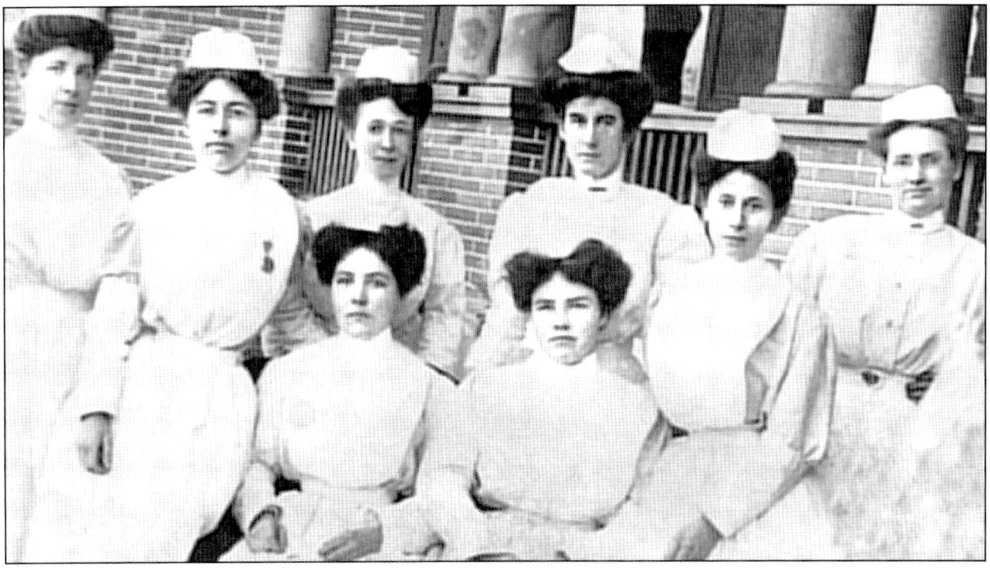

WINGED CAPS OF LOVE. With its roots back to 1897, Peninsula Regional Medical Center provides substantial employment for the Eastern Shore. Nursing has always played a significant role in providing patient care. That tradition continues today. This 1908 photograph shows a graduating class of nurses from the Training School of Nurses that opened in 1905. It was later called PGH (Peninsula General Hospital) School of Nursing. The hospital changed names again to Peninsula Regional Medical Center or PRMC. (*A Heritage of Caring: Peninsula Regional Medical Center 1897–1997.*)

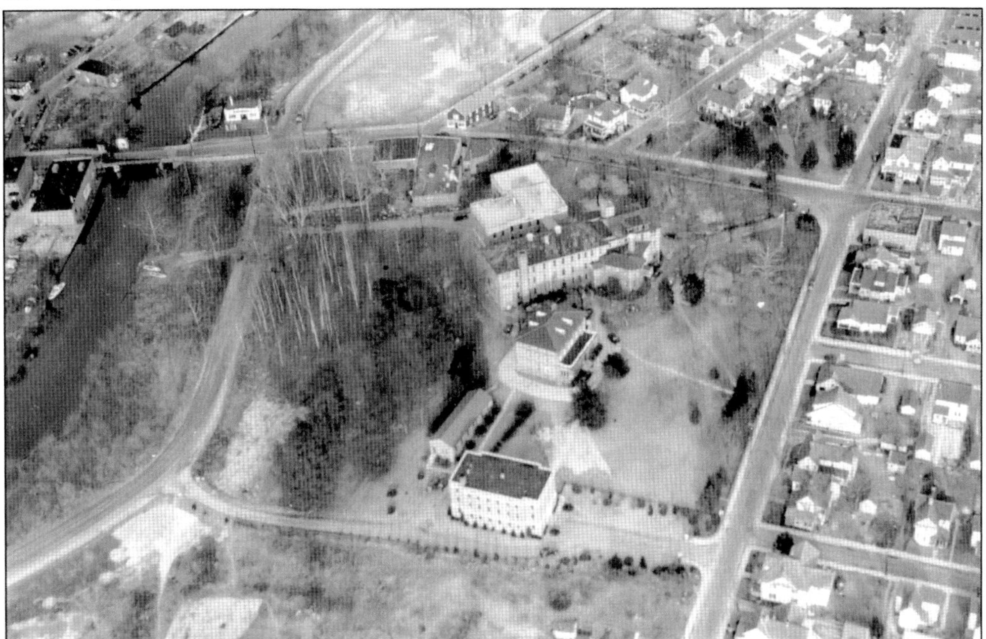

ROOM TO GROW. This aerial shot of the hospital looks almost idyllic with the buildings surrounded by woods and open space, but all that changed within 30 years, as the facility grew and needed more parking area. Landscaping around the building is the only evidence of the greenery that once formed a restful view for patients (Courtesy of Salisbury Chamber of Commerce.)

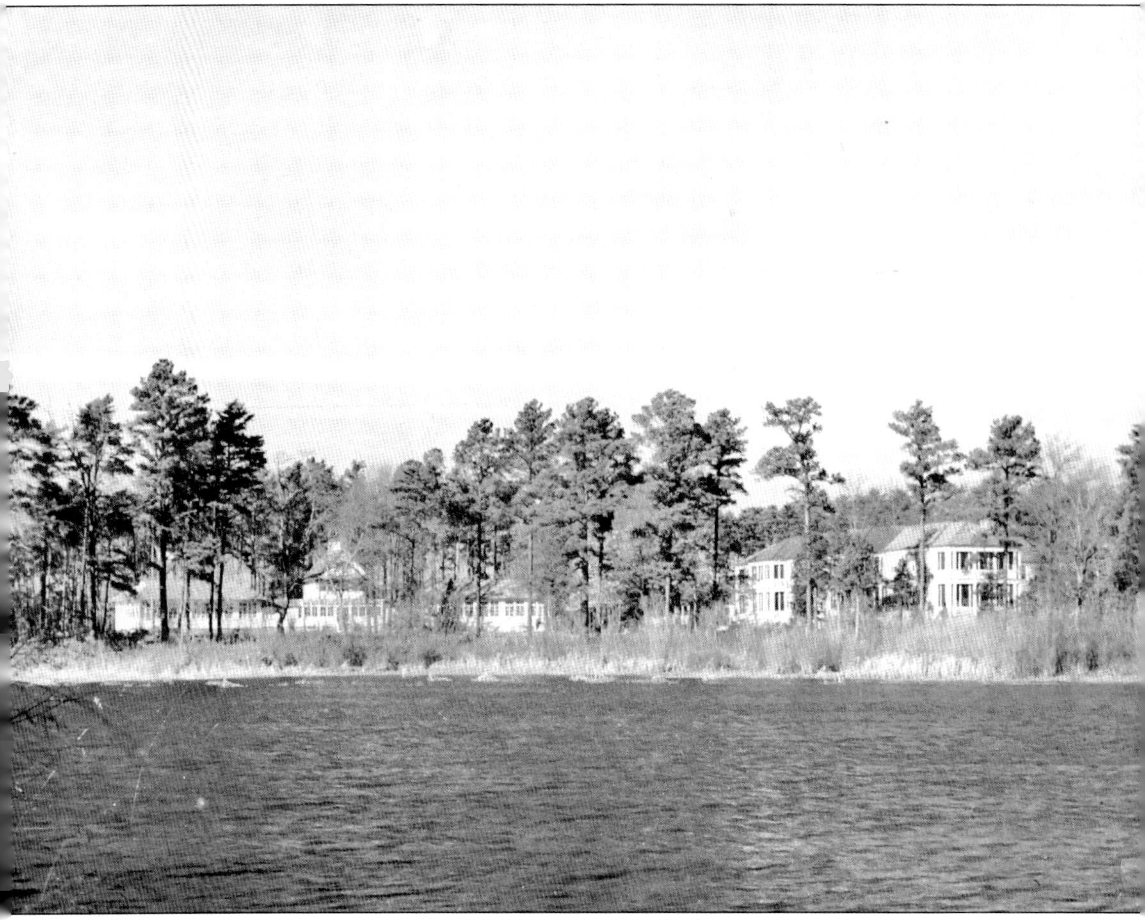

SANITARY SANITARIUM. In this mid-1940s image, Pine Bluff State Hospital was a private institution run by Superintendent Edward Ritchings, M.D. It had two wings—one for males and the other for females. It opened in 1912 but became state owned in 1928. Its Wicomico County telephone was Pioneer 9-6503. It had 65 patients and a staff of 42. The complex is no longer a hospital but is now a Maintaining Active Citizens (MAC) center, a non-profit organization dedicated to maintaining the quality of life for older adults. (*A Survey of Salisbury, Maryland.*)

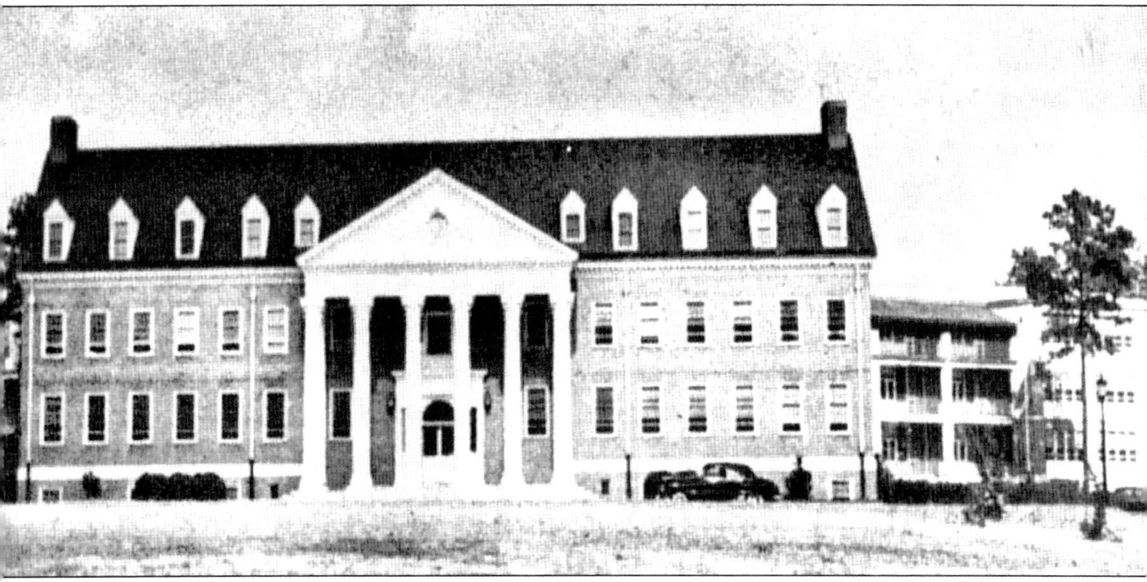

HUNTING DEER'S HEAD. Built around 1950 for $2.5 million, Deer's Head State Hospital—now called Deer's Head Center—was built for the chronically ill and was state-of-the-art for its time. It's setting boasted water on three sides and housed 284 beds staffed by three full-time physicians and 262 employees. Today there are 90 beds with a full-time, highly recognized dialysis center. (*A Survey of Salisbury, Maryland.*)

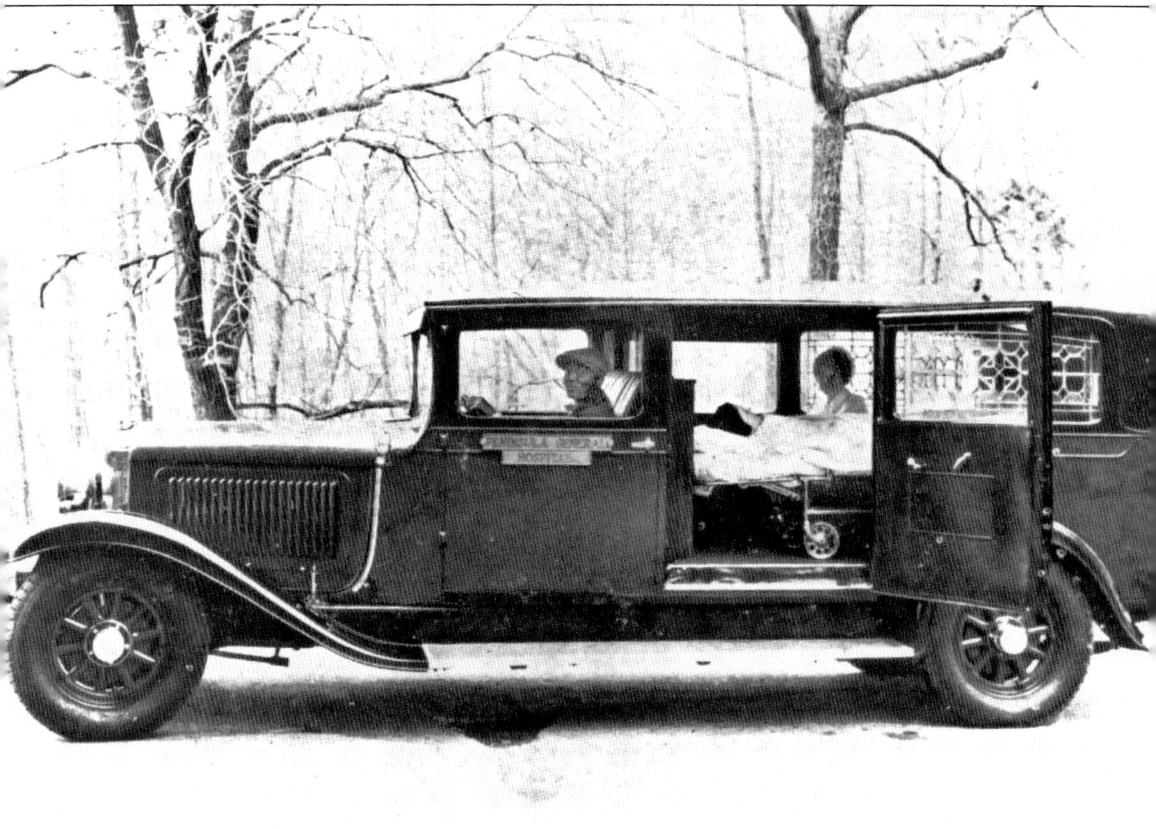

THERE GO THE SIRENS. Peninsula Regional Medical Center was originally called Peninsula General Hospital, and today, with nearly 400 beds, it's considered to be one of the larger and top hospitals in the nation, in spite of its modest roots. Originally a horse-drawn ambulance was used, but this was replaced with a motor vehicle in 1919. This image shows a c. 1925 ambulance. (*A Heritage of Caring: Peninsula Regional Medical Center 1897–1997.*)

Three

READING, WRITING, 'RITHMETIC

Wicomico County has a rich history of educating its residents, from one-room schools holding no more than a handful of students to imposing, massive structures enlightening thousands. In this chapter, there are rare images of schools composed of six or seven young people to segregated and minor schools, to major, colossal universities. Public institutions—except for higher education—were governed by the county and not by individual communities as of 1867. A dilemma that faces the taxpayers is the overcrowding of schools because of unprecedented population growth. There are over 15,000 students and 21 schools operating on a $120-million-plus budget. School for boys began in Salisbury in 1818 and for girls around 1823. The first newly constructed high school cost $15,000 in 1905. Today a modern high school is underway to be built for over $73 million, and it will be overcrowded before the ribbon is even cut. Currently there are four high schools in the county, each holding about 1,300 students—way beyond capacity.

Though most schools need updating, they do offer commendable high-tech equipment and teaching. There are several remarkable preparatory and private schools as well. The Maryland State Normal School—now Salisbury University—opened on 20 acres in 1925 to train teachers. Today there are over 7,000 students representing 49 countries and 33 states or territories in 42 undergraduate programs, 13 graduate programs, and 5 post-baccalaureate certificate programs. The university has gone through several names changes and expanded many times in its 82-year history and is presently undergoing construction of larger buildings. Sojourner-Douglass College has a satellite campus here, offering a baccalaureate and a master's degree. Wor-Wic College has seen wild growth because of its popular vocational and associate degree programs. Founded in 1975, it initially operated as a "college without walls" but now has its own campus and buildings. Currently there are over 3,000 students. Many changes have taken place in the educational realm in the county, and many more are on the horizon.

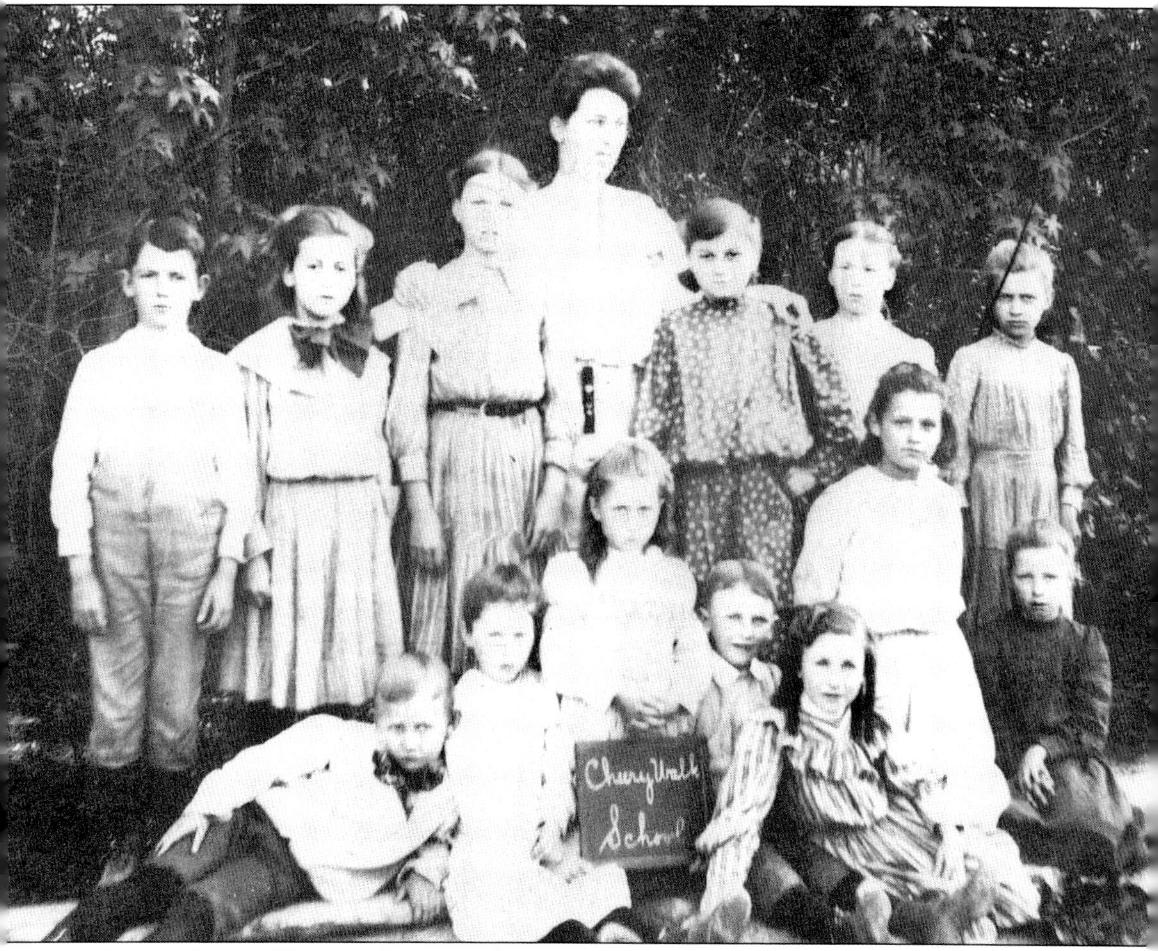

JUST A CHERRY WALK TO SCHOOL. This is an image from the John E. Jacob Collection via Nabb Research Center featuring a small school located west of Quantico, Maryland, that is in the area of Bivalve and Nanticoke. It was named School No. 5 and had a small enrollment since the water towns on the west side of the county were bedroom communities. (Courtesy of Nabb Research Center of Salisbury University and Preservation Online and the John E. Jacob Collection.)

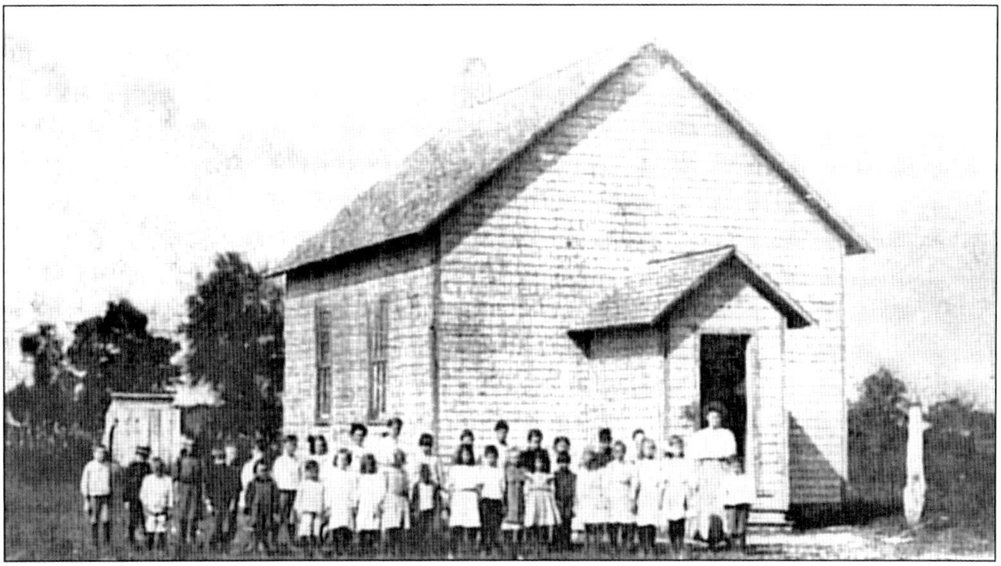

ONE ROOM ONLY. The teacher in the image (far right) shows the type of dress that dates the photograph to around 1905. The outhouse is to the left; the old-fashioned pump is to the right. The location of this school is unknown. Some historians believe it was in Clara, Maryland. During this period, one-room schools were common. In some places, only boys went to school, while the girls stayed home. (Courtesy of Sylvia Taylor.)

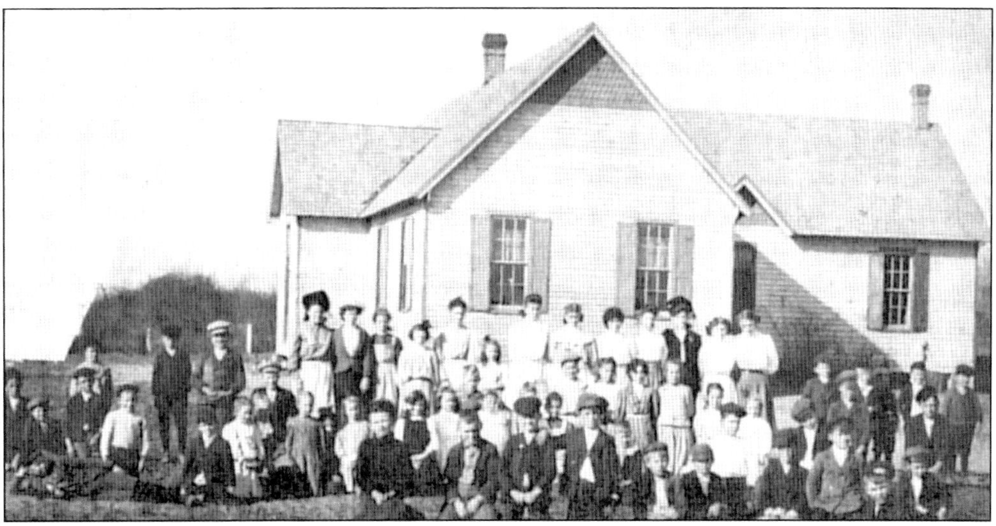

BIVALVE SCHOOL. This is a postcard of 1907 showing Bivalve school students, teacher, and their three-room schoolhouse. The town runs along the eastern banks of the Nanticoke River, accessed by Route 349. In 1883, the town was called Waterville, today it is still known as Bivalve, since it was a major watermen town. (Courtesy of the John E. Jacob Collection.)

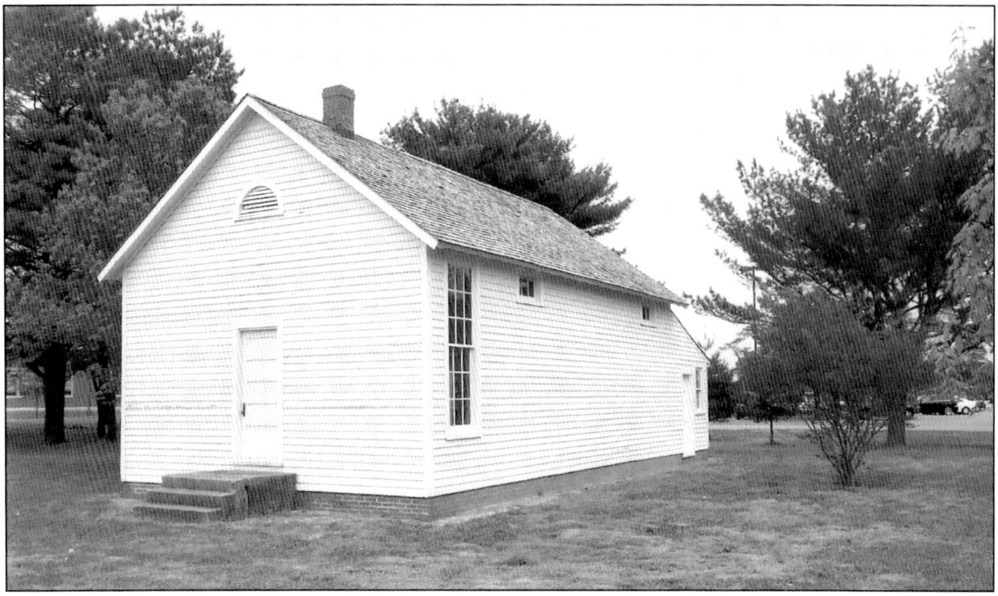

NO ROCK "A'WALKIN" TO THIS SCHOOL. The eponymous school existed in this tiny mill hamlet of Rockawalkin as far back as the mid-1800s. Historians believed it ran from 1872 to 1939, serving the then-rural needs of the west side of the county. The building pictured is on the grounds of the current Pemberton Elementary School at the crossroads of Pemberton Drive and Ellegood Street, where it's been restored. (Photograph by Andy Nunez.)

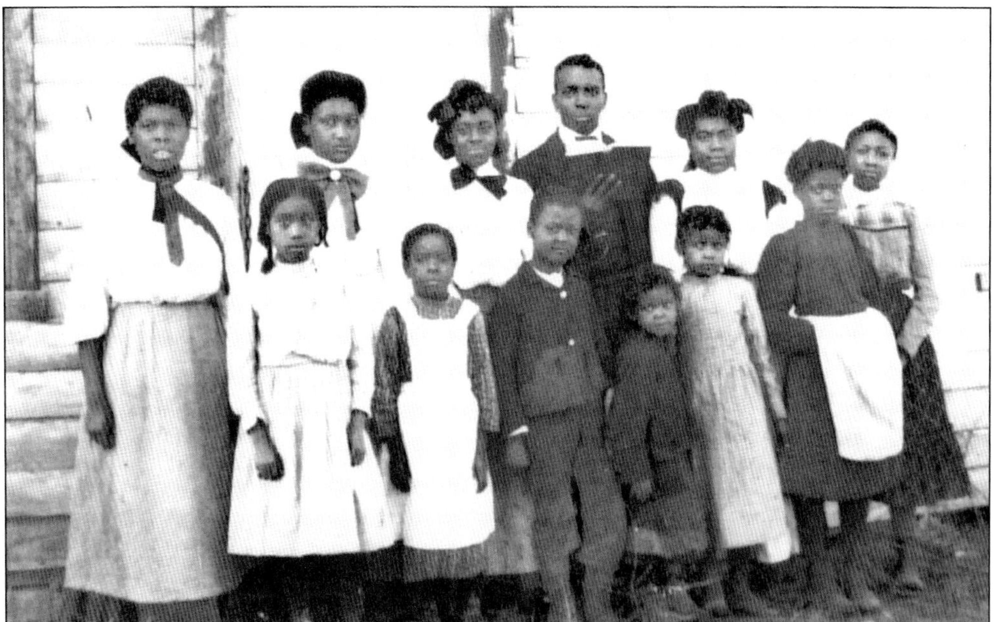

ROSENWALD. Built in 1919 in the tiny community of San Domingo, this school was founded by James Brown, a former slave. The community was named after the Haitian slave revolt of the 1790s. In 1820, the town boasted 1,000 inhabitants, but its population has greatly dwindled. However, the people have garnered a grant to renovate the old school. (Courtesy of Nabb Research Center at Salisbury University and Preservation Online and the John E. Jacob Collection.)

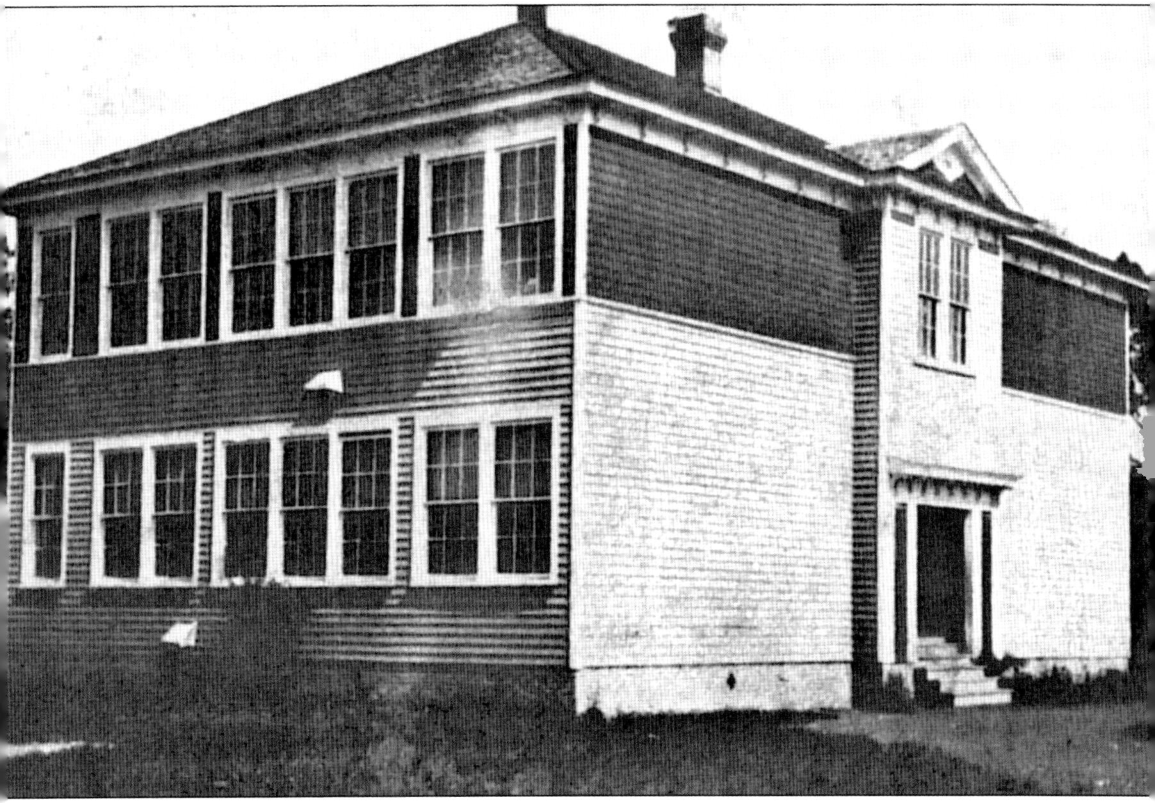

NANTICOKE HIGH SCHOOL. Notice the box architecture—the easiest and cheapest to build, especially around 1914, when this school was erected. The class of 1948 was the last to graduate from here, as then it became an elementary school until 1967, when it closed. Students were then sent to Quantico and Hebron schools. Currently the town has 423 residents, and the name means "tidewater people" in Algonquian. (Courtesy of Sylvia Taylor.)

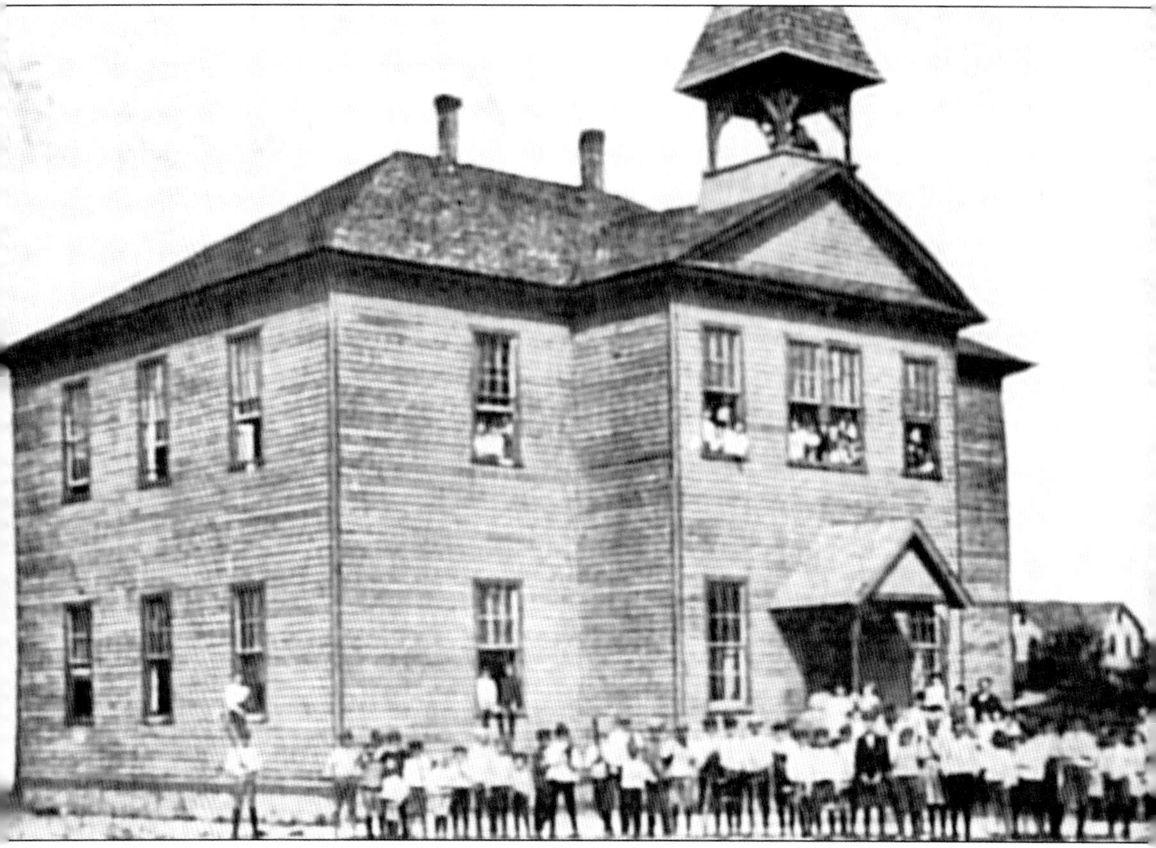

SHARPTOWN HIGH SCHOOL. This postcard was issued about 1905, though the school was built in 1896 and remained in existence until the mid-1930s. There were less than 150 students, most of whom look as though they're peering out of windows if not assembled in front of the building. (Courtesy of the John E. Jacob Collection.)

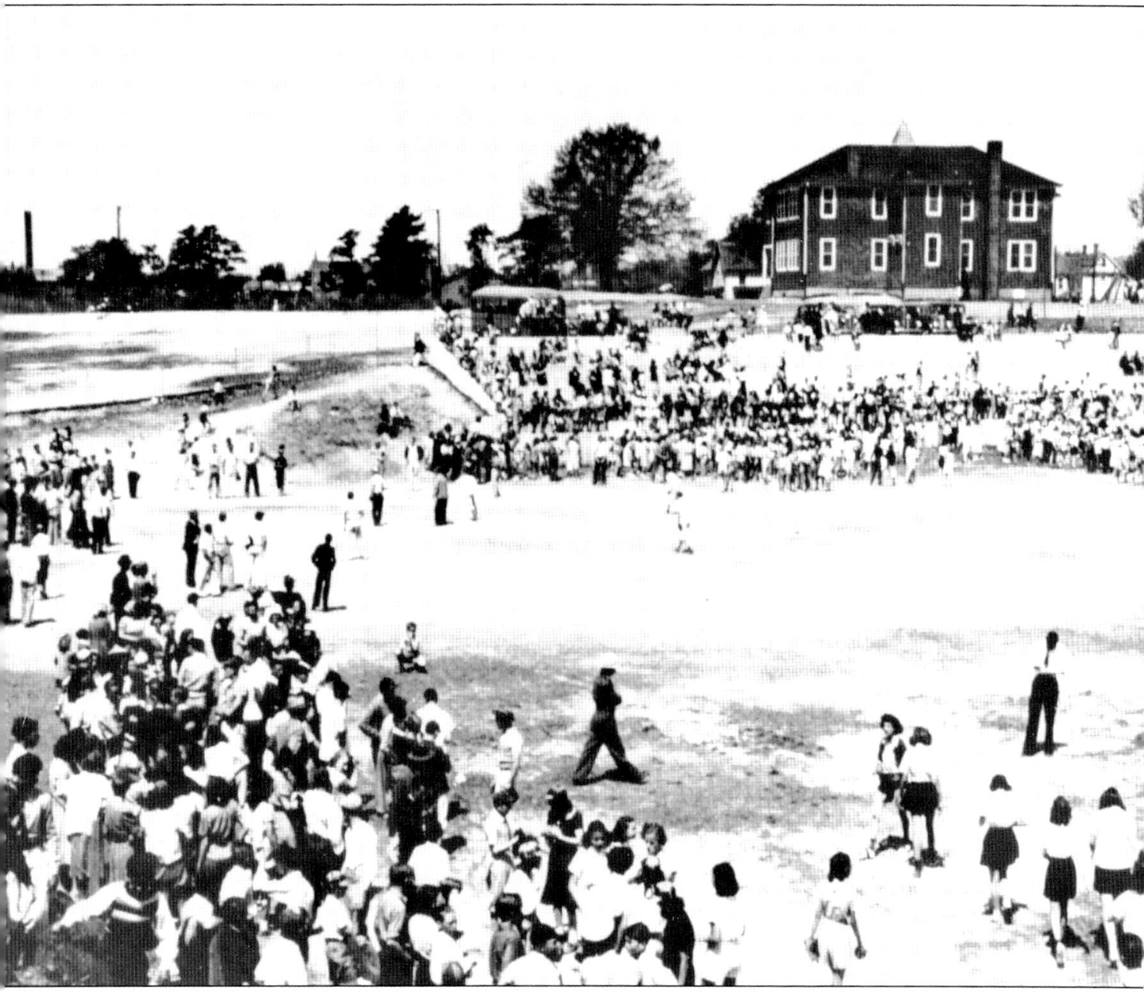

GOOD OLD WICOMICO HIGH SCHOOL. This building is across from the park, and though it may have been imposing during its era (around 1900), it had only about four classrooms and reading/oral rooms on the first two floors, along with a library that doubled as an office. The basement housed the heating system and bathrooms. In 1930, the school was renovated and expanded, and it was later turned into a middle/junior high school. A new structure was built in the 1950s in a different location. Actors John Glover and Linda Hamilton are alumni, as is Mike Seidel of the Weather Channel. (Courtesy of the Palmer Gillis collection.)

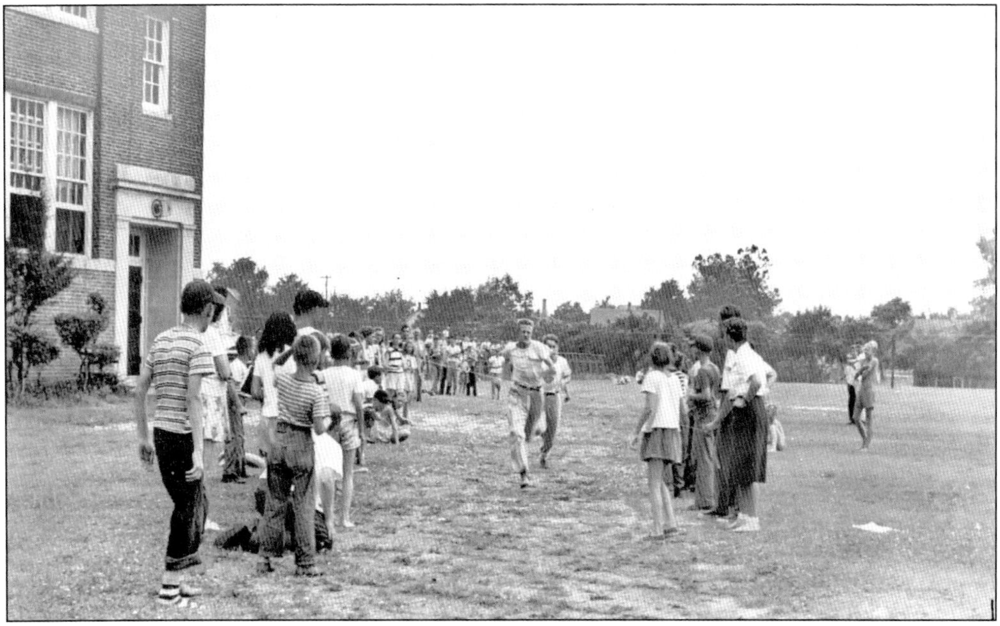

UNDETERRED BY WORLD WAR. This action shot is of the Wicomico High 1942 school Olympics and was taken at the East Main Street location, which is now Wicomico Middle School, though it had served as the high school before a new one was built. It's one of four secondary schools in the county. With so much growth in the Salisbury metropolitan core, new, high-tech, deluxe high schools are being built and older ones remodeled. (Photograph by James Perry; courtesy of Salisbury Chamber of Commerce.)

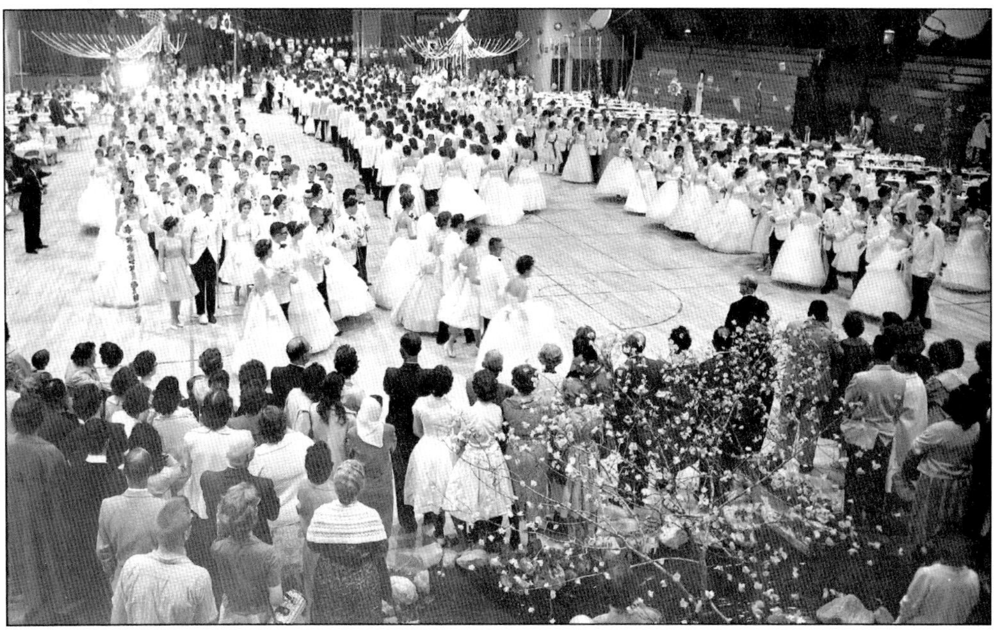

FROM SCHOOLBOOKS TO PROM DRESSES. Here are happy couples at the Wicomico High School prom of 1963, which was held in the old civic center. The 1960s were the years of the Beatles, train wrecks, and the assassination of Pres. John F. Kennedy. (Photograph by Orlando Wooten; courtesy of Salisbury Chamber of Commerce.)

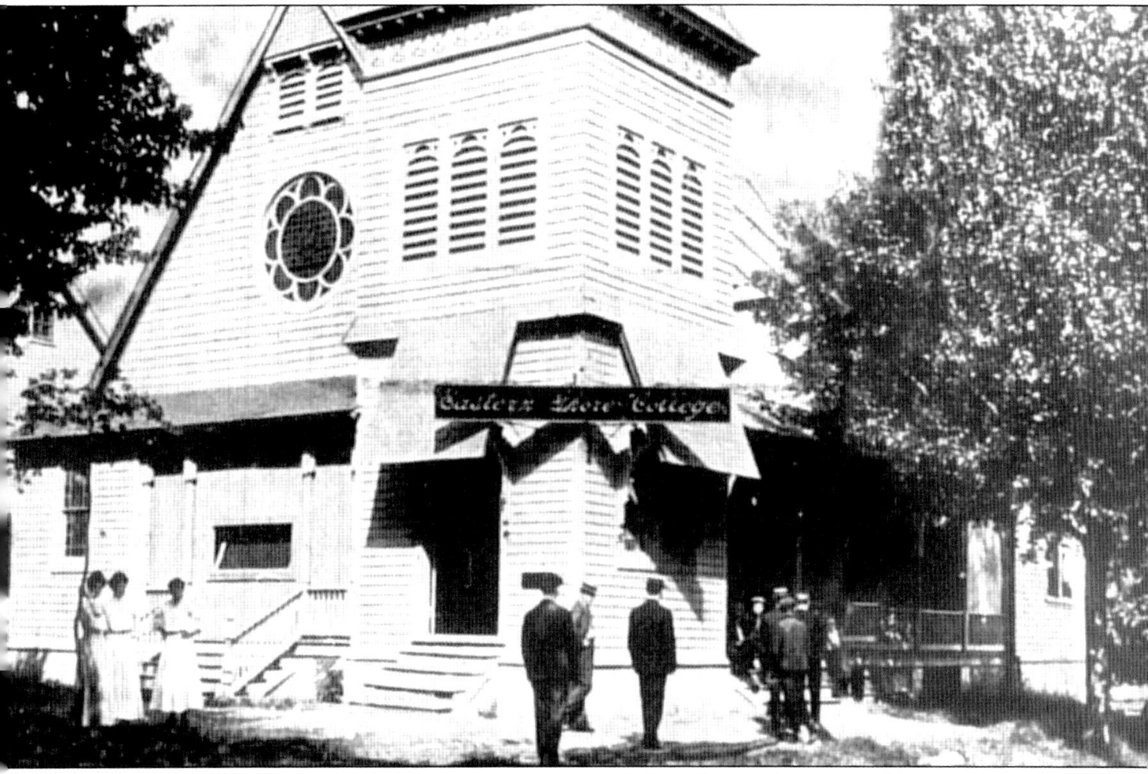

EASTERN SHORE COLLEGE. This building transitioned from being the original hospital, to St. Francis church, and finally to the Eastern Shore College, which was a business school around 1910. The young enrollees were well dressed, with the men in suits and the women in dresses. The college, no longer in existence, was on Calvert and Bond Streets. (*Salisbury, Maryland: The Central City of the Eastern Shore.*)

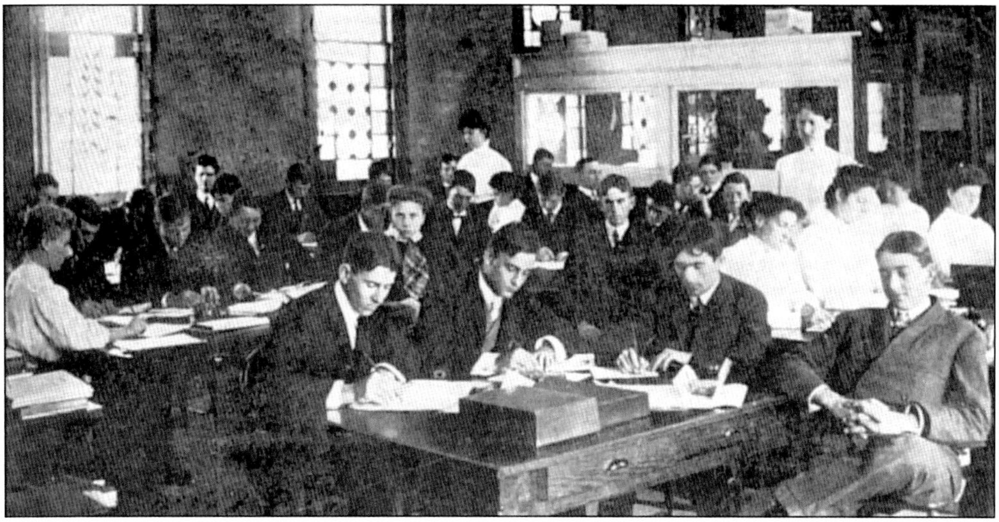

AMERICA'S FUTURE PROFESSIONALS. These business students at the Eastern Shore College were dressing for the future. Two key courses were accounting and bookkeeping. Most business schools today either have been absorbed by other four-year colleges or have reinvented themselves as baccalaureate institutions. The Perdue School of Business of Salisbury University is nationally ranked. (Courtesy of the Jessica Anderson collection.)

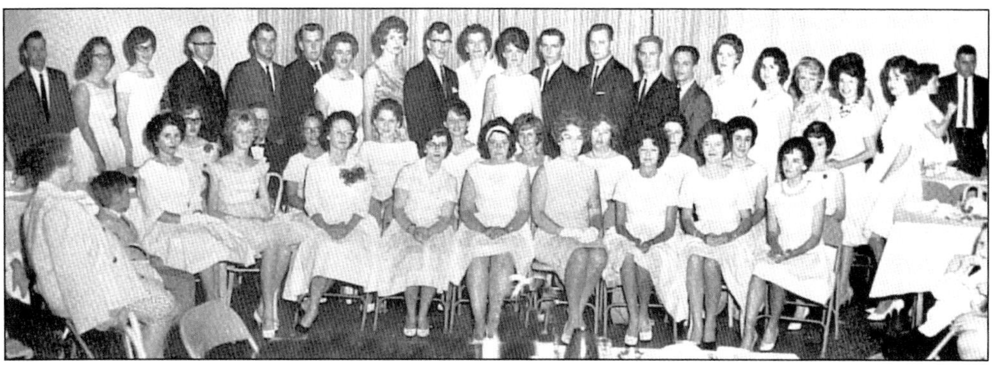

MORE FUTURE BUSINESS LEADERS. This image gives a good sense of the size of the college. Jefferson School of Commerce had started in 1959 with 14 students and two teachers and grew until it became its own independent entity. Notice the hairstyles and attire that dates the image to 1963. (Jefferson Yearbook, *The Independent*.)

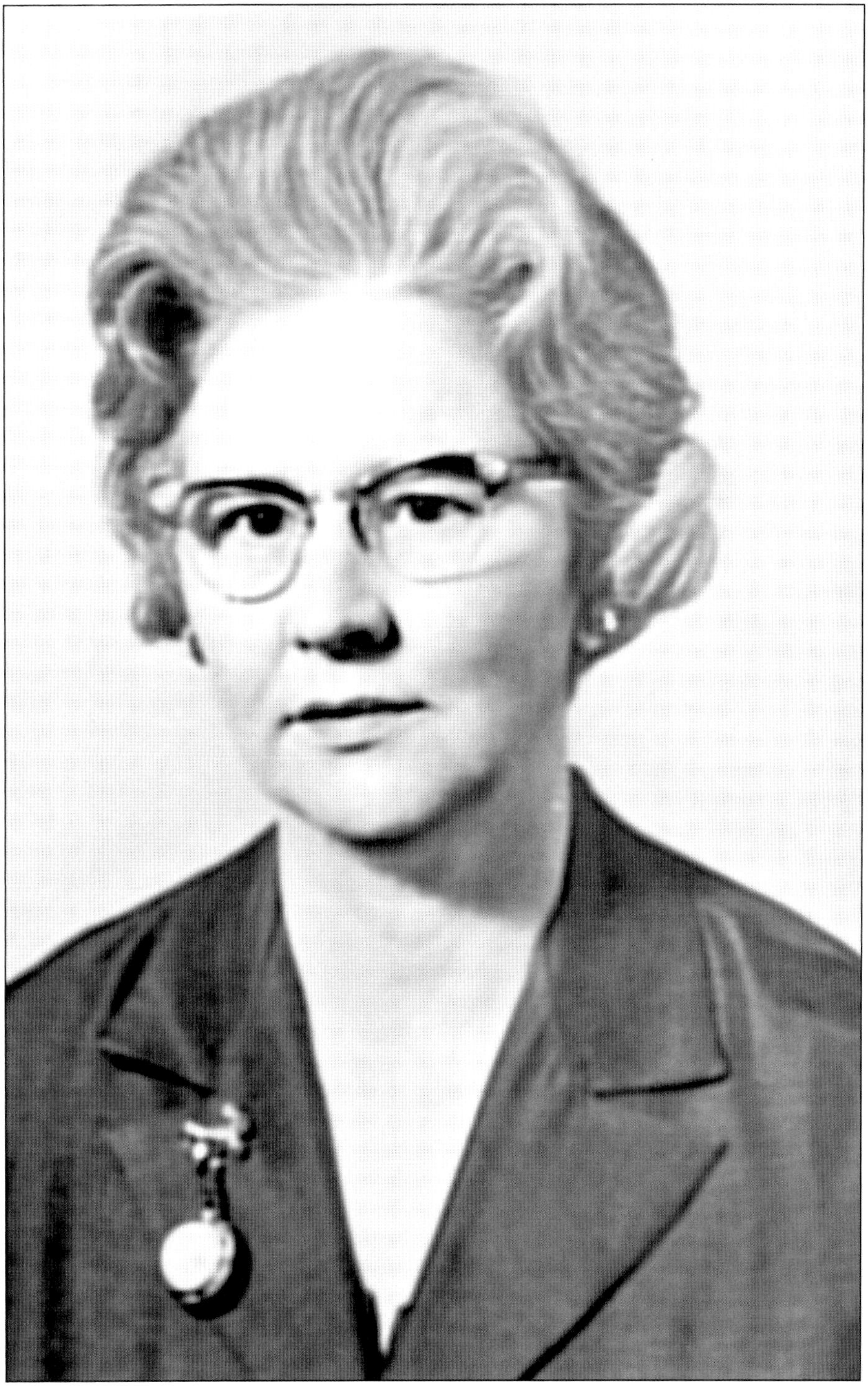

BOSSY BAUSERMAN? Lucille Bauserman served as president of Jefferson School of Commerce in Salisbury and taught accounting, shorthand, and business math. It became chartered in Maryland and independently owned in 1960. It no longer is in existence. Its curricula consisted of stenographic, secretarial, and general business courses. (Jefferson Yearbook, *The Independent*.)

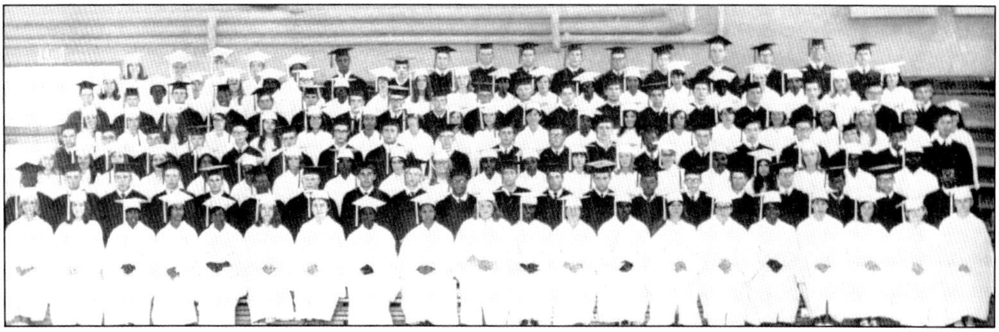

WICOMICO HIGH SCHOOL CLASS OF 1969, SECTIONS I AND II. This two-part image was taken from the *Tom Tom* yearbook of 1969, when principal Kenneth Smith and vice principals Mrs. Samuel Graham and Franklin Waller oversaw the school. This image shows the first class to ever attend Wi-Hi for four years; thus it was this class that chose many of the firsts for the school, such as homecoming queen Debbie Hastings, the first winning school float, and the first student council. Today Wi-Hi houses over 1,200 students from 9th through 12th grades. (Courtesy of Robert Culver; 1969 Wicomico High School yearbook.)

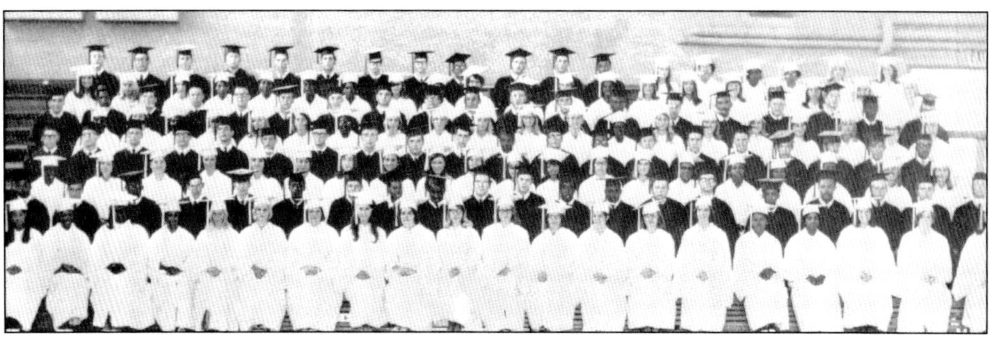

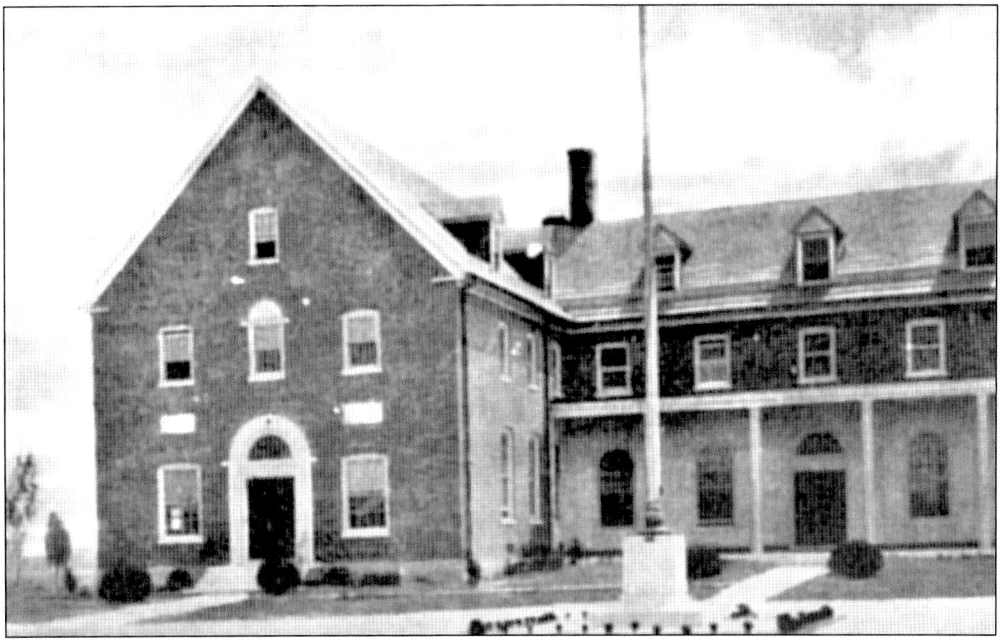

THE MARYLAND STATE NORMAL SCHOOL. Founded in 1925, it served as a teachers' college that later merged with Holloway Hall of Salisbury University, with about 2,800 students. From its transition from a normal school to a university of about 7,000 students, it's still expanding physically as well. Holloway Hall remains a focus of the campus on Camden Avenue. The university has a tunnel for students to walk underneath Route 13 South, a major city artery, to get to other streets where the campus has blossomed. (Courtesy of Salisbury Chamber of Commerce.)

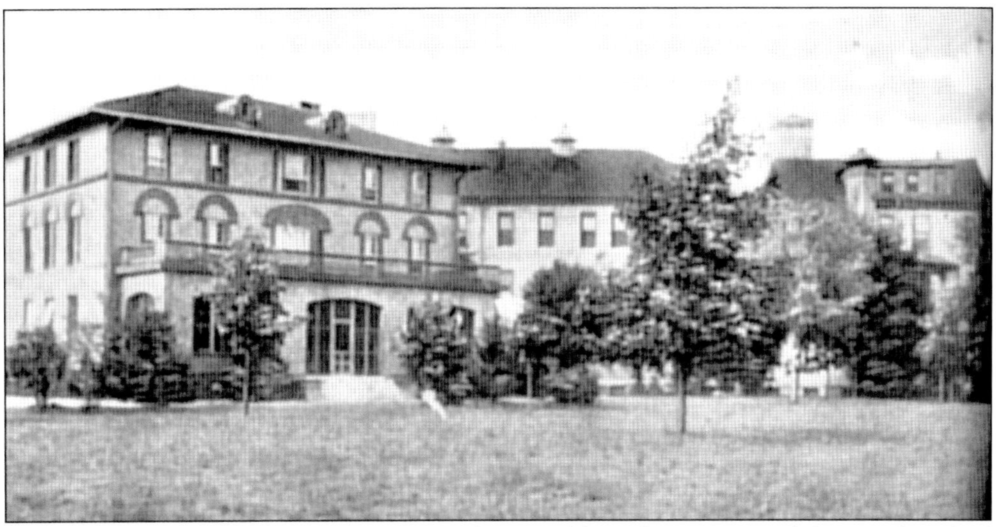

NURSING SCHOOL. In 1904, Peninsula General Hospital (PGH), now Peninsula Regional Medical Center, provided residences for nurses in its new Central Wing; the same year, a horse-drawn ambulance was donated. It wasn't until 1905 that the hospital opened its Training School for Nurses (later called the PGH School of Nursing) under the direction of Helen VanDevanter Wise. The first class graduated in 1908. (*A Heritage of Caring: Peninsula Regional Medical Center 1897–1997.*)

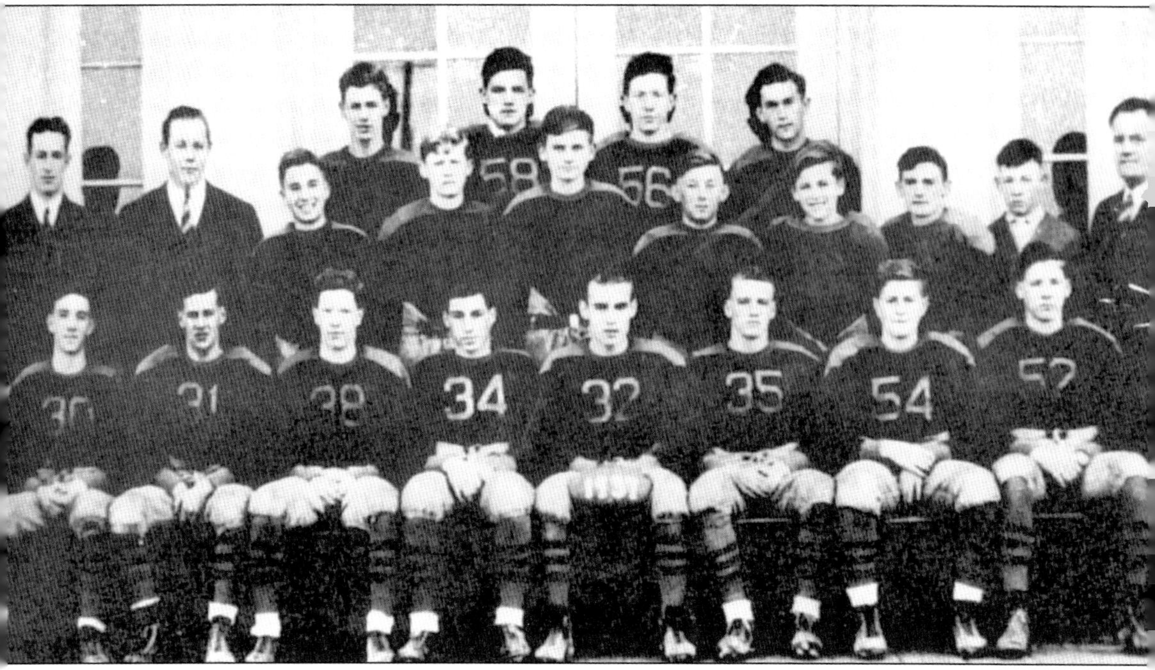

DELMAR TEAM. This is how the coaches dressed and style of the uniforms football players wore around 1937. Not all the players' names are known, but Coach Mitchell is at left in the second row wearing a suit and tie. At right in the second row is principal Harold Whiteside. The players' uniforms are not the heavy protection provided for today's athletes. (Courtesy of Walter Sullivan.)

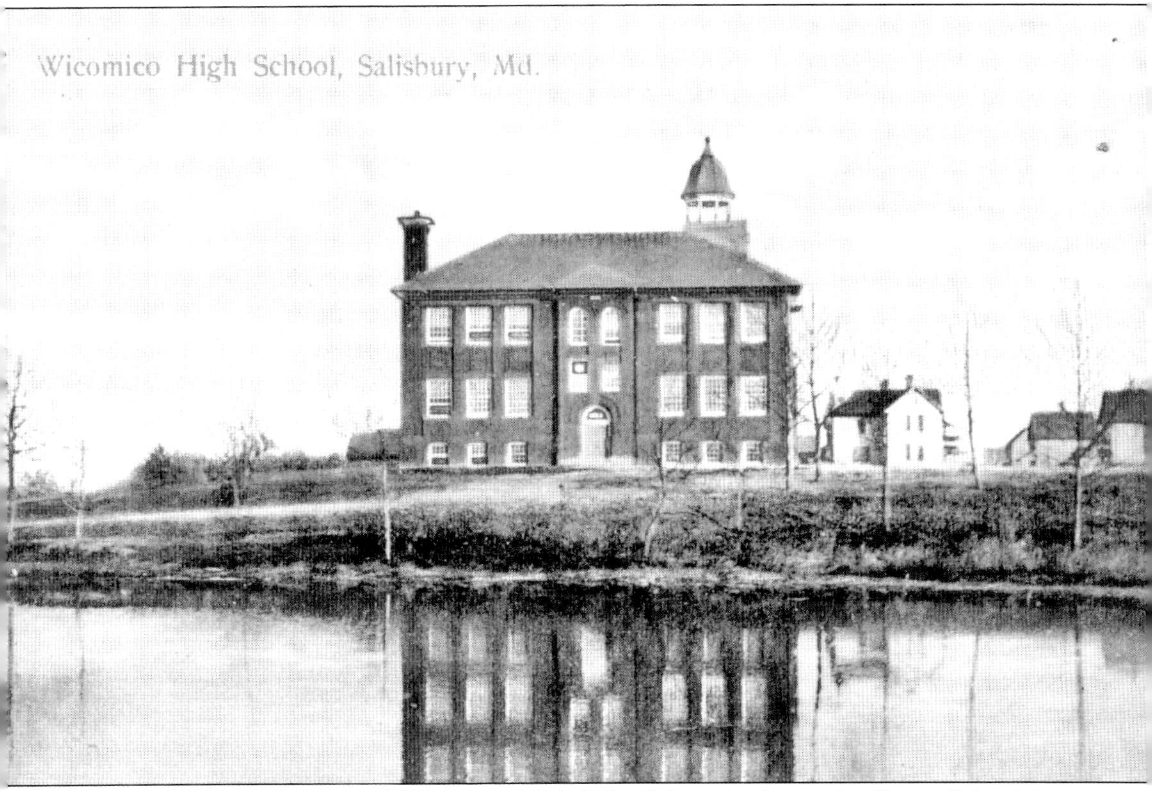

UPSCALE UPTON. The original Wicomico High School, known also as the Upton School, is shown from across Humphrey's Lake. It opened in September 1905 just before the Humphrey's Lake dam broke. Later razed for the next Wicomico High School, it was built across from the park. The *Daily Times* building now stands there. (Courtesy of George Chevallier.)

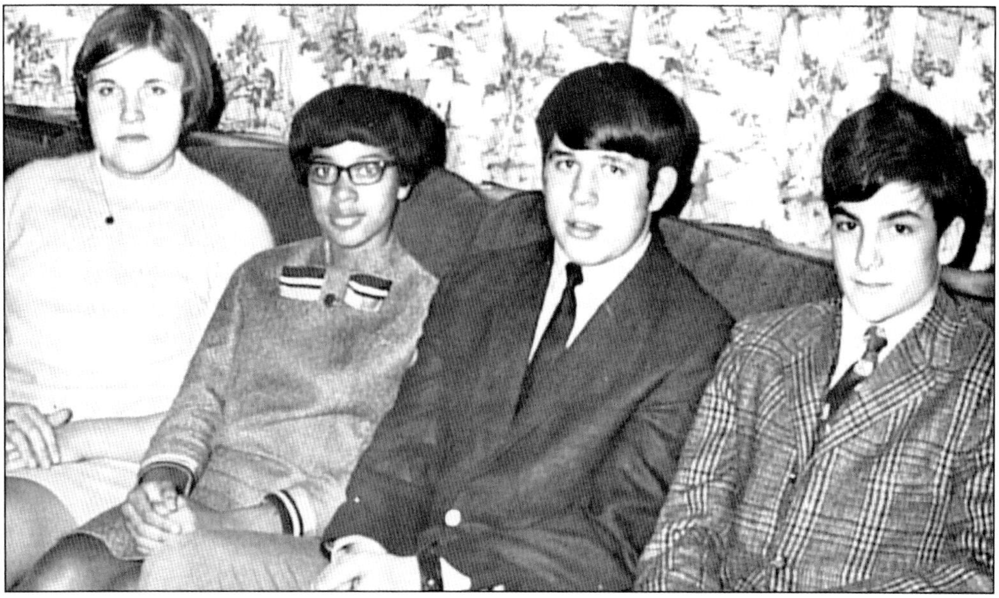

FIRST GRADUATING CLASS OFFICERS. Following on the heels of the first graduating class of Wicomico High School in 1969, this image shows the officers of the 1971 sophomore class. From left to right are Bonnie Lokey, treasurer; Debbie Teagle, secretary; Brian Austin, vice president; and Chip Veise, president. Notice the coats and ties on the guys. (Courtesy of Robert Culver; Wicomico High School Yearbook.)

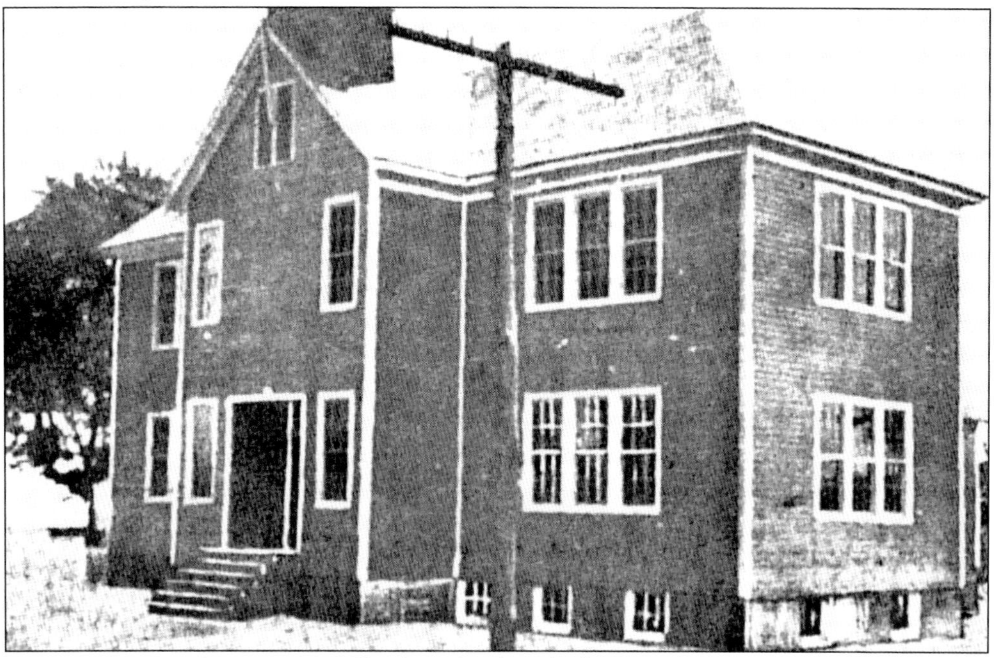

BEYOND THE 1936 SCHOOL. Pittsville's first school was built in 1836, serving as both the elementary and high school. A new school was built in 1930, enrolling over 280 students, containing nine classrooms and ancillary rooms and offices, and served only elementary and middle school children. The Pittsville community was named after railroad president Dr. H. R. Pitts, with an estimated population of 1,200. (Courtesy of the John E. Jacob Collection.)

Four

Foundations of the County

People and places make a city and its county what they are. Wicomico County has been fortunate to have such a high number of well-intentioned public servants, from politicians to the neighbors next door. Some are high-profiled entrepreneurs and/or philanthropists; others are just Jane and Joe from the mom-and-pop store down the corner, or they're teachers who aren't always showered with proper gratitude, or nurses who give long, loving hours, or the sheriff who risks his life day after day. There are too many to name, and too few who rightfully thank them. Some are risk-takers, others are shy, and still others give so often that we sometimes take them for granted. It is to these people and the many not named in this chapter that we take off our hats.

Though there are remnants around the county that remind us of the former tranquil, soft, sparsely populated area, there are more now than ever that tell us the county and its Salisbury metropolitan core is blossoming into a mini-Baltimore, where pavement seems to spread farther than farmlands, where corn and soy fields are now expensive subdivisions boasting two-story homes with pools and boats, where once-silent streets now effervesce with too many cars and the hustle and bustle of traffic. This chapter visits those idyllic days where railroad stations served as a hub, mills shared the rivers, canning factories provided continuous employment, and family-owned restaurants served the best food with the widest smiles while remembering every customer's name. Big-box stores were unheard of, and undeveloped land was inexpensive to buy. Those days are now long gone. But stored in the following pages are soothing and inspiring images to behold.

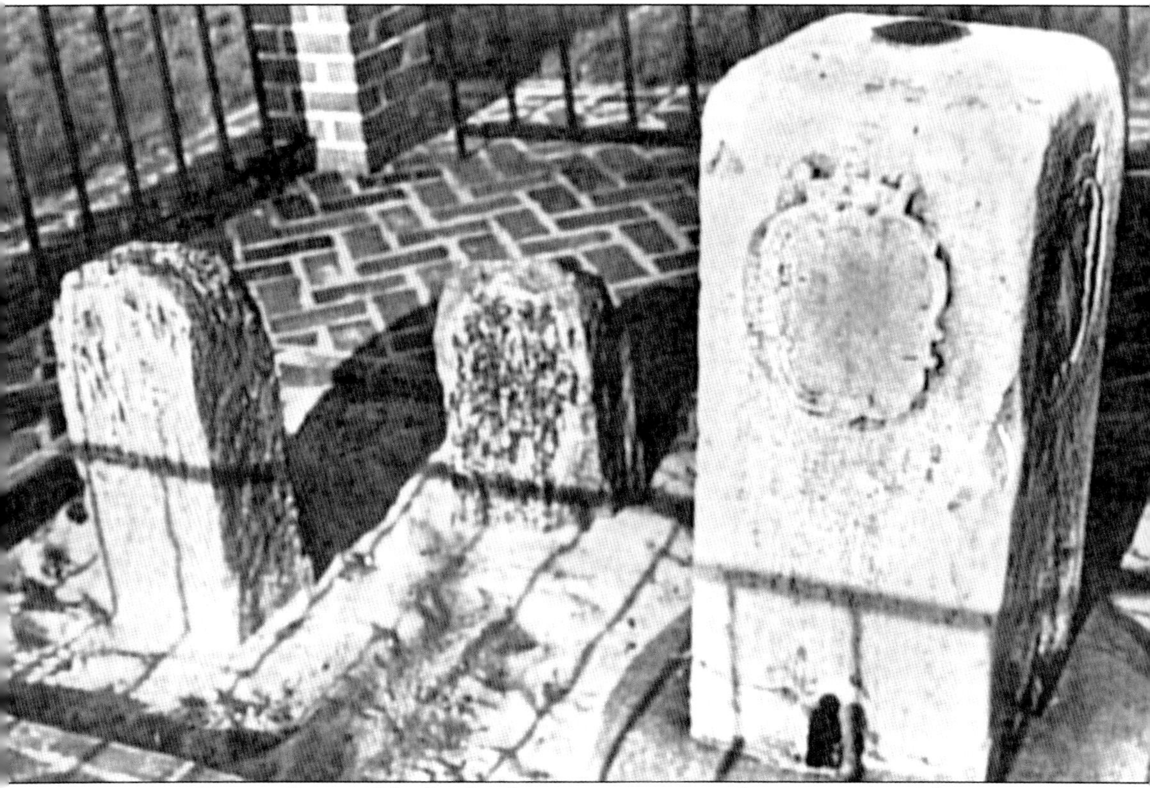

North Versus South. The borders between states were always a matter of dispute. In 1751, surveyors established the bottom of the Maryland-Delaware line. Starting at its westernmost point, near Mardela, the famous surveyors Mason and Dixon finished the boundaries between Maryland, Delaware, and Pennsylvania between 1763 and 1767. Today three stones mark the corner of the state line, each a replacement for worn and vandalized ones. The stone shows the coat of arms of the Calvert family and William Penn. (Courtesy of Salisbury Chamber of Commerce.)

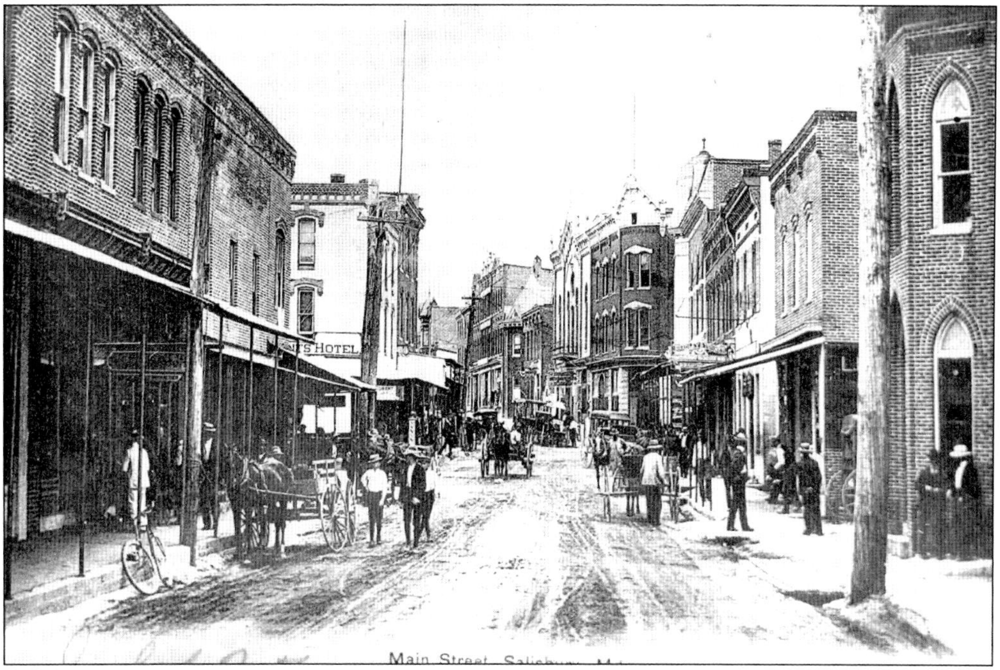

A NEW WIND BLOWS INTO SALISBURY. This photograph of downtown Salisbury is dated 1906 and shows the still-unpaved streets of the future "Hub of Delmarva." (Courtesy of Salisbury Chamber of Commerce.)

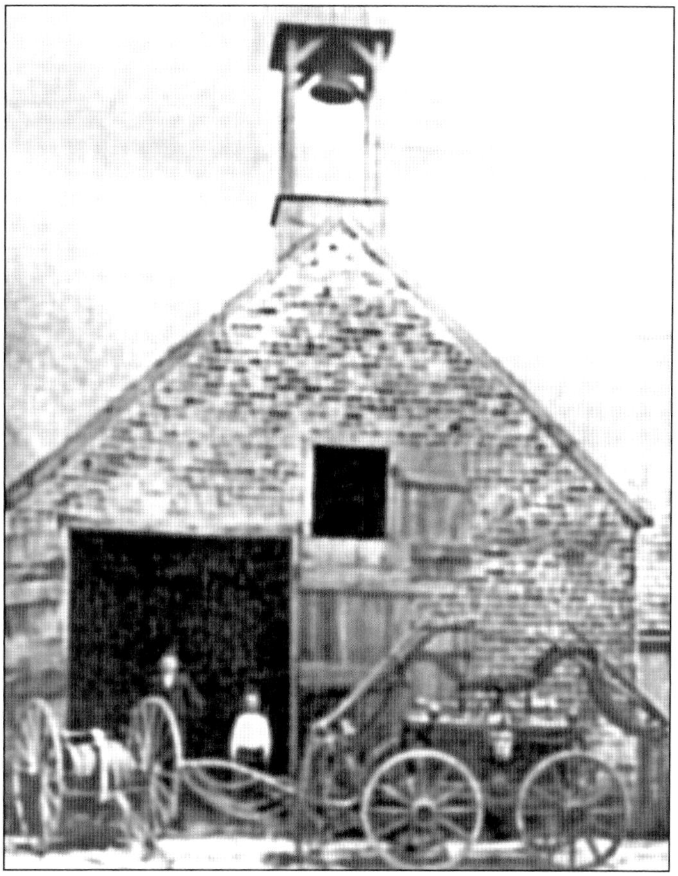

OLD STONE FIREHOUSE HEADQUARTERS. This is the original fire company building on Humphreys Pond. The fire department originated in 1872 as a result of a major fire in 1860, when flames spread through wooden buildings on Main and St. Peter's Streets. Local citizens suddenly became volunteer firefighters. The fire engine was burned, and the cost was estimated at $150,000. (*Our Anniversary: Salisbury Fire Department 1872–1972.*)

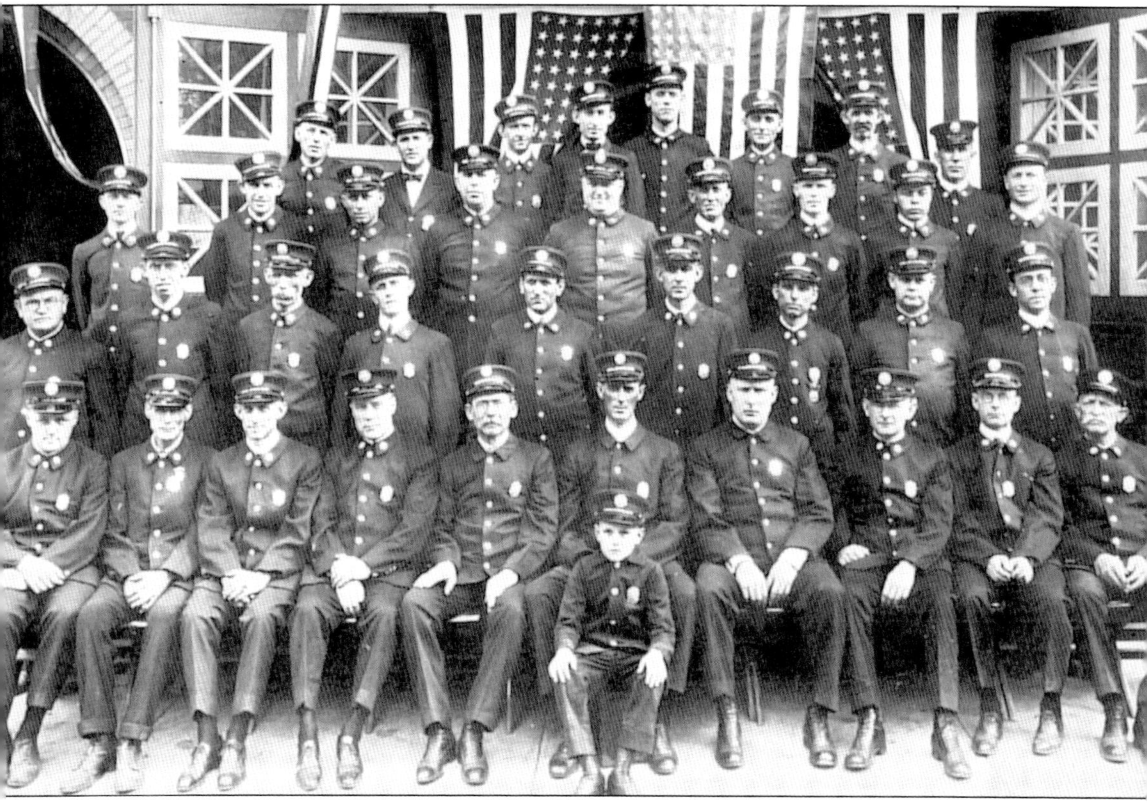

1922 FIREMEN. This shows how the firemen of Wicomico County dressed 85 years ago. They sat for the portrait to celebrate their 50th anniversary. Made up of predominantly volunteers, the company was moved into new headquarters on South Division Street in 1928. Two years later, another firehouse was built. At this time, fire prevention laws were enacted. Today Salisbury's fire department is 135 years old. (*Our Anniversary: Salisbury Fire Department 1872–1972.*)

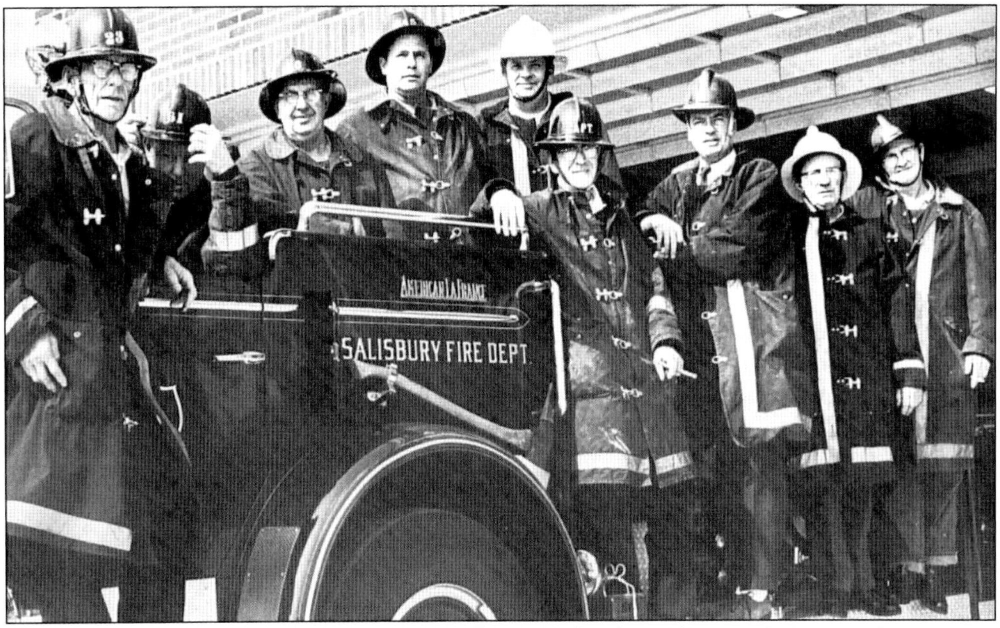

WILLIAMS FAMILY. All these men are from the same family, and in combination, they present a record 230 years of service. Based on the style of the truck and uniforms, this is a mid-1960s photograph. The men represent a span of ages, with the gentleman on the left, No. 23, apparently the oldest. The captain is in the middle holding something in his left hand. (*Our Anniversary: Salisbury Fire Department 1872–1972.*)

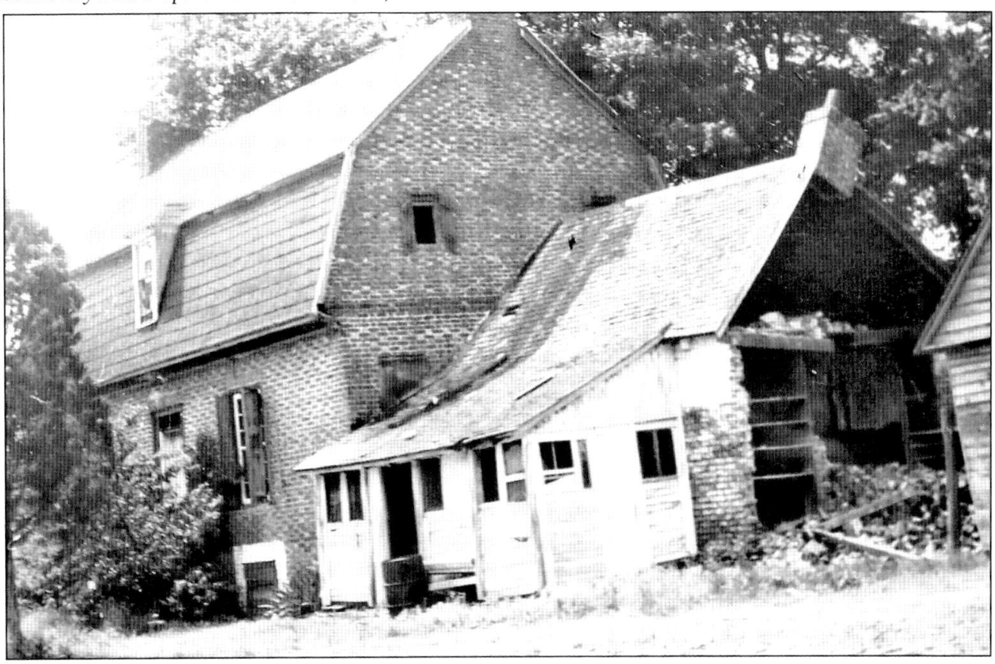

LORD OF THE MANOR HOUSES. This photograph shows Pemberton Hall in the 1960s before the Pemberton Hall Foundation purchased and restored this 1741 manor house. It was built by Col. Isaac Handy, an energetic individual of many skills and founder of Handy's Landing (later named Salisbury). (Courtesy of the Pemberton Hall Foundation, Inc.)

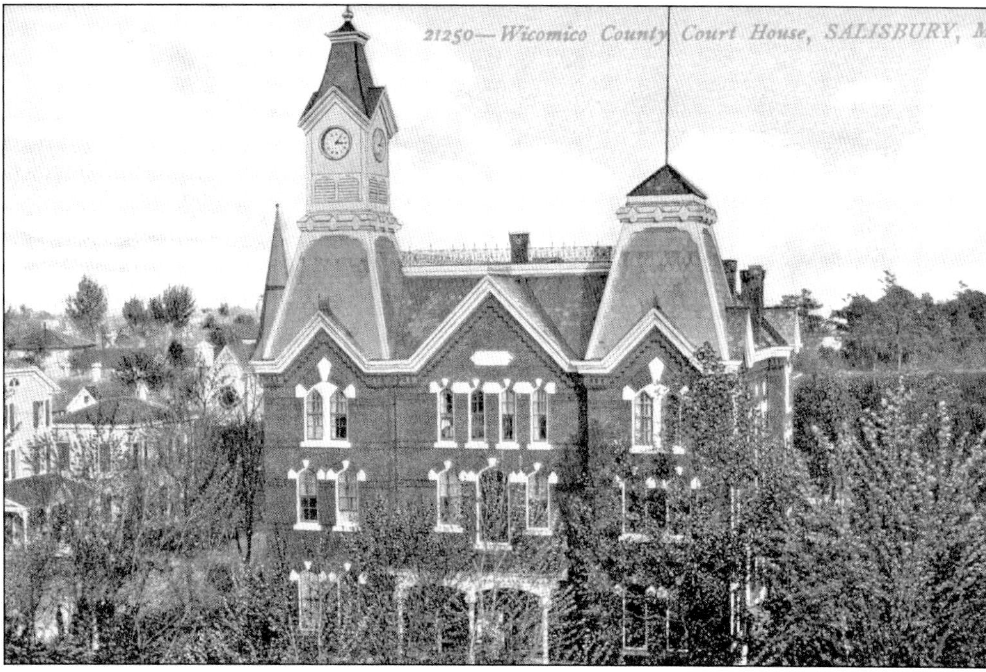

STILL HOLDING COURT. The current Wicomico County Court House was originally constructed in 1878, as seen in this 1911 photograph, and has been added to on several occasions. It is registered with the Maryland Historic Trust. (Courtesy of George Chevallier.)

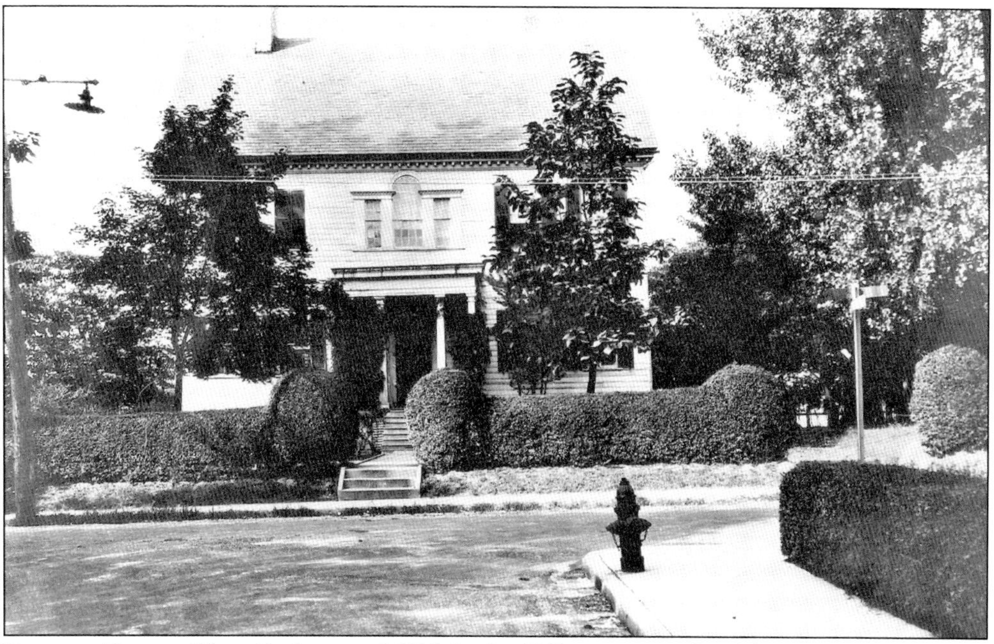

POPULAR POPLAR HILL. Built around 1795, Poplar Hill mansion is the oldest dwelling in the city limits of Salisbury. It was built by Maj. Levin Handy and is a large-frame, double-pile, Federal-type structure. Unfortunately, the major was unable to enjoy the house, because it had to be sold to pay his debts in an uncompleted state. Since 1974, it has been owned by the City of Salisbury as a historic museum. (Courtesy of Salisbury Chamber of Commerce.)

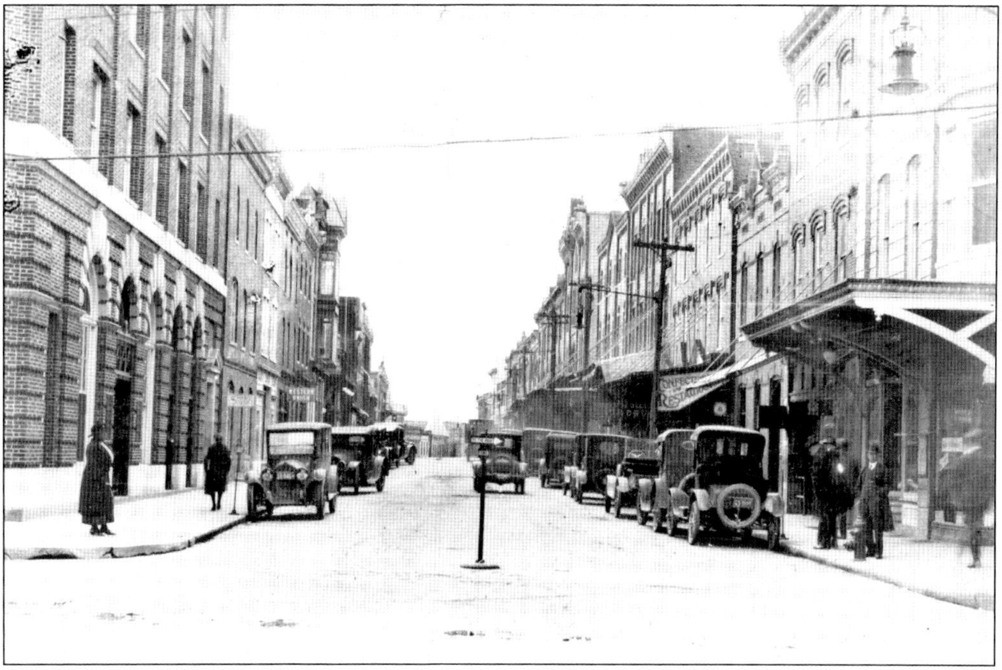

MACHINE AGE COMES TO SALISBURY. This 1923 shot of downtown shows that horse and buggies had been swept away by automobiles. The storefronts are still predominantly brick, something that would change in another 20 years after a series of fires. (Courtesy of George Chevallier.)

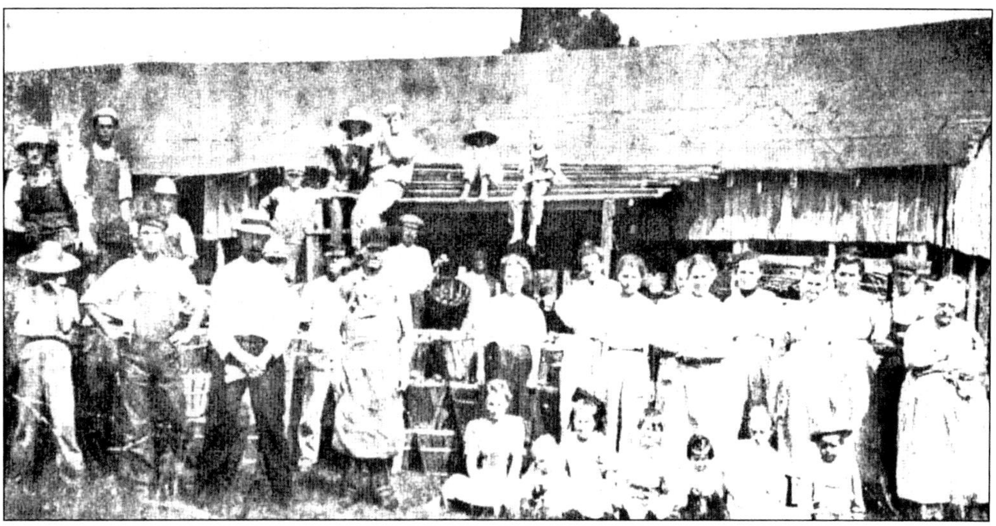

PACKING IT AWAY. Built on a human grave in Sharptown, this packing business was a result of three merged companies. The building burned in 1953 and wasn't rebuilt. It became a subsidiary of Atlas Plywood Company. This canning factory had 100 personnel. At one time, canning and packing were such major industries that every community in the county had at least one packing/canning factory—a total of over 33 in their heyday. (Courtesy of the Hilda Fowler Collection.)

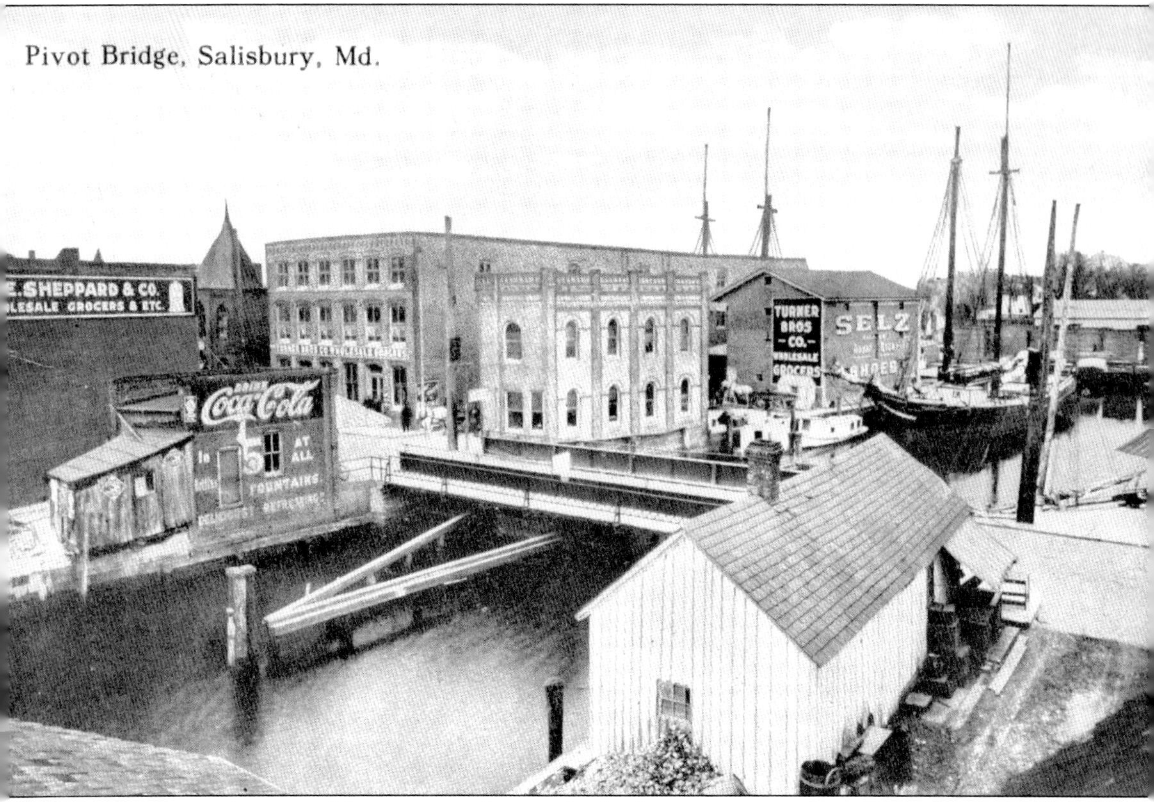

PIVOTING AROUND. Unique in its design, the bridge was too ingenious for its own good. The photographer was standing on the pivot branch, which would be below the foreground of the photograph, and snapping the scene. The pivot bridge moved sideways by a pair of tong-like arms. This is a *c.* 1905 postcard taken before the bridge was swept away in 1926 and had to be replaced with a lift bridge. (Courtesy of George Chevallier.)

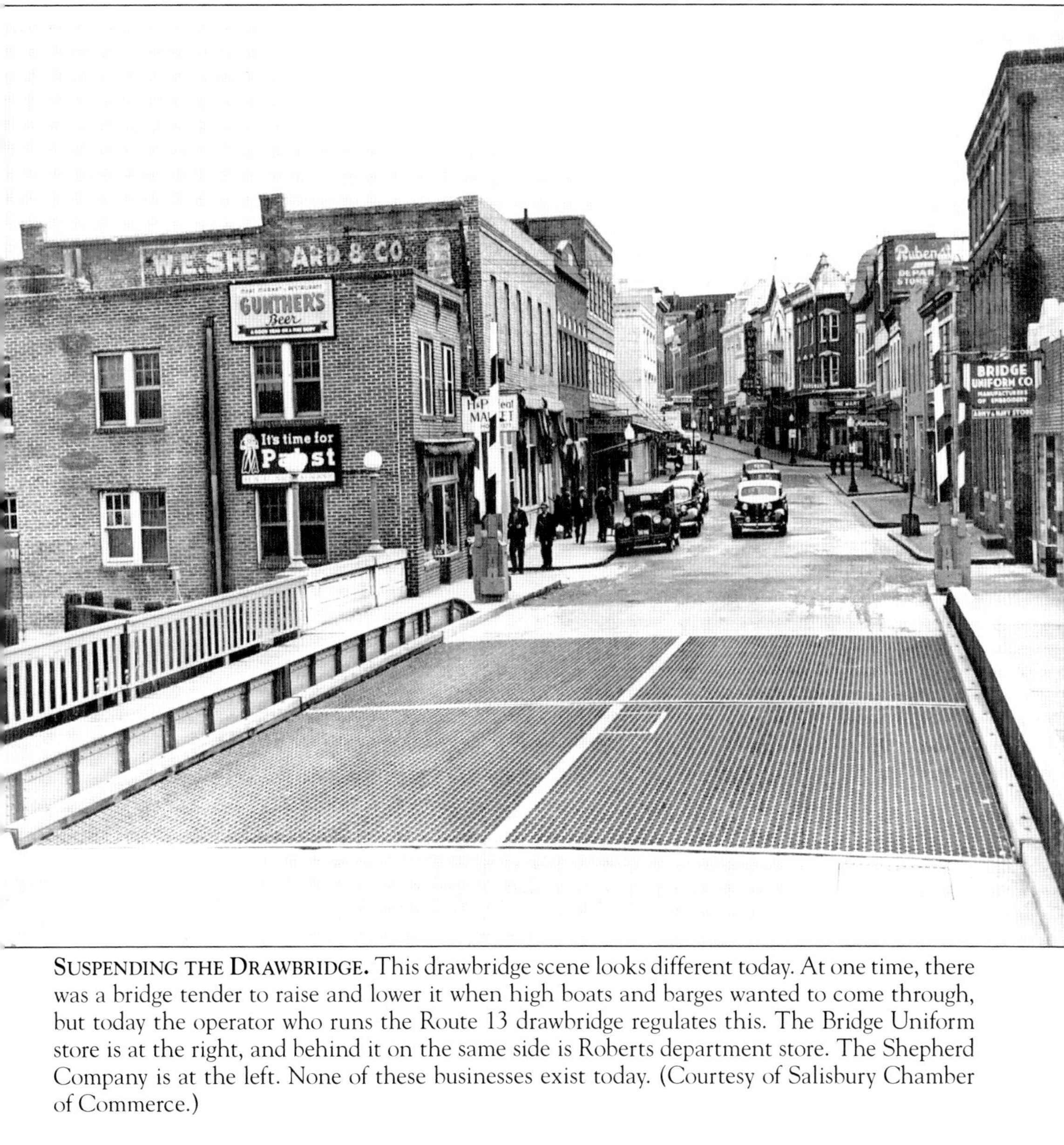

SUSPENDING THE DRAWBRIDGE. This drawbridge scene looks different today. At one time, there was a bridge tender to raise and lower it when high boats and barges wanted to come through, but today the operator who runs the Route 13 drawbridge regulates this. The Bridge Uniform store is at the right, and behind it on the same side is Roberts department store. The Shepherd Company is at the left. None of these businesses exist today. (Courtesy of Salisbury Chamber of Commerce.)

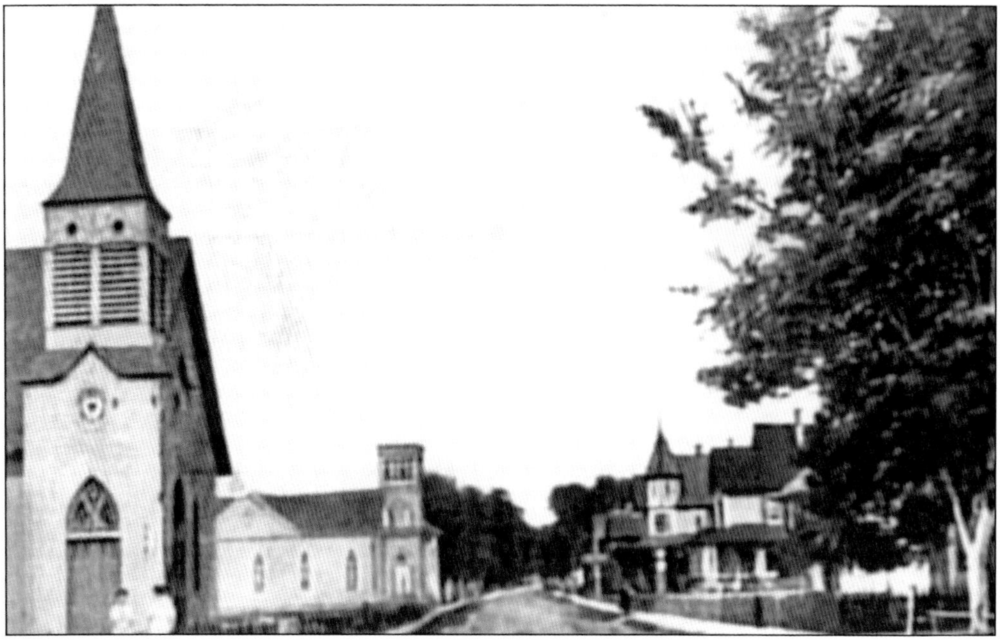

DIVIDING LINE DELMAR. Division Street splits Delmar into Maryland and Delaware. It features old homes, churches, and some businesses. The side of the street a telephone call is placed on determines if it is local or long distance. With Salisbury's growth, the little town is becoming part of the metropolitan core. This image shows the Methodist Episcopal and the Methodist Protestant churches. (Courtesy of the Frank Holloway Collection.)

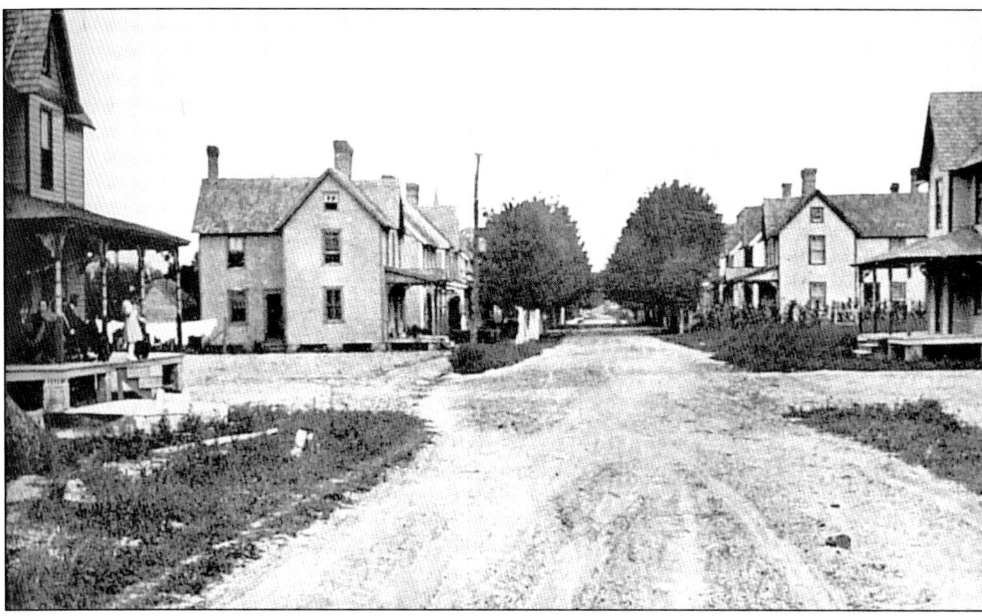

LITTLE HEBRON. Hebron is on the west side of Wicomico County, with a population of 807 in 2000. This sleepy town has been jolted awake by developers buying up land and building homes on the once-pristine farmlands. This image reflects the town from the angle of West Church Street, showing residences of then-longtime families. The road is not paved, but in the background, stately pear trees line the street. (Courtesy of the John E. Jacob Collection.)

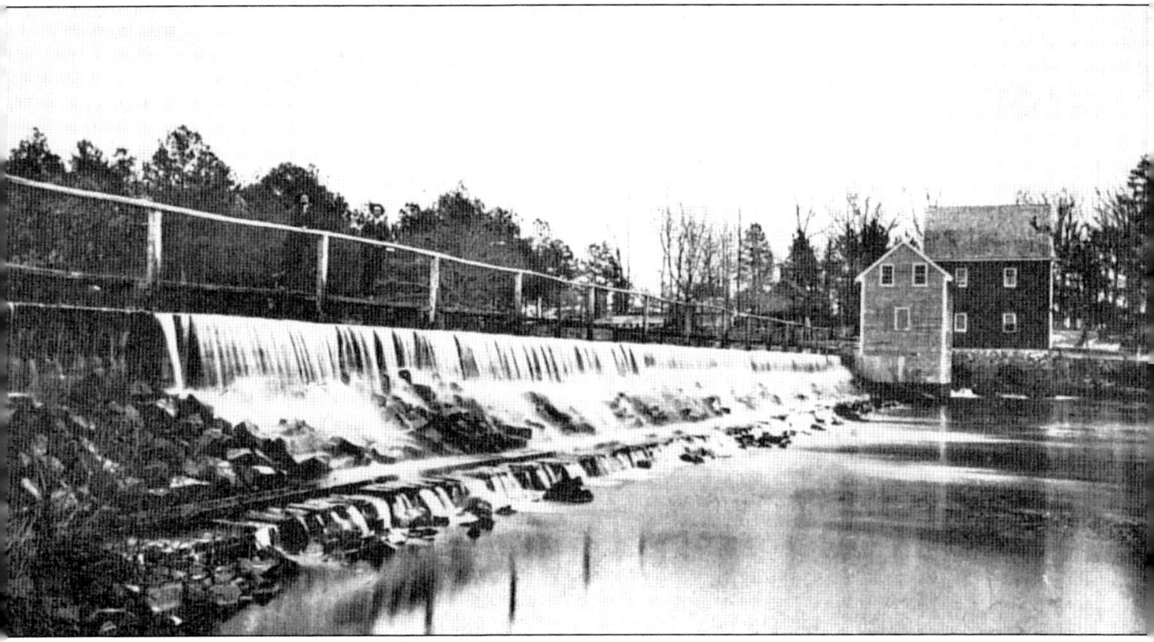

TUMBLIN' DOWN. There are two walkways in this old photograph of Wicomico Falls. It appears to have been taken near the park around Division Street. One walkway is above the dam with a handrail; this was for people. The other ran along side the bottom of the dam and was for horse and buggies. At the far end is some type of mill. (Courtesy of the John E. Jacob Collection.)

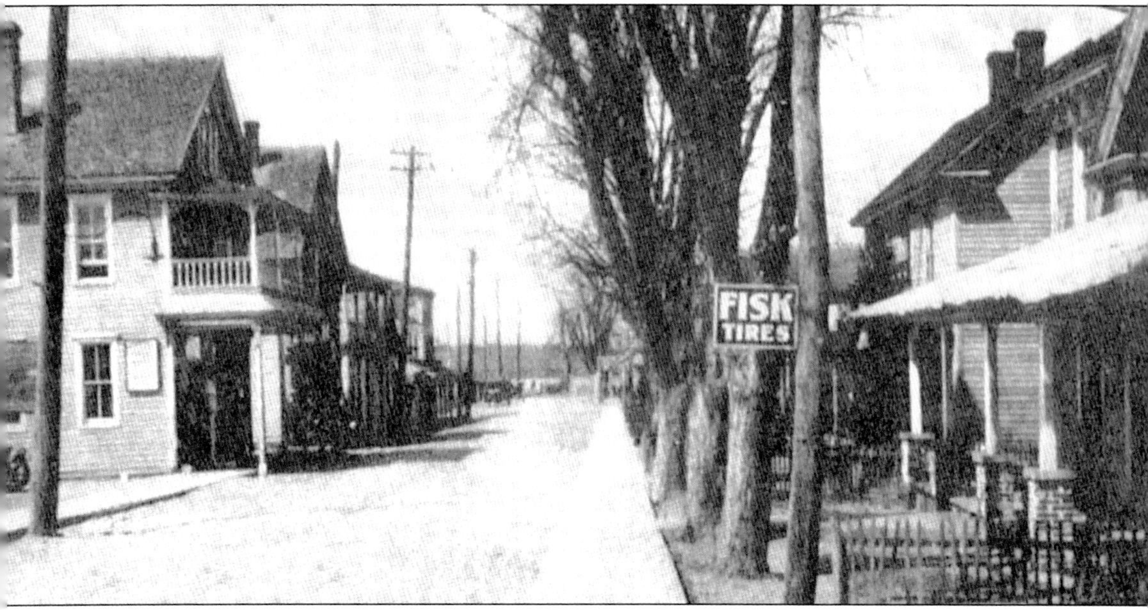

STROLLING SHARPTOWN'S MAIN STREET. The Fisk Tires sign jumps out in the image because it appears to be the only business on the street, though other stores did line this Main Street, such as the drugstore on the left and a gas station on the right. The Nanticoke River is in the background. It's difficult to date this photograph, but it is reminiscent of the 1940s. (Courtesy of the John E. Jacob Collection.)

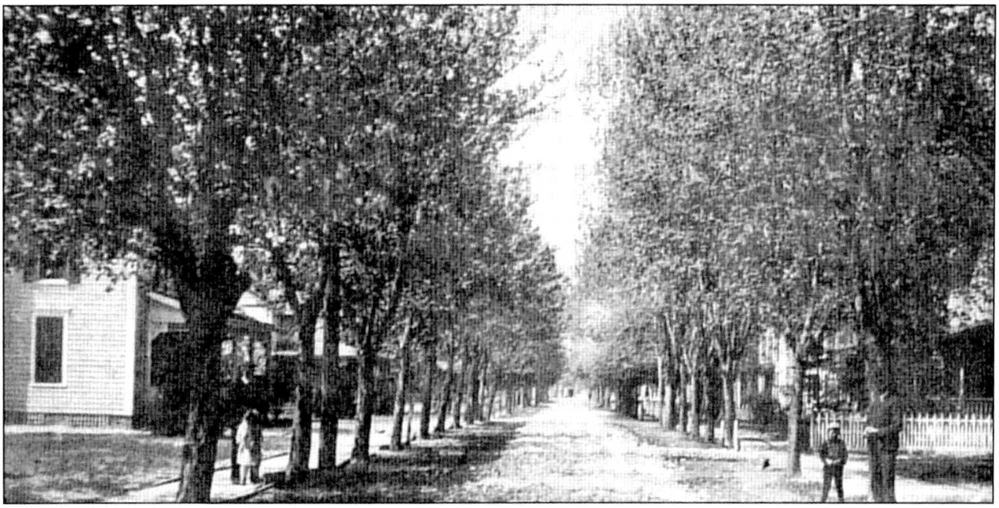

MARDELA: MARYLAND, DELAWARE. Though quaint looking in this image, the trees and picket fence no longer exist. Two figures are standing on each side of the street. Transportation to this town was by train back in the early 1900s. Mardela remains charming, but extensive growth in the county is bringing it to the foreground as a quiet, rural place to live where everybody knows everybody. (Courtesy of James Jackson.)

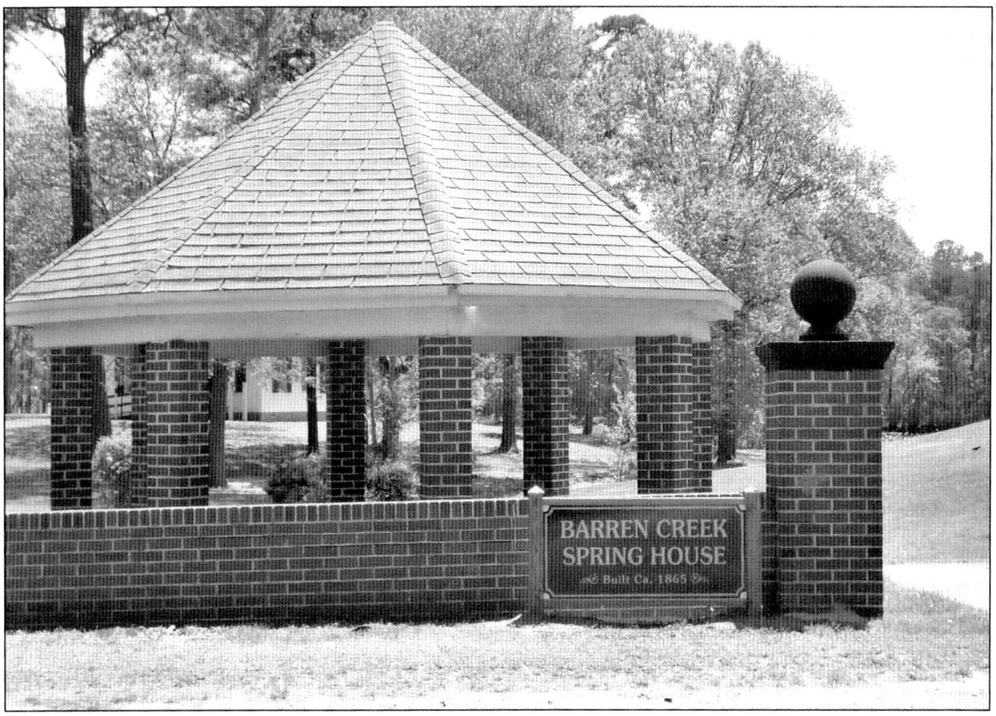

BARREN, BUT NOT WITHOUT CHARM. Nearby on a hill stands a stately brick mansion where a hotel once overlooked the natural springs that flowed from Barren Creek. Water still flows through a pipe in the spring house today and was considered to have curative powers. People came from far and wide to drink and bathe in the supposedly miraculous liquid, including such notables as future-president William Henry Harrison. Today it stands as a reminder of simpler times, when purity was seen as a cure for many ills. (Courtesy of Sylvia Bradley.)

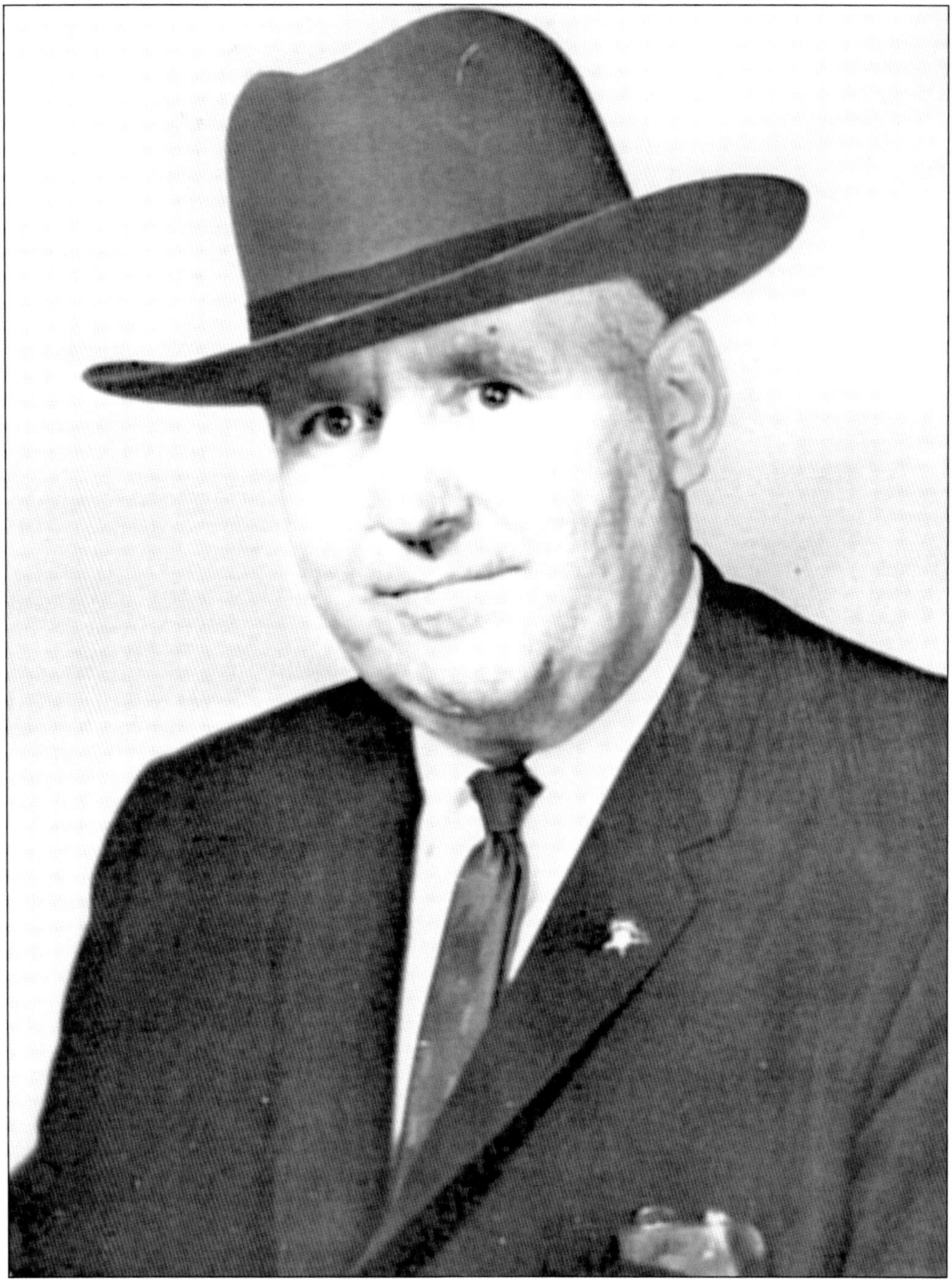

WHO SHOT THE SHERIFF? On December 8, 1968, Deputy Albert Kelley was killed after an inmate—who had a gun smuggled into his cell hidden in a box of candy—forced him to open all cell doors. Sheriff Samuel A. Graham, who resided in a jail apartment, was fatally shot when he went to investigate. His watch ended after 11 years of service to Wicomico County and contributed to a double tragedy in one night. (Courtesy of Wicomico High School yearbook.)

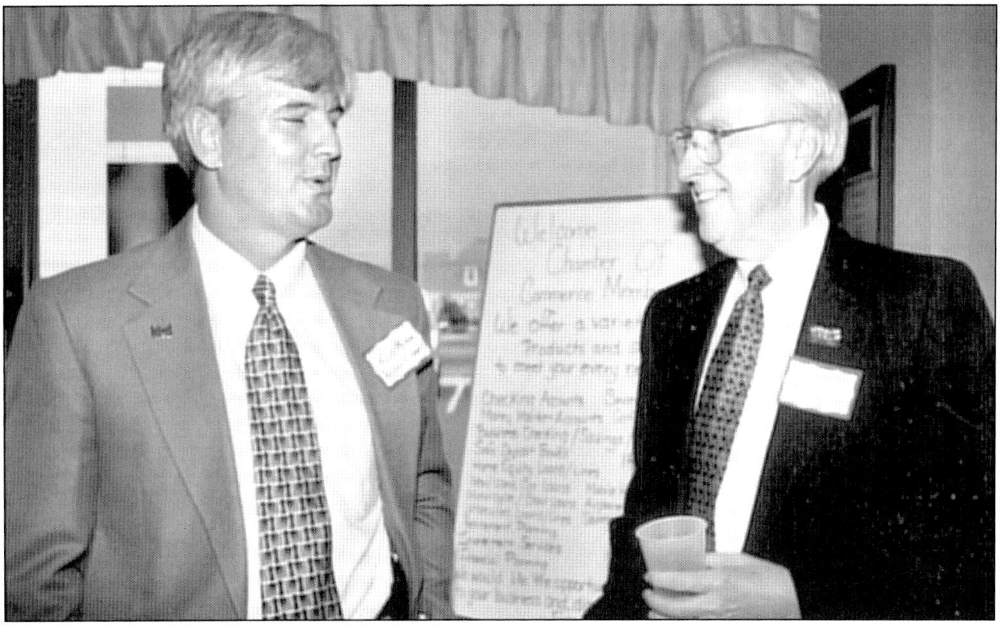

LAYING FOUNDATIONS. "Rusty" Molnar, former county councilman, discusses a chamber of commerce topic at a major chamber event with longtime Wicomico County public schools superintendent William Middleton, who gave 40 years of service to the school system before he retired in 2002. Through his guidance, the county schools advanced in all areas. (Courtesy of Salisbury Chamber of Commerce.)

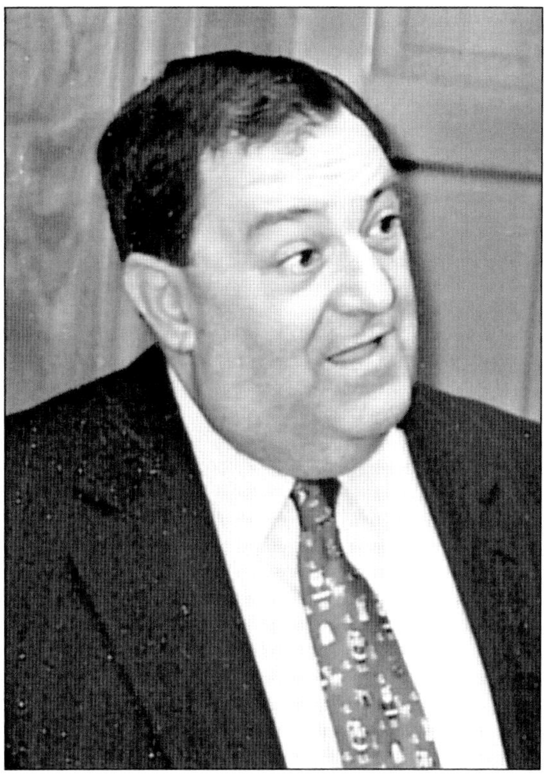

PUBLIC FIGURE NO. 1. Norman Conway has served in the public sector since the mid-1960s as a teacher and administrator. In January 1987, he was elected as a member of the Maryland House of Delegates from District 38 (Wicomico and Worcester Counties) and remains in that capacity in 2007. He is a recipient of many awards and serves on various state committees. He is a familiar and friendly face to the area. (Courtesy of Salisbury Chamber of Commerce.)

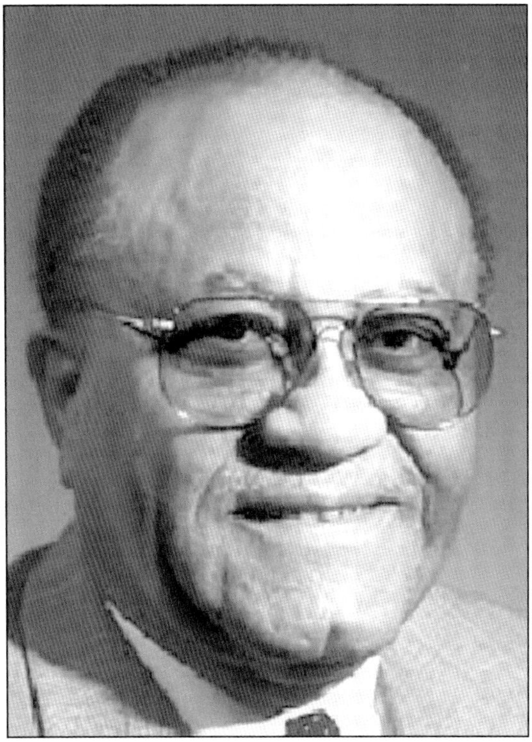

He Has a Dream. Respected by many and born in Marion, Maryland, of May 23, 1934, Delegate Rudolph C. Cane makes himself available to help all in Wicomico and Dorchester Counties and works at consolidating differences among others. He has served in the Maryland House of Delegates since 1999 and serves on various task forces and committees. He resides in Wicomico County with his wife and is the father of two. (Photograph by Delegate Cane's office.)

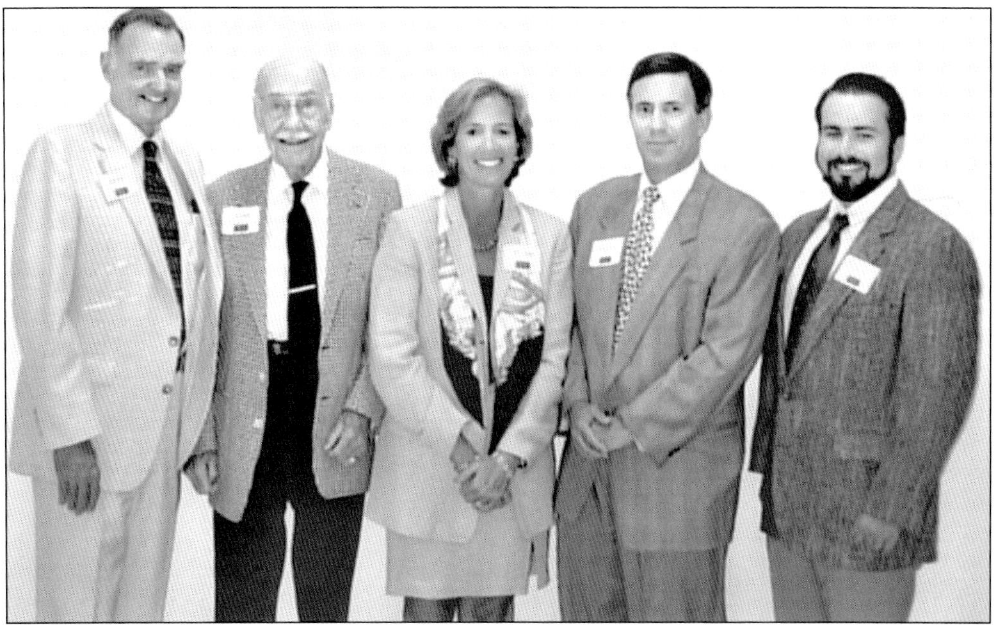

The Influentials. These five influential people are, from left to right, Dr. Arnold Maner, president emeritus of Wor-Wic College; the late Richard Henson, a philanthropist and founder of Henson/US Airlines; Cathy Guerrieri and her brother Michael, who are major philanthropists, especially to educational institutions; and Morgan Hazel, former owner of the Pepsi bottling plant in Salisbury. He and his family are key benefactors in the county as well. (Courtesy of Salisbury Chamber of Commerce.)

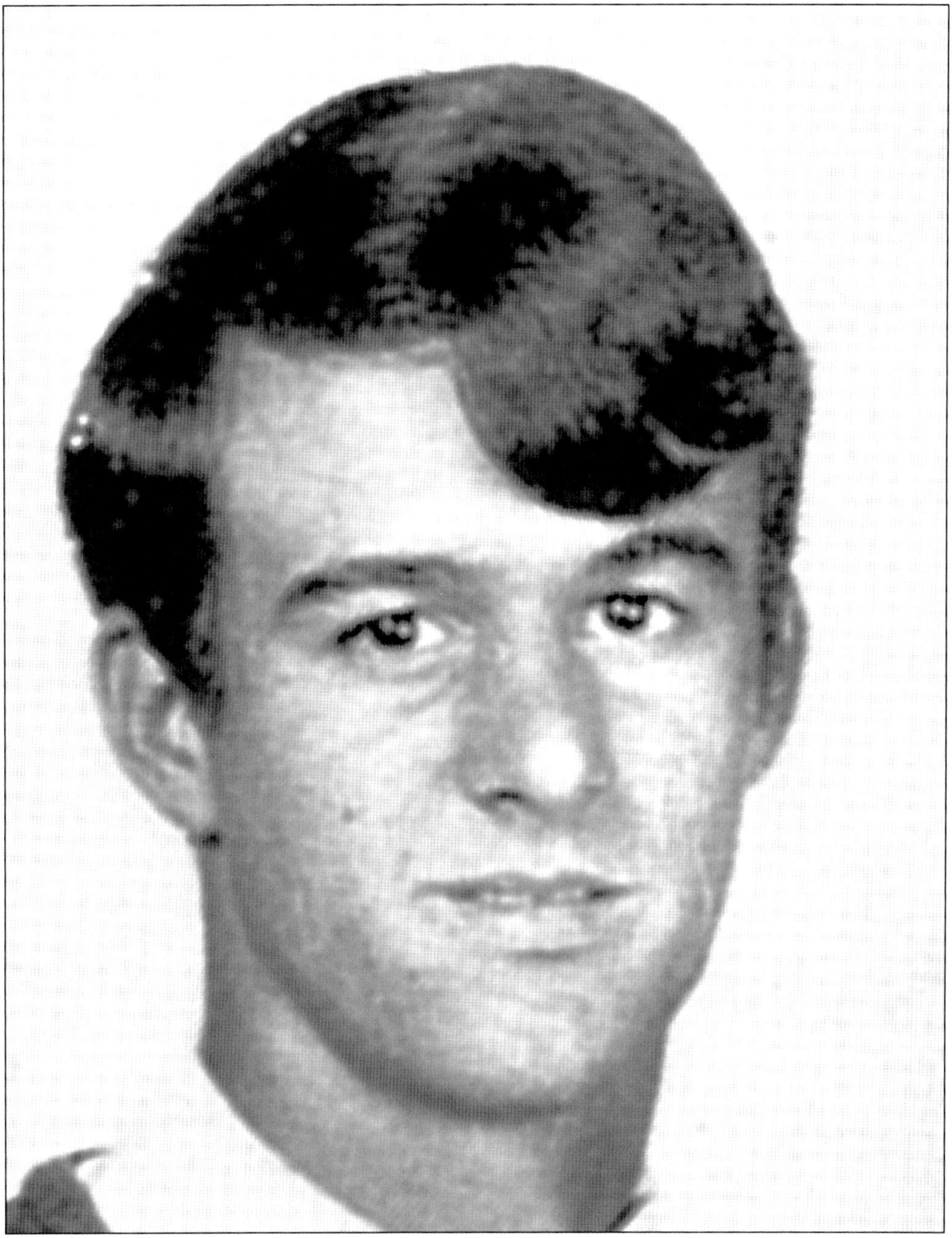

CUTTING-EDGE CULVER. The Culvers' roots go back to 1856, and over the generations, they have become a prominent family in the area, with many of them serving in the construction industry. Because of this, they have left their footprints all through the county in the many buildings and developments they have created. Bob Culver, pictured, is an innovative real estate developer, having built many projects when others shied away. This is a 1969 photograph from the *Tom Tom* yearbook. (Courtesy of Wicomico High School yearbook.)

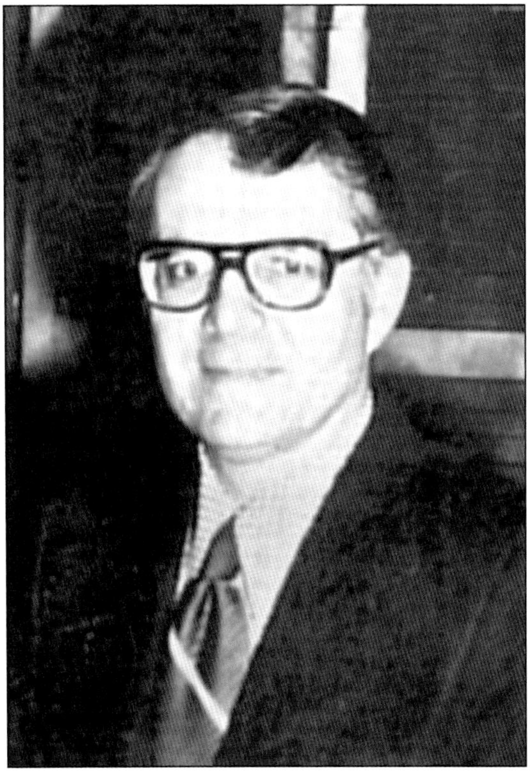

WORKING TEAM. Though popular and locally famous Jack Purnell has passed away, his wife, Anna, thrives knowing that the Kuhn's Jewelry store has been handed over to their daughter Susan Purnell, who runs the operation professionally and smoothly. Susan has gone on beyond college to earn her certification in specialties in gemology. Kuhn is the sixth-oldest fine-jewelry store in the nation and is nationally known as well. (Courtesy of the Susan Purnell archives.)

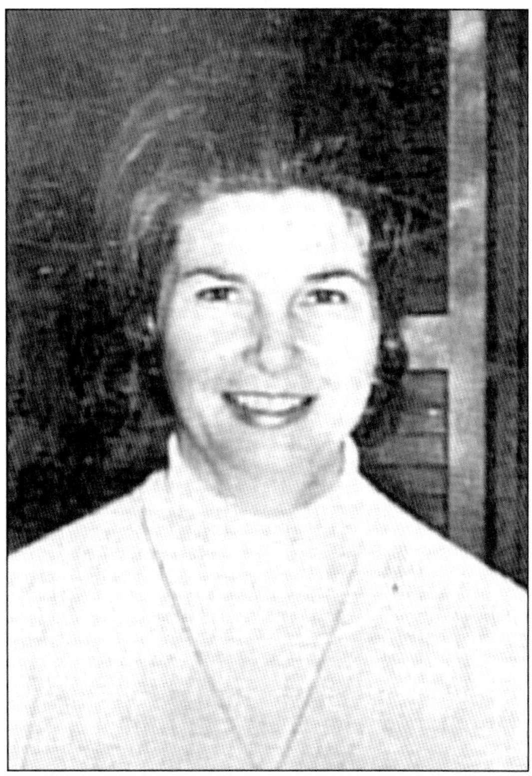

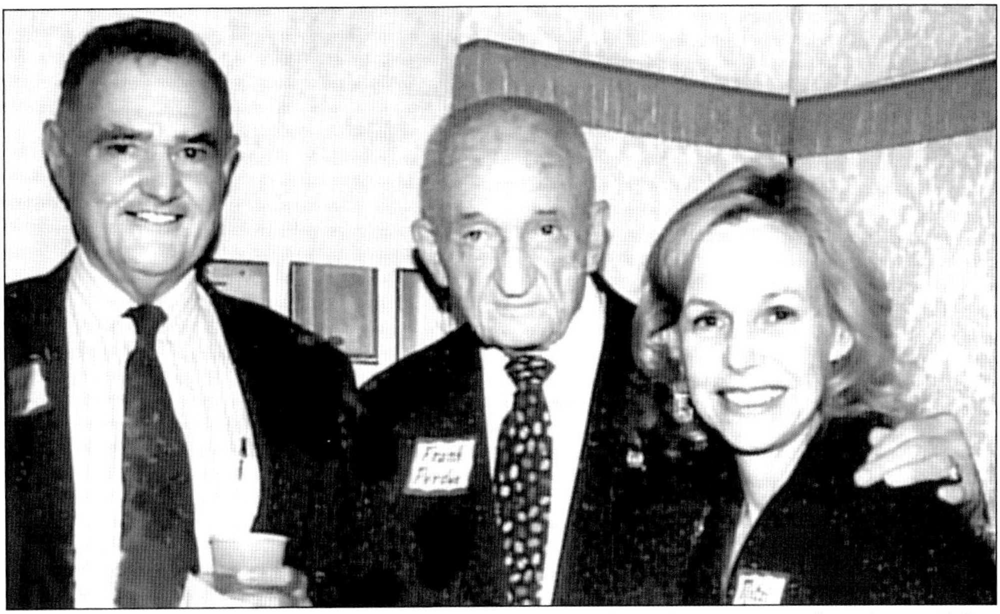

Three Bigwigs. Dr. Arnold Maner (left) served as president of Wor-Wic College from 1975 to 2000. Frank (center) and Mitzi Perdue owned Perdue Farms, which is now run by Frank's son Jim. Frank has passed away, but the family-owned poultry industry has spread nationally and internationally. Mitzi is known for her handcrafted Fabergé eggs ("Eggscapes") and for founding Healthy U—an organization promoting good health in personal and professional environments. (Courtesy of Salisbury Chamber of Commerce.)

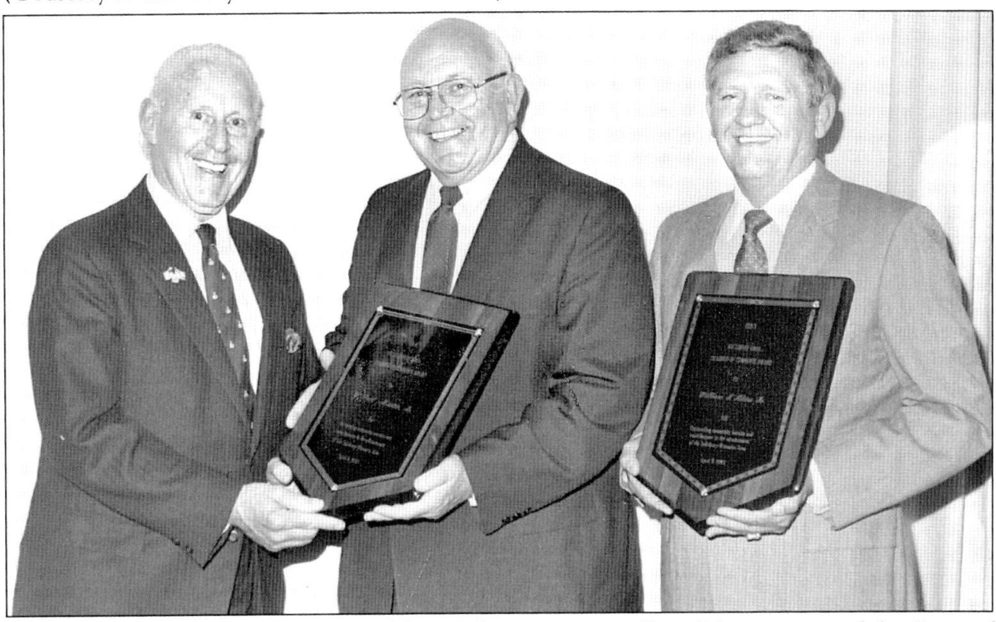

Big Men. At left, the late Louis Goldstein, former comptroller of the treasury of the State of Maryland from 1959 to 1998, hands the late Salisbury mayor W. Paul Martin (center) and real estate developer William Ahtes the Salisbury Chamber of Commerce award for their unending years of service. Mayor Martin served Salisbury from 1982 through 1998. (Courtesy of Salisbury Chamber of Commerce.)

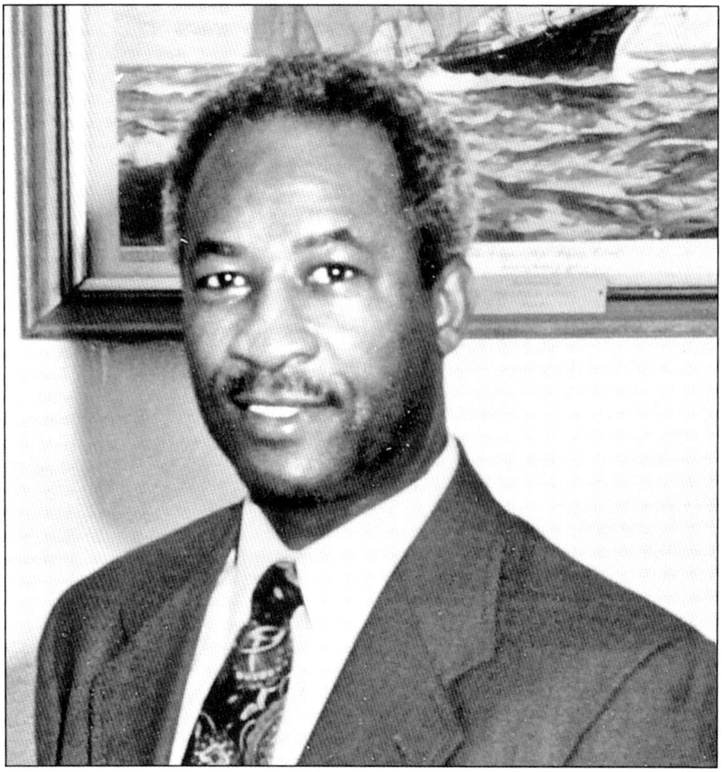

PRINCIPLED PRINCIPAL. Daniel J. Savoy was a familiar figure walking along not only the halls of Bennett Middle School but also the sidewalks, watching over students boarding school buses for home at dismissal. After a long service in the classroom and behind the principal's desk, Savoy moved on to serving on the Wicomico Board of Education. His many former students look fondly upon him. (Courtesy of Salisbury Chamber of Commerce.)

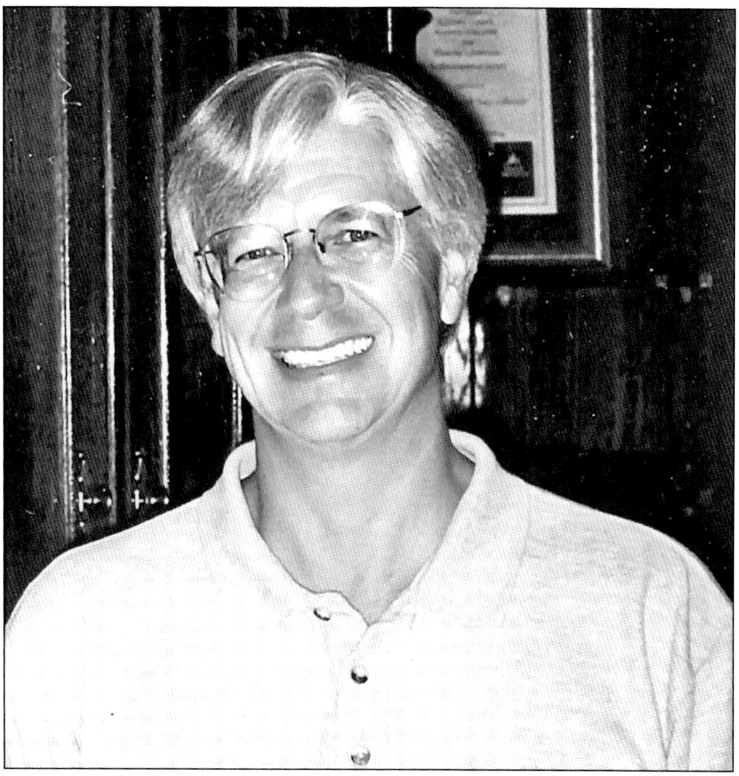

WICOMICO IN PALMER'S PALMS. A well-known figure in the county and throughout the region, Palmer Gillis starred as a councilman, developer, and visionary who has managed to almost single-handedly renovate much of downtown Salisbury with his partner Gillis Gilkerson, Inc. They concentrated on turning the former Woolworth's building on the downtown plaza into an office complex with an investment of $2.2 million. (Courtesy of the Palmer Gillis collection.)

Five

County Cornerstones

Calvin Coolidge said that the business of America was business. This also became the mantra for Wicomico County. Founded as a landing for ships to carry on trade, the wharves along the Wicomico soon found themselves ringed by warehouses and then the supporting businesses that complemented such industry. Doctors, lawyers, and even Native American chiefs were joined by stores and shops offering a variety of goods and services. Fires destroyed them in turn in 1860 and 1886, but the business owners of Wicomico County and Salisbury were undeterred. Salisbury, as the center axle in the wheel of Wicomico commerce, boasted chain stores like Woolworth, Montgomery Ward, Sears, and others, but they competed with local entrepreneurs like Hess, Benjamin, Kuhn, Powell, and many more. Main Street in Salisbury bustled with shoppers during Christmas season, and buildings went from wood to brick to granite and marble to show the town's prosperity.

Then came downtown's doom. In 1968, the Salisbury Mall opened, drawing name-brand stores from the downtown area to its central location; the downtown area died a slow death that continues today, and the once gaily decorated storefronts are now full of banks, lawyers, and restaurants. The Salisbury Mall, in its turn, was eclipsed by the rise of big-box stores like K-Mart and Wal-Mart and its own bigger brother, the Centre at Salisbury. Building in every direction has caused Salisbury to lose much of its rustic charm, and now its corridors are filled with the staple businesses of any average American city. While the goods and services offered are the equal of any other area, some of the nostalgic thrill of shopping in the centuries-old downtown area is gone, perhaps for good.

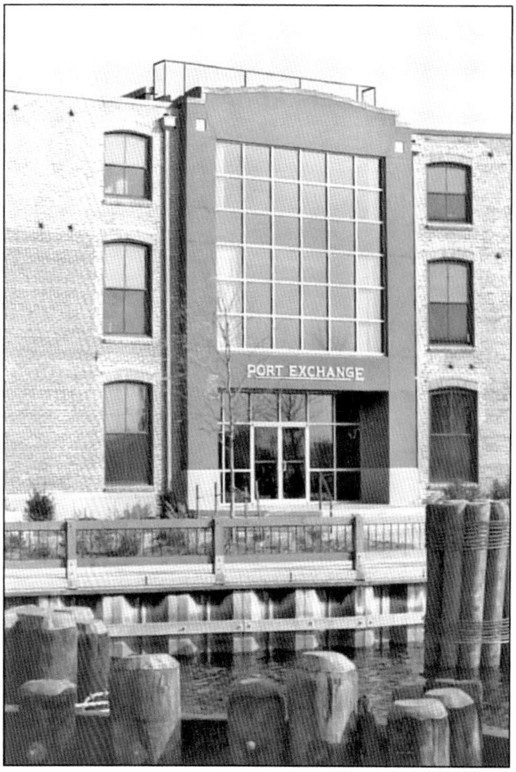

PORT EXCHANGE. This building dates back to the Civil War, when it was two distinct buildings, and soldiers would arrive in Salisbury—some by boat on the Wicomico River—and enter the building for stay and munitions. In the early 1990s, the Becker Morgan Group architects purchased the buildings, totally renovated them, restructured and reinforced them, connected them, and turned the structure into an office center with long windows highlighting the flowing river and its traffic. It sits at the corner of Main and Mill Streets with one entrance opening on the side of the suspension/ old pivot bridge. (Courtesy of Salisbury Chamber of Commerce.)

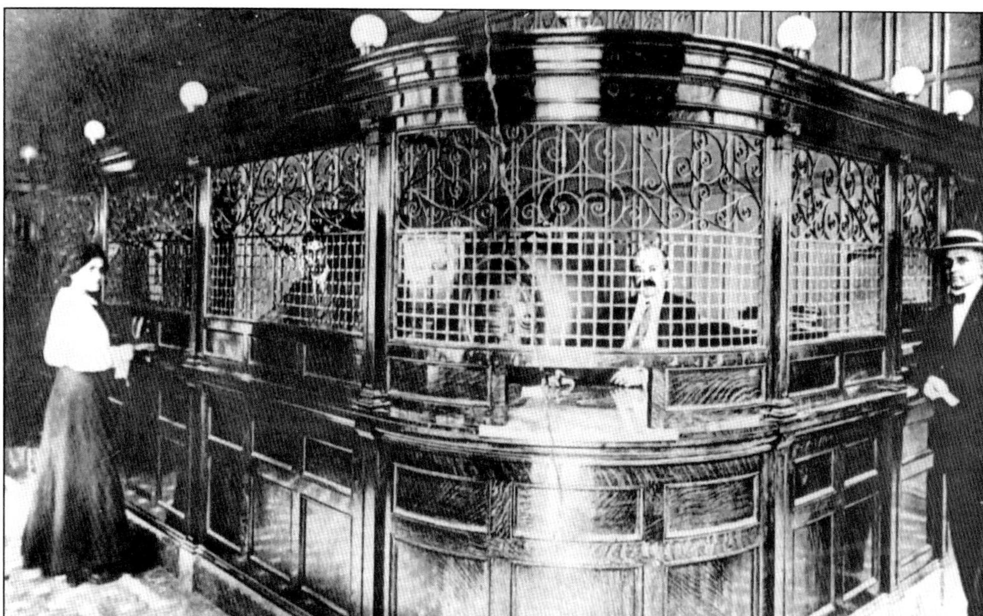

IN PENINSULA WE TRUST. Likely an early-1900s image based on the type of attire, this bank was popular during its glory days and used by many Wicomico County residents. It was located in downtown Salisbury and boasted a capital of $100,000 and a surplus of $10,000. Notice the cage around the tellers. The balloons may indicate opening day. (Courtesy of the Palmer Gillis collection.)

SALES RECEIPT. This 1921 bill of sale confirms the purchase of the building and all its fixtures by John A. Kuhn for $6,000 from Guy Fisher to open a jewelry store that became the sixth-oldest fine-jewelry store in the nation. John Kuhn's daughter, Anne, inherited the business, which was then run by her husband, John Purnell. Their daughter, Susan Purnell, now runs it. (Courtesy of the Susan Purnell archives.)

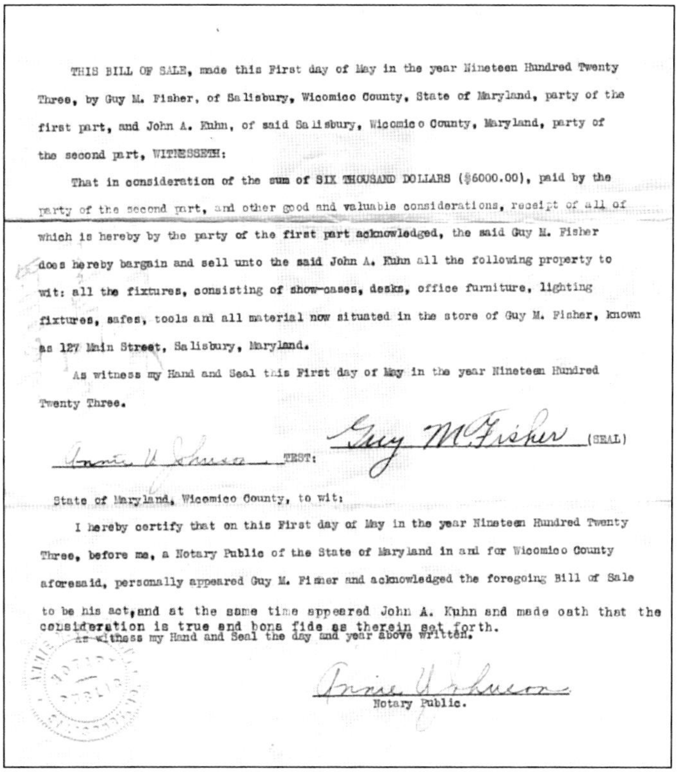

THIS BILL OF SALE, made this First day of May in the year Nineteen Hundred Twenty Three, by Guy M. Fisher, of Salisbury, Wicomico County, State of Maryland, party of the first part, and John A. Kuhn, of said Salisbury, Wicomico County, Maryland, party of the second part, WITNESSETH:

That in consideration of the sum of SIX THOUSAND DOLLARS ($6000.00), paid by the party of the second part, and other good and valuable considerations, receipt of all of which is hereby by the party of the first part acknowledged, the said Guy M. Fisher does hereby bargain and sell unto the said John A. Kuhn all the following property to wit: all the fixtures, consisting of show-cases, desks, office furniture, lighting fixtures, safes, tools and all material now situated in the store of Guy M. Fisher, known as 127 Main Street, Salisbury, Maryland.

As witness my Hand and Seal this First day of May in the year Nineteen Hundred Twenty Three.

Guy M. Fisher (SEAL)

TEST:

State of Maryland, Wicomico County, to wit:

I hereby certify that on this First day of May in the year Nineteen Hundred Twenty Three, before me, a Notary Public of the State of Maryland in and for Wicomico County aforesaid, personally appeared Guy M. Fisher and acknowledged the foregoing Bill of Sale to be his act, and at the same time appeared John A. Kuhn and made oath that the consideration is true and bona fide as therein set forth.

As witness my Hand and Seal the day and year above written.

Notary Public.

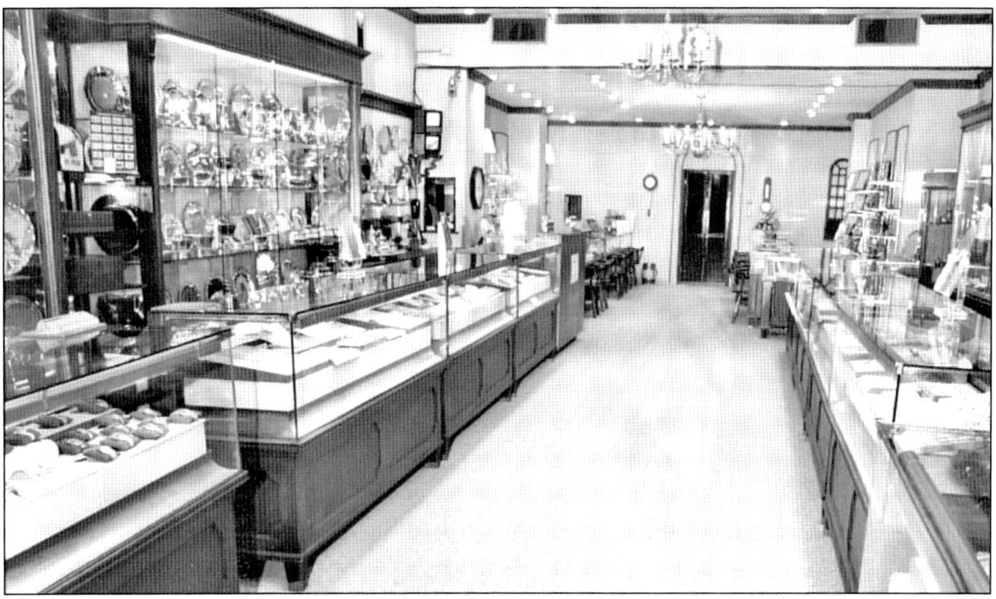

FINE AND REFINED. This is how Kuhn's store's interior looked on a postcard in its early days, though it has the same elegance today. Since 1853, it has established itself as a seller of classy giftware and guild jewelry, which signifies top-of-the-line quality. In 1953, the late John R. "Diamond Jack" Purnell, John A. Kuhn's son-in-law, took over the business. His daughter, Susan, who is active in the community, became co-owner of the firm in 1995. (Courtesy of the Susan Purnell archives.)

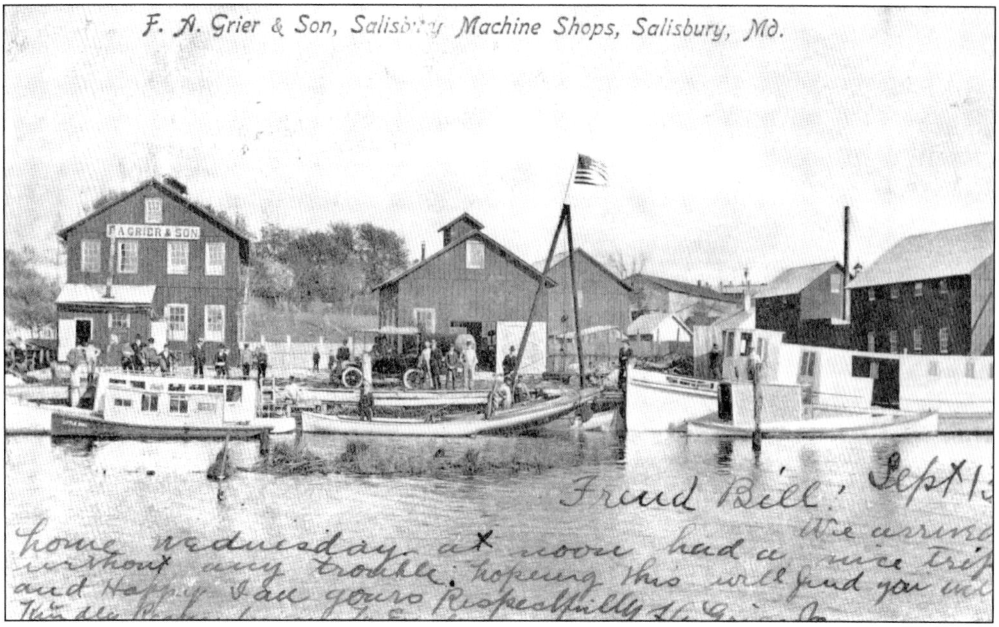

F. A. Grier. The Grier brothers did most of the machine work in the county since 1888, when the city council granted them permission to build their Salisbury Foundry at the docks. The *Salisbury Advertiser* reported in 1890, "George McBriety, notorious . . . for his diabolical conduct and general cussedness, was severely horsewhipped . . . by R. D. and F. A. Grier, whose families he was abusing in the most insulting manner." This postcard was sent from Ansonia, Connecticut, by F. A. Grier himself in the early 1900s, as seen by the inscription. The Grier name became associated with more than one business over the years. (Courtesy of George Chevallier.)

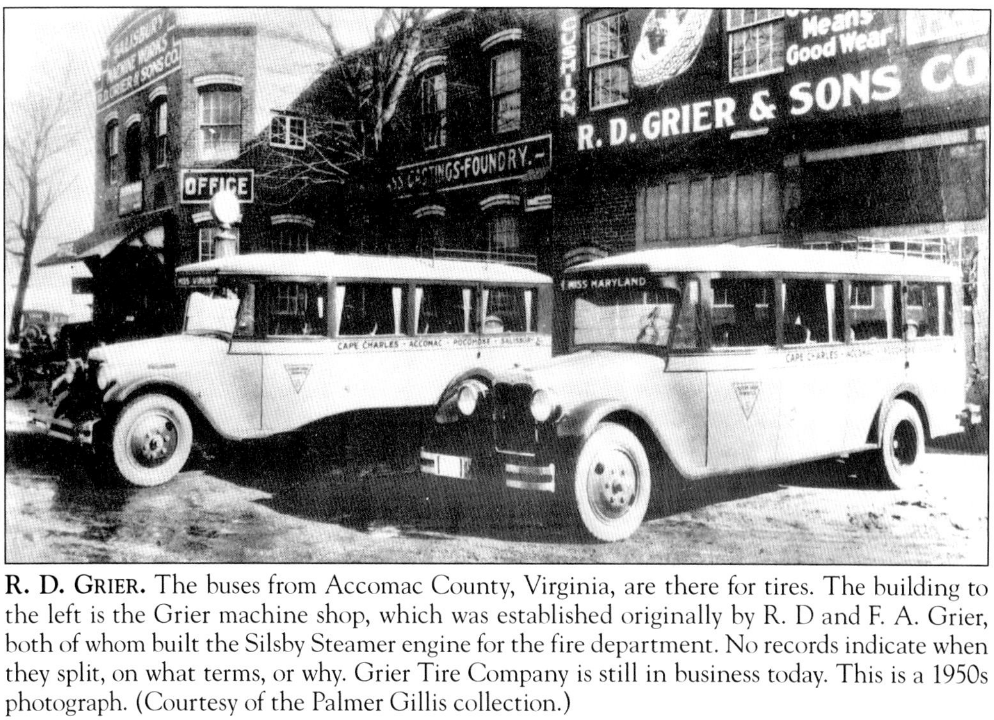

R. D. Grier. The buses from Accomac County, Virginia, are there for tires. The building to the left is the Grier machine shop, which was established originally by R. D and F. A. Grier, both of whom built the Silsby Steamer engine for the fire department. No records indicate when they split, on what terms, or why. Grier Tire Company is still in business today. This is a 1950s photograph. (Courtesy of the Palmer Gillis collection.)

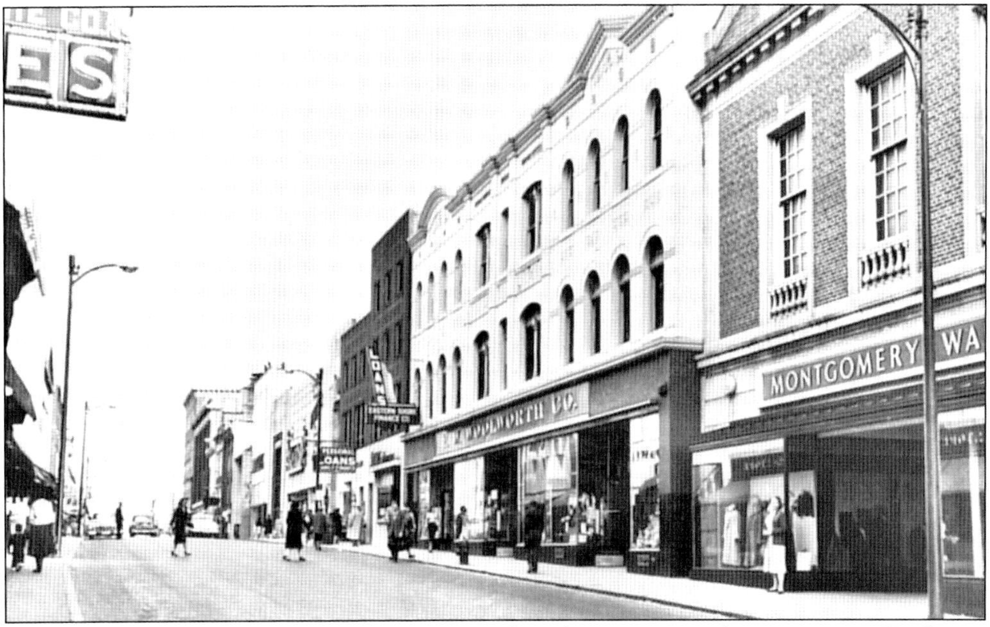

PRE-MALL SHOPPING AT ITS FINEST. F. W. Woolworth Company and Montgomery Ward were two of the top retail stores in Salisbury for close to a century. Both starting downtown, they boomed. Wards boomed so much that it eventually opened a larger store south on Route 13. Woolworth's closed in the 1970s, choked off by the Salisbury Mall, but a Woolco store existed near the old mall for a few years before the entire chain succumbed to the rising tide of big-box stores. (Courtesy of the Palmer Gillis collection.)

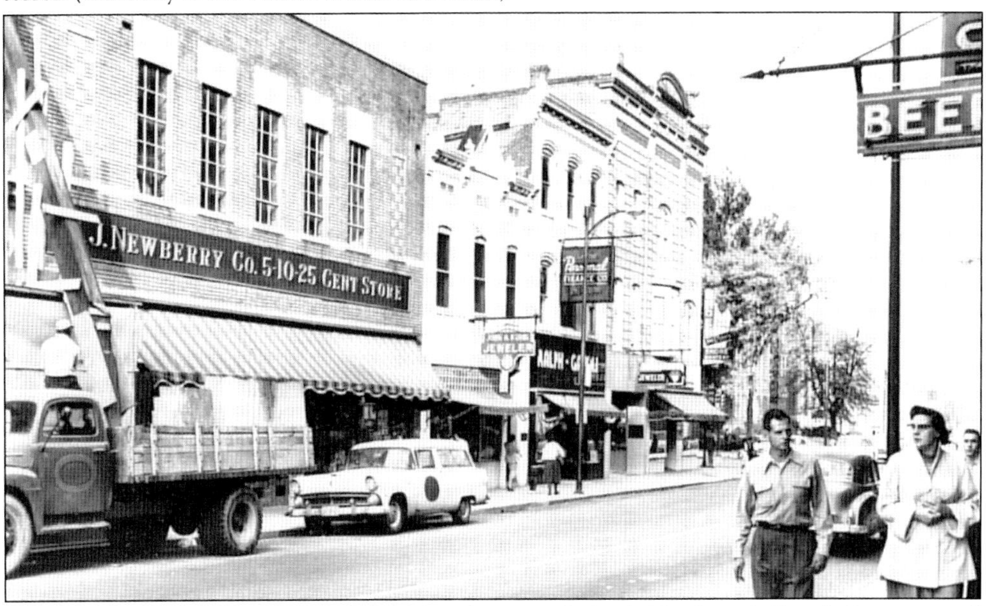

PLACES, OLD "NEW"BERRY. In this 1950s photograph, both Newberry's 5-and-10¢ store and Woolworths shared customers. McCrory's also emerged. Next to Woolworth's was Montgomery Ward, which eventually moved to Route 13 then to the Centre at Salisbury before it went out of business. At one point, downtown was filled with inexpensive department stores. Next to Newberry is the John A. Kuhn jewelry shop. (Courtesy of Salisbury Chamber of Commerce.)

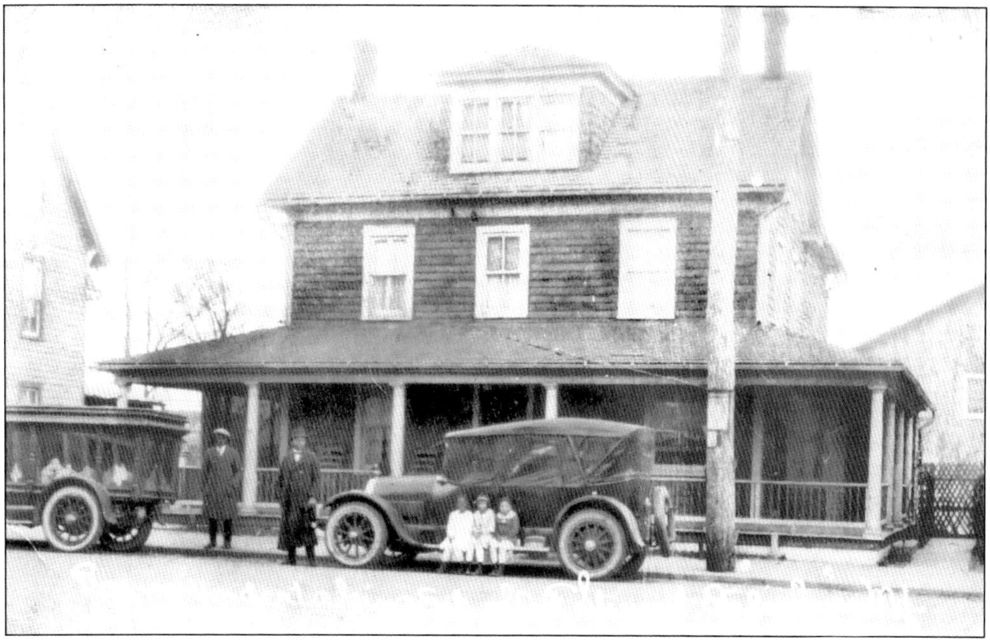

DEATH KNOWS NO COLOR. James F. Stewart Funeral Home is pictured in this 1920s shot. Stewart was one of the first African Americans to operate a funeral home in the area, and his business was located at 402 East Church Street, since renumbered to 324. (Courtesy of George Chevallier.)

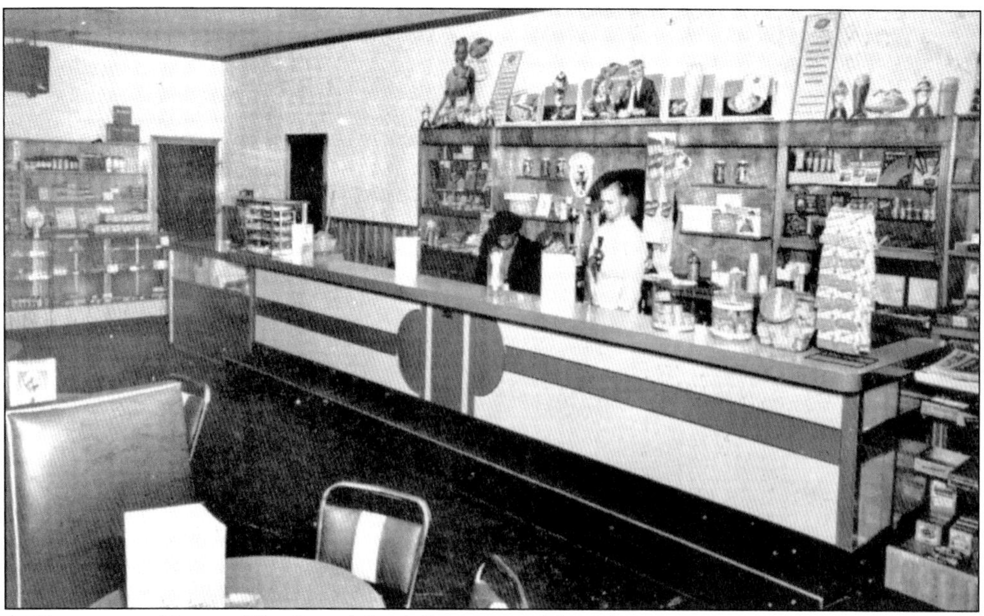

A HAPPENING PLACE. The Postal Card Shop, owned by African American entrepreneur James Weatherly, sat at 219 Lake Street and had a meeting hall upstairs for community functions. It was later turned into a pool hall. (Courtesy of George Chevallier.)

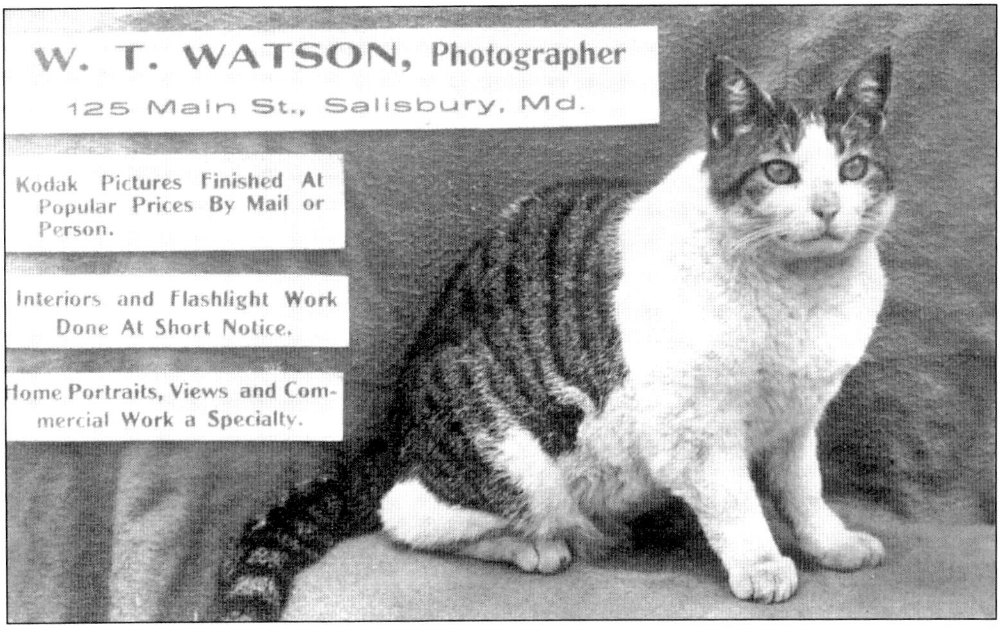

CAT GOT YOUR TONGUE? This postcard was an advertisement for W. T. Watson, a local photographer, and is from around 1918. Watson took a number of photographs that were later turned into postcards. (Courtesy of George Chevallier.)

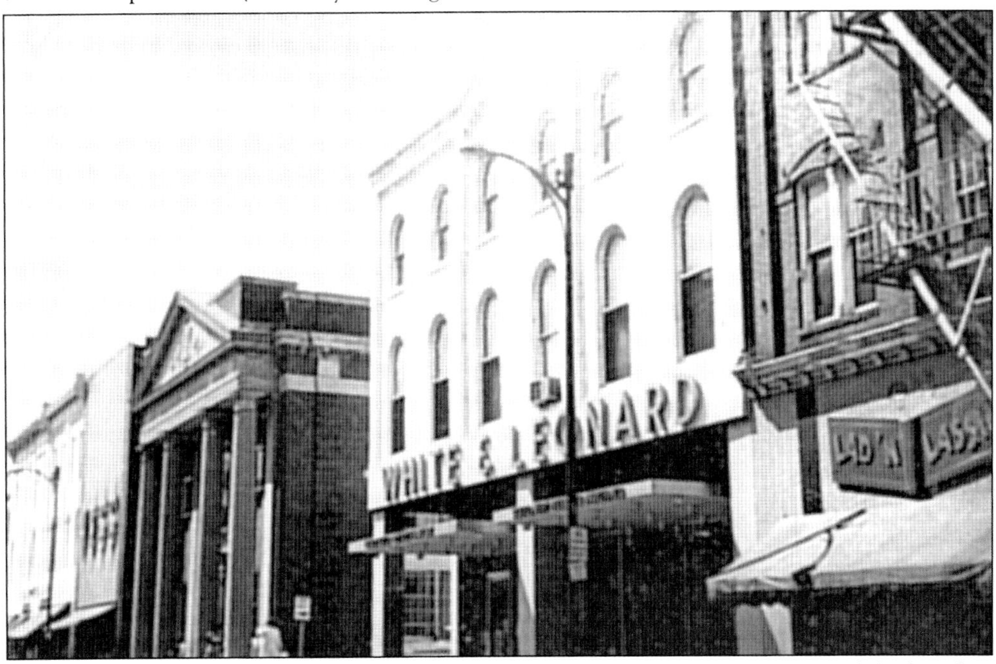

MEMORABLE DOWNTOWN BUILDINGS. White and Leonard drugstore was one of the last four pharmacies in Salisbury in the early years until it was purchased and remodeled into a furniture/stationery store The businesses surrounding it—Lad N Lassie, Powell, Hess—have all since closed. The beauty of these old buildings can be seen in their ceilings, floors, molding, and woodwork. Though White and Leonard ceased being a drugstore, it did evolve into a business supply shop. (Courtesy of Salisbury Chamber of Commerce.)

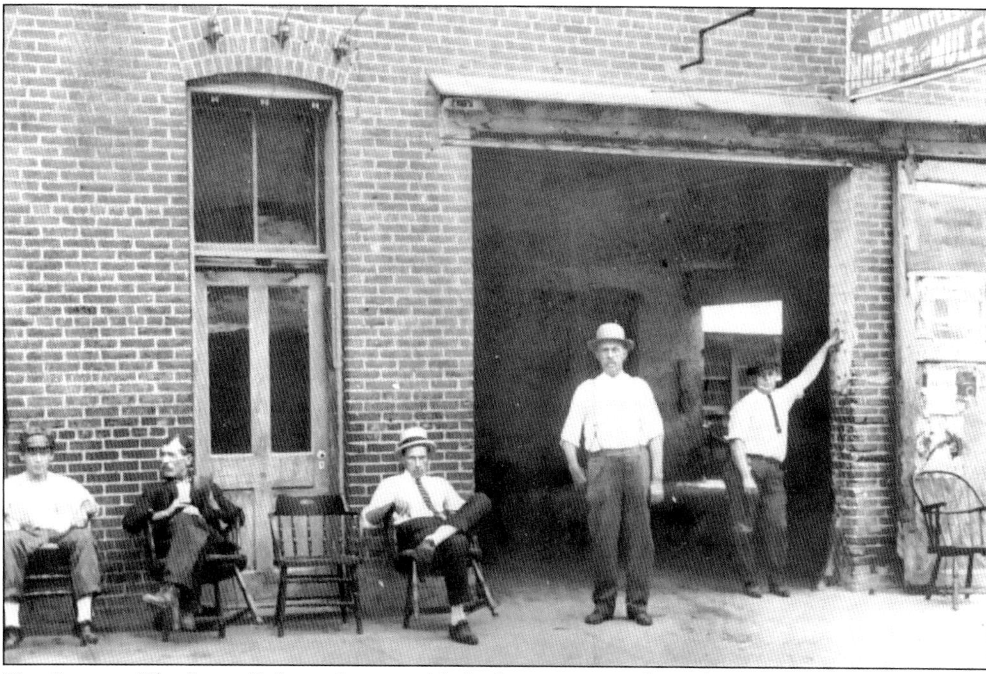

THE LIVERY. The James R. Lowe Livery is likely the same one where the spark for the catastrophic Sunday, October 17, 1886, fire (known as the Great Fire) initiated that wiped out the entire downtown and resulted in over $1 million in damage. The sign to the right of the image reads "Sale & Exchange Stable; Horses and Mules." The Livery was at the docks where present-day Market Street is. (Courtesy of Palmer Gillis collection.)

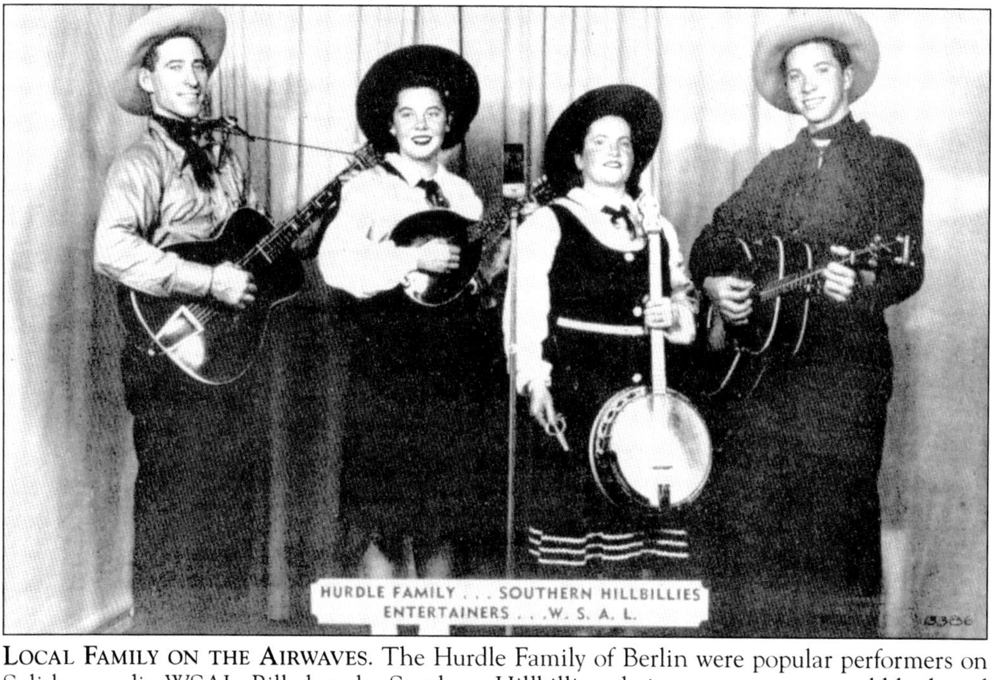

LOCAL FAMILY ON THE AIRWAVES. The Hurdle Family of Berlin were popular performers on Salisbury radio WSAL. Billed as the Southern Hillbillies, their country twang could be heard from studios downtown. (Courtesy of George Chevallier.)

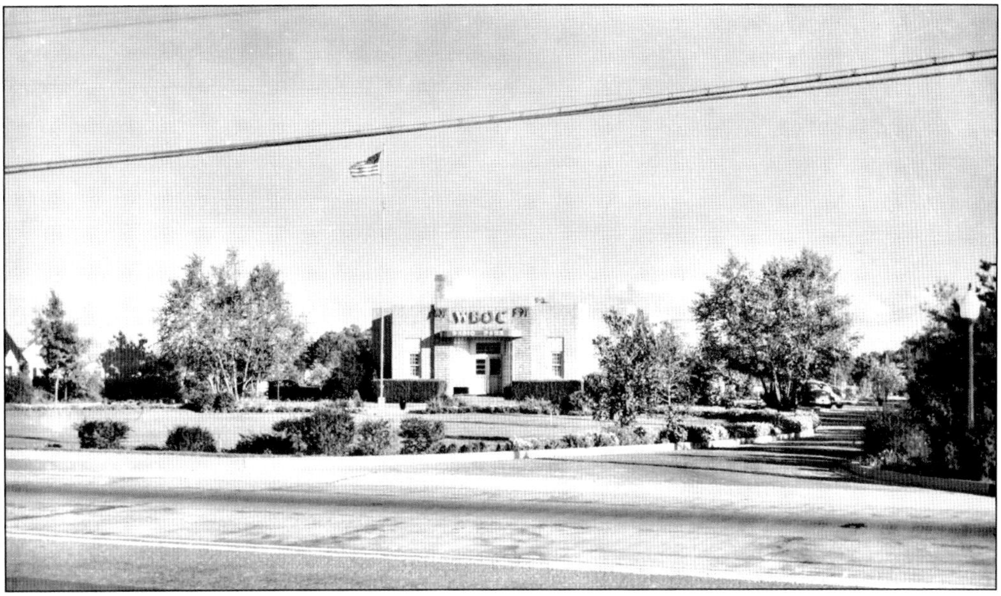

PICTURES OUT OF THE AIR. Wicomico County boasted the first television station on the lower Shore, WBOC-TV, an outgrowth of its Salisbury radio station. It has withstood the test of time as a CBS affiliate for over 50 years and has now expanded to include a Fox affiliate. Though greatly expanded, the station remains in its original location along Route 13, just north of downtown. (Courtesy of Salisbury Chamber of Commerce.)

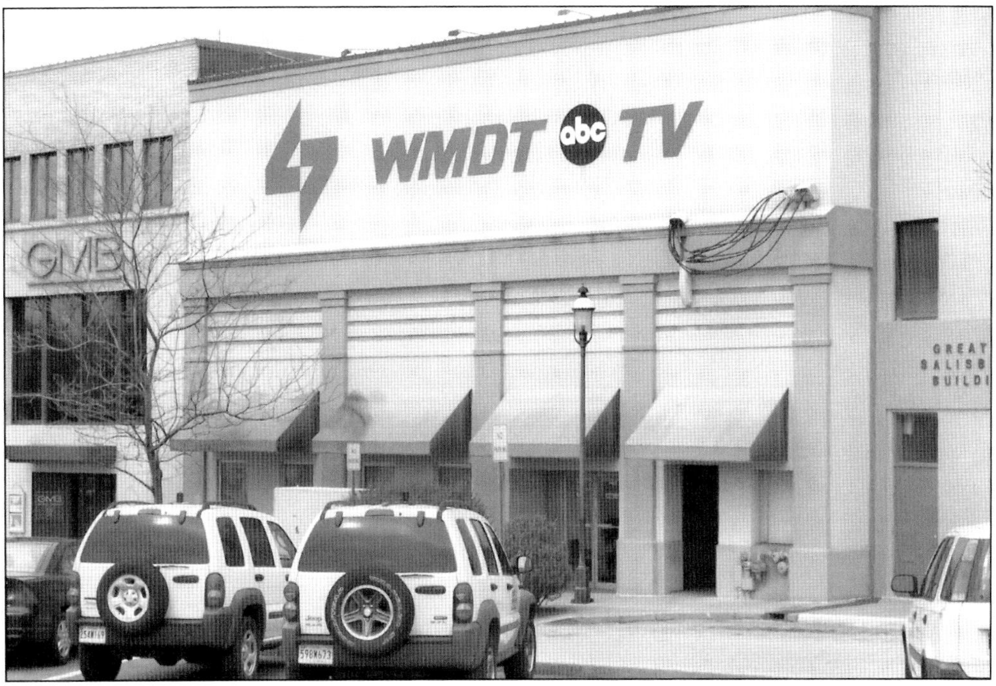

COUNTY TOO BIG FOR ONE TV STATION. In 1980, WMDT-TV Channel 47 began broadcasting from its headquarters in a downtown building that formerly housed Read's Drug Store. It began as an ABC affiliate and grew substantially. Now it also provides its own CW affiliate as well. (Photograph by Andy Nunez.)

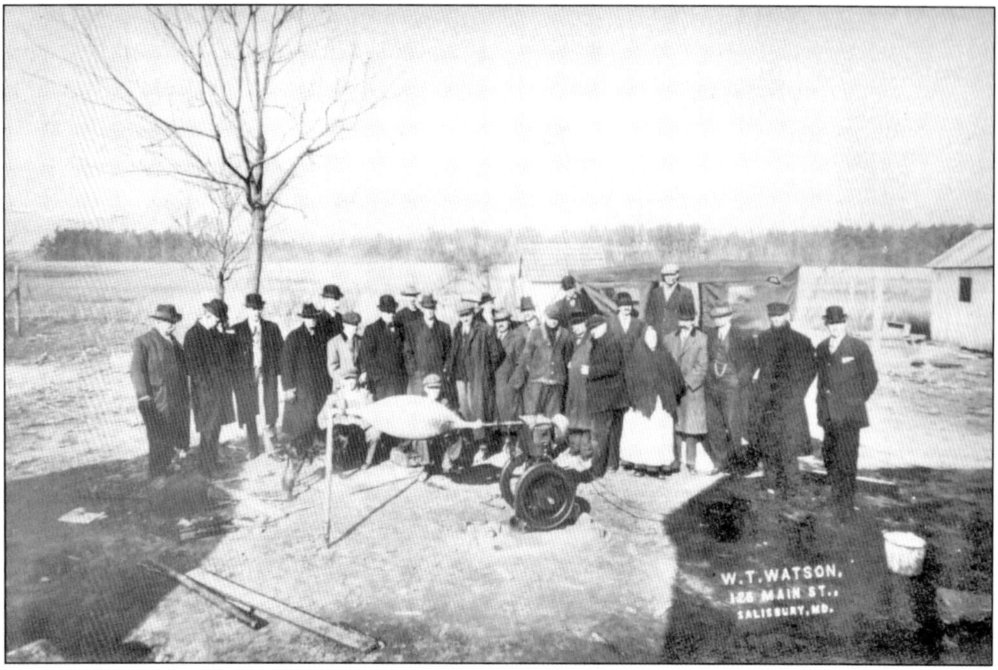

FULL OF HOT AIR. This is Wicomico County Gas and Oil Company. This early 1900s photograph shows the officers next to their pumping station. Unfortunately, this pocket of natural gas near Parsonsburg on the east side of the county was so small that it quickly ran out, and the company went broke. (Photograph by W. T. Watson; courtesy of George Chevallier.)

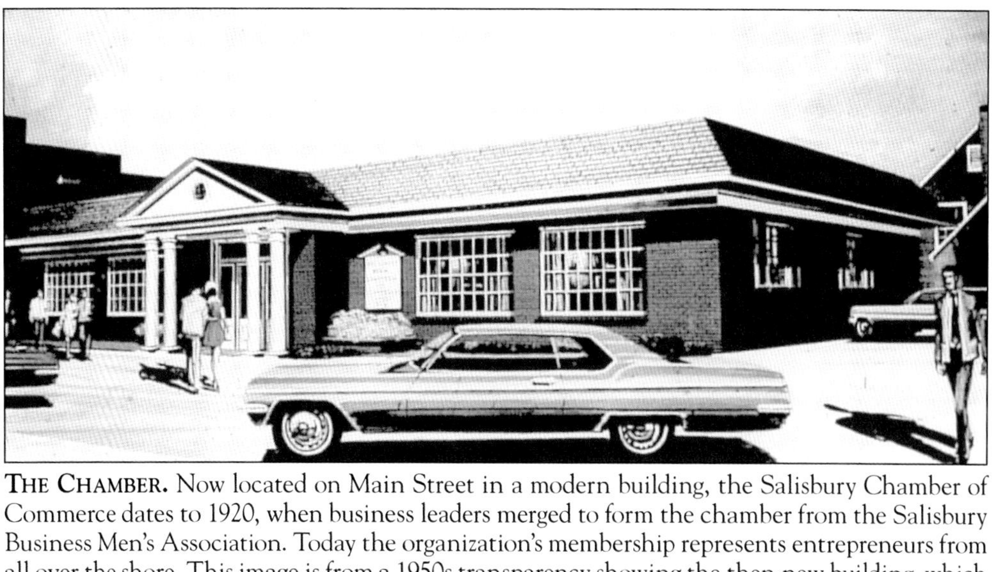

THE CHAMBER. Now located on Main Street in a modern building, the Salisbury Chamber of Commerce dates to 1920, when business leaders merged to form the chamber from the Salisbury Business Men's Association. Today the organization's membership represents entrepreneurs from all over the shore. This image is from a 1950s transparency showing the then-new building, which was likely a sketch. (Courtesy of Salisbury Chamber of Commerce.)

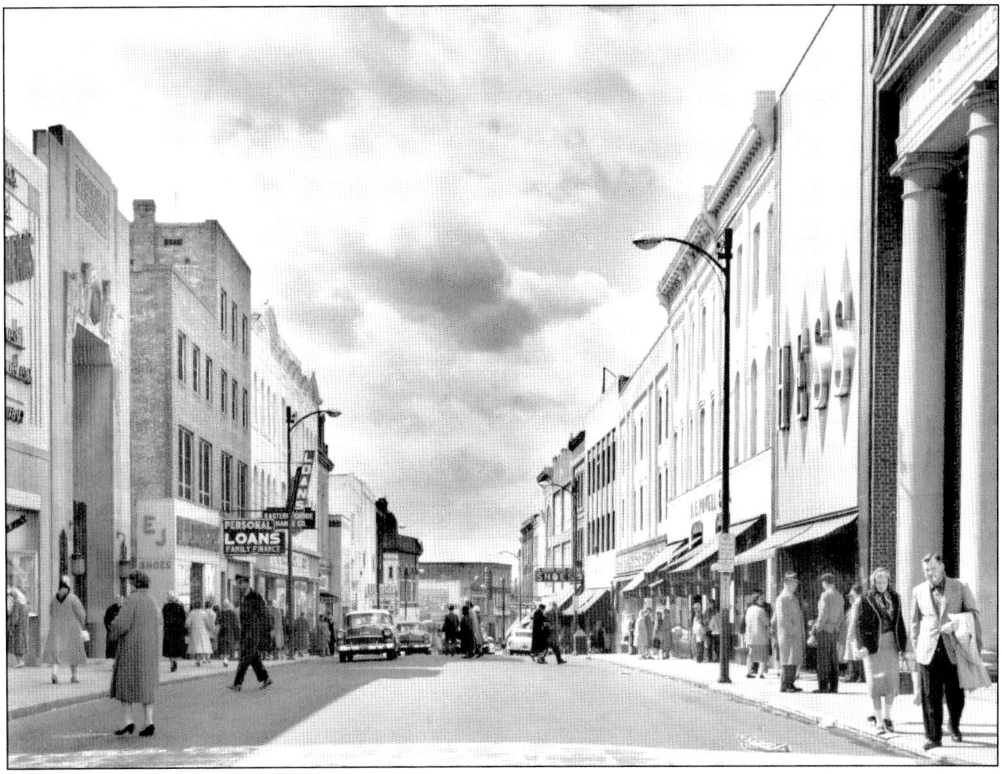

DOWNTOWN. This 1957 photograph of downtown Salisbury shows the changes that two major fires had wrought on the downtown area. Both the Kennerly Building and the Arcade Theater had gone up in flames, and now marble and granite gleamed as Salisbury became the premier city on Maryland's Eastern Shore. At the Ullman, *Under Fire* with Rex Reason was playing. Lady shoppers show the headscarf that was fashionable in that day. (Courtesy of Salisbury Chamber of Commerce.)

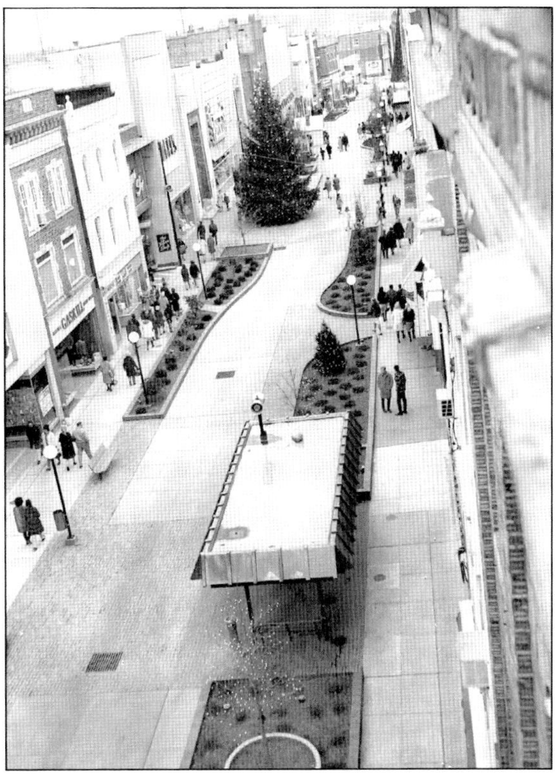

BEGINNING TO LOOK A LOT LIKE CHRISTMAS. In order to give downtown more atmosphere, a section of Main Street was turned into a plaza. As inviting as it was, it didn't lure people from the mall. Still, there were lots of shops open downtown, and Read's Drug Store had moved across the street by then. The Ullman had burned, leaving only two theaters open downtown, the Wicomico and the Boulevard. (Courtesy of Palmer Gillis collection.)

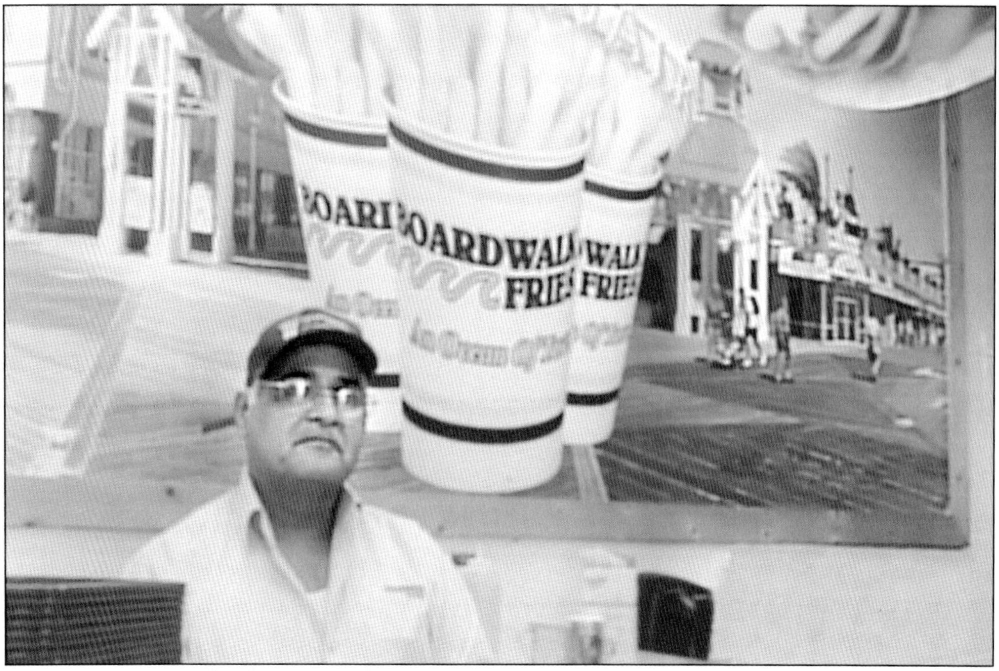

DILIP'S FRIES. Boardwalk Fries are famous on the Delmarva Peninsula. People run to Ocean City to order large basketfuls. But Wicomico County now has its very own, as offered by Dilip Jeswani of Bombay, India, who moved to this country 12 years ago. As a business entrepreneur, he also owns two major printing companies in India. This store is located in the Centre of Salisbury. (Courtesy of James R. Hayes.)

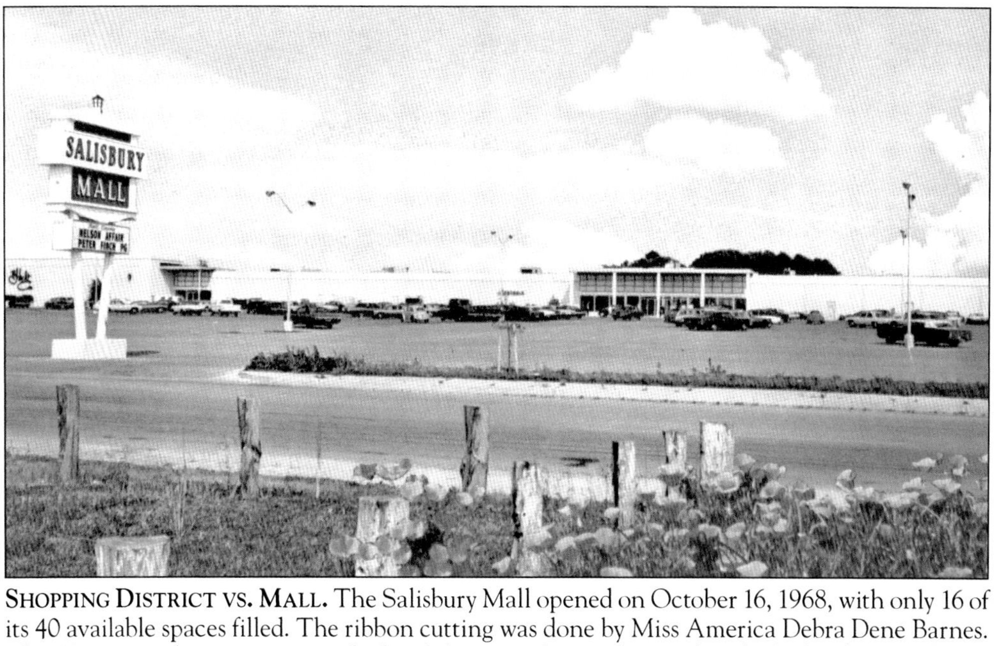

SHOPPING DISTRICT VS. MALL. The Salisbury Mall opened on October 16, 1968, with only 16 of its 40 available spaces filled. The ribbon cutting was done by Miss America Debra Dene Barnes. The 80-acre site became a mecca for local shopping for nearly two decades before being eclipsed by the more recent Centre at Salisbury. Long closed, the "old mall," as locals call it, is set for demolition for a planned retail/housing community. (Courtesy of George Chevallier.)

Six

Another Day's Labor

While agriculture has always been the primary industry in the county, as the population and urbanization of the area increased, so has the diversity of trades across the county. Farmers still till thousands of acres, and watermen still make their living from the rivers and bays, but they are fewer today. Overall, the principle industry in the county was the raising and feeding poultry and the rendering of them for consumption. Perhaps the most famous face in the poultry industry, Frank Perdue, took his father's business from a local concern to a global corporation. Besides agriculture, early business was in shipbuilding and lumber. With the demise of the use of small ships for transport, textiles and machinery employed residents. Companies like R. D. Grier, Salisbury Steel, and Wayne Pump rose and fell.

Today Salisbury has an industrial park with several big businesses, and on the riverfront, large cruise ships are once again under construction. Electronics firms show the current trends toward an increasingly computerized world. Besides industry, retail has outgrown the small downtown area of Salisbury and has spread along Route 13 from Maryland's northern state line almost to the border with Somerset County and slowly creeps east and west along Route 50. What was once farmland now glitters with strip malls, auto dealerships, and big-box shopping centers. What people 30 years ago had to travel to Baltimore to purchase can now be had within a short drive from their homes. Route 13 alone is filled with Wal-Mart (the one on 13 North is the largest on the East Coast), Sam's Club, Kohl's, Macy's, Marshall's, Uno's, Chilli's, Texas Roadhouse, Outback Steakhouse, and much more. It's a veritable bulging conurbation.

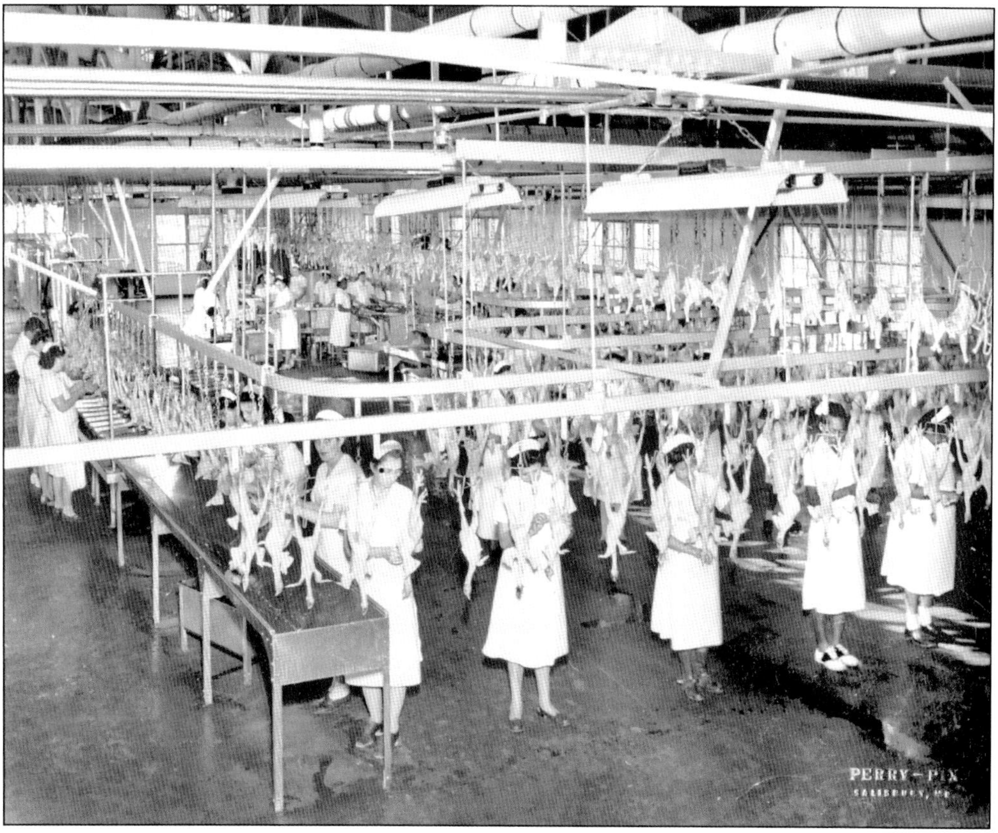

It Takes More than a Tough Man. This photograph of a chicken plant was taken in the 1940s and used by a New York newspaper showing the premier industry of the Eastern Shore. (Photograph by James Perry; courtesy of Salisbury Chamber of Commerce.)

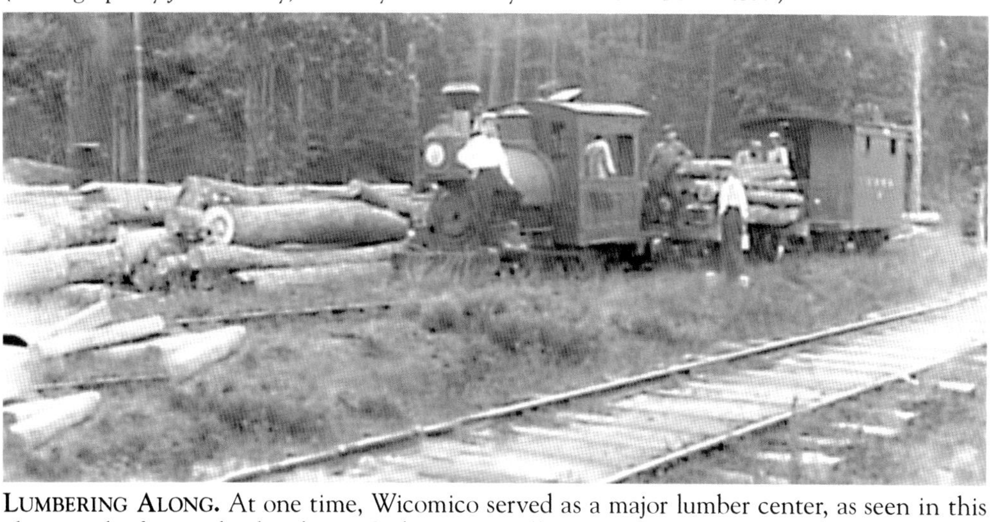

Lumbering Along. At one time, Wicomico served as a major lumber center, as seen in this photograph of a train hauling logs in Hebron. Sawmills and planing mills sprang up and interlaced with barges, railroads, trucking, and shipbuilding. The area was once covered with a heavy growth of oak, chestnut, pine, beech, and cypress trees that came from clearing the land for farming. (Courtesy of the Pamler Gillis collection.)

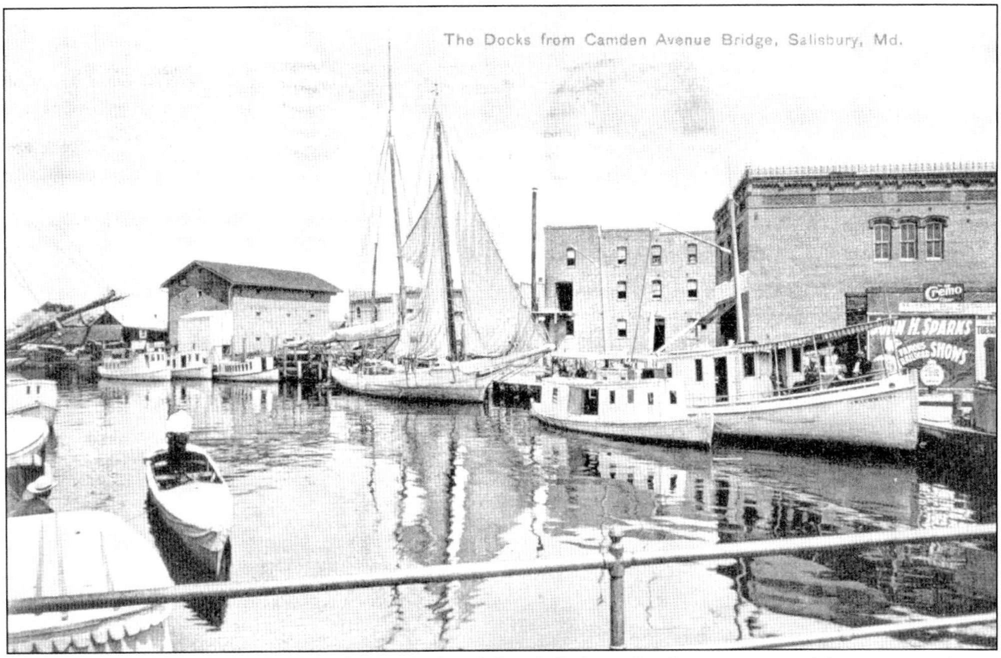

BUSINESS AFLOAT. This 1909 photograph of the Salisbury harbor is unusual because it shows ships with sails unfurled and was taken from the Camden Street Bridge. The rivers were the original highways of the county, and there is still considerable waterborne cargo plying county waterways. (Courtesy of George Chevallier.)

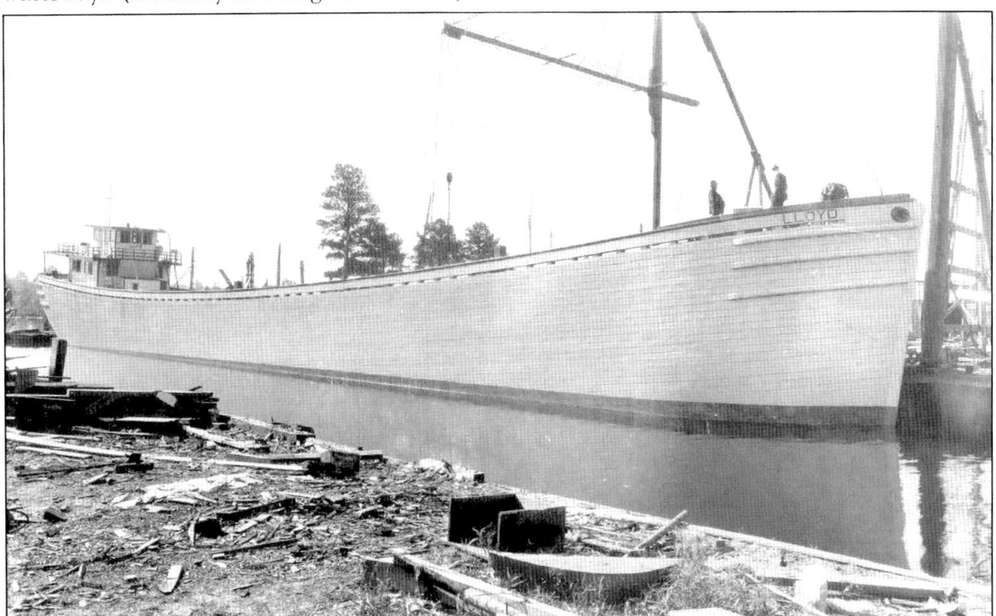

BUILD IT, THEY SAIL. Shipbuilding has been a staple of Wicomico County's economy for centuries. Dockyards similar to this sprang up in Sharptown, Whitehaven, and Salisbury, building everything from simple rowboats to powerful schooners and rams. However, the barges and sailing ships of the past have been replaced by luxury cruise ships. (Courtesy of Salisbury Chamber of Commerce.)

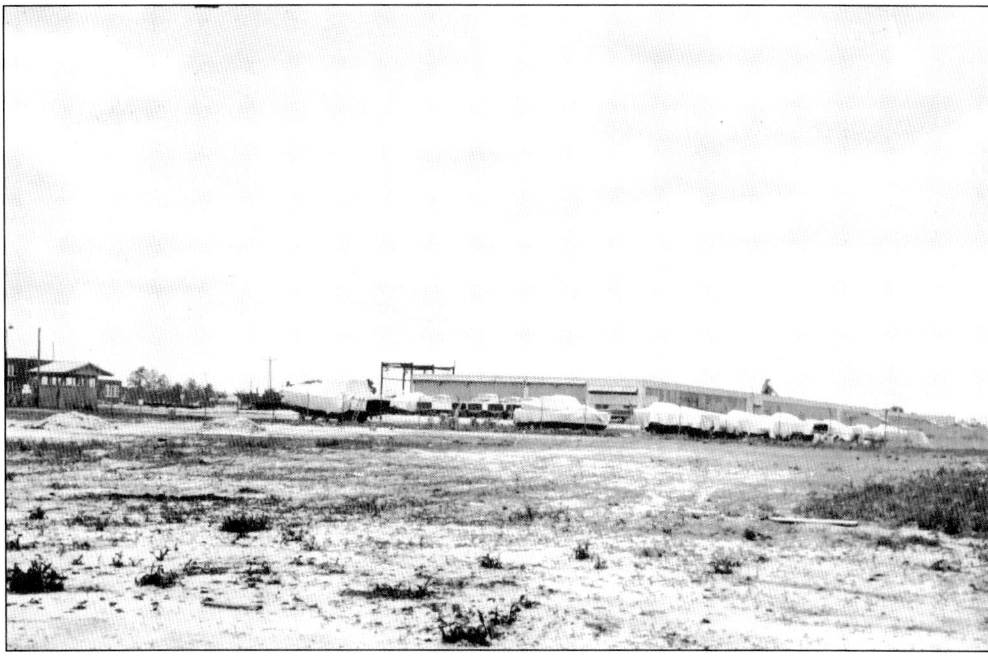

Sporting Luxury. By the beginning of the 20th century, Chris Craft was building a line of sport craft and speedboats that set the gold standard in the industry. Started by Chris Smith and his brother, factories opened around the country, including one in Salisbury. As the demand diminished, the plant was sold four times. (Courtesy of Salisbury Chamber of Commerce.)

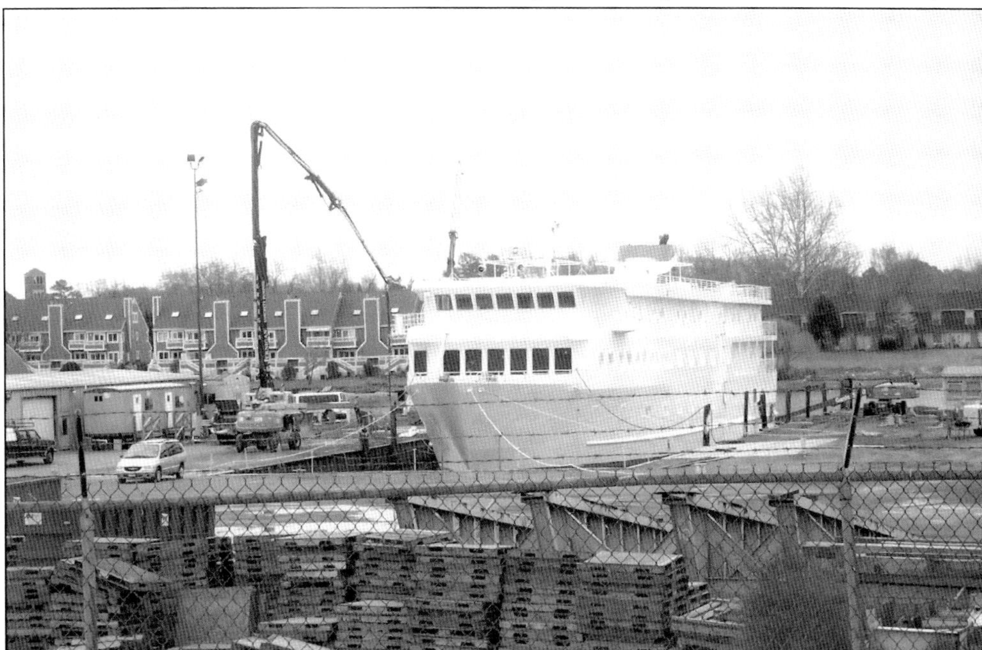

Rebirth of an Industry. Shipbuilding never completely died out in the county, and even now Chesapeake Shipbuilding turns out car ferries and gigantic hulls for luxury cruise boats that travel up and down the coast. (Photograph by Andy Nunez.)

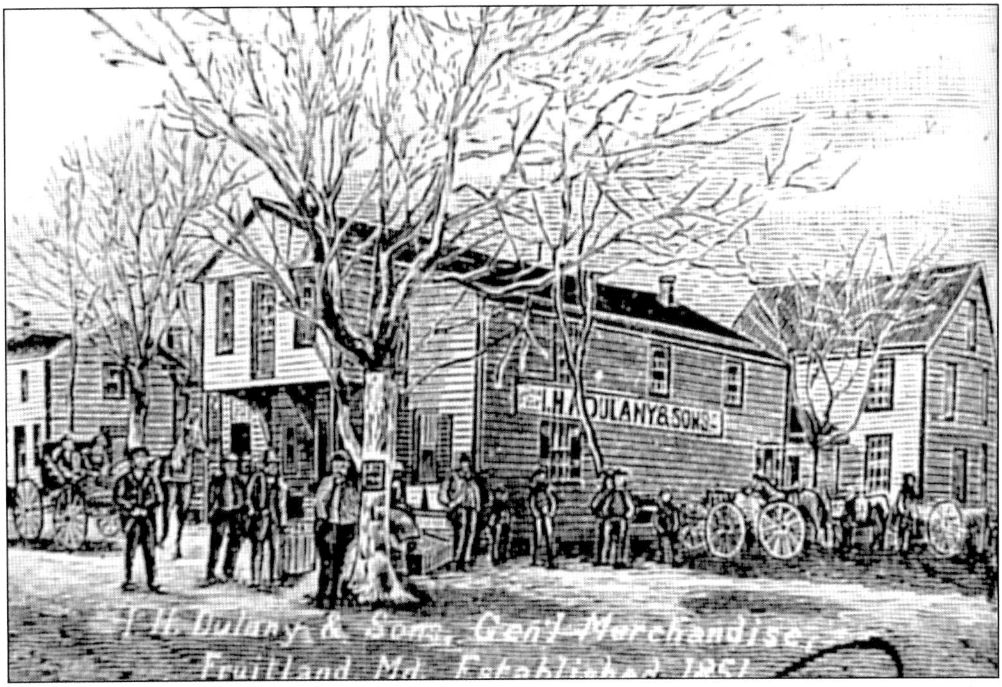

GENERAL STORE. This is a postcard rendition of a pen drawing of the general store on Camden Avenue in Fruitland. It was established in 1861. Dulany's became famous for canned tomatoes, which eventually led the family into the canning business after they closed the store. Before it was sold, it had been a major employer in the town. (Courtesy of the John E. Jacob Collection.)

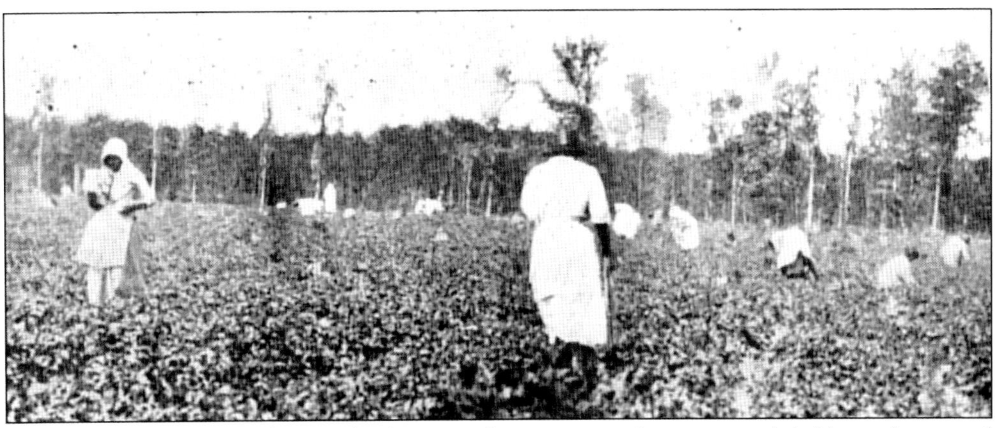

OH, MY ACHING BACK. Thousands of migrant farmers—mostly women and children—harvested strawberries, as seen in this 1919 photograph, at which time 13 million quarts of strawberries were produced. Trucking was an important aspect of the industry. Strawberries are still a vital crop on the shore, as are other produce such as corn, watermelon, and vegetables. (Courtesy of Delmarva Eastern Shore Association.)

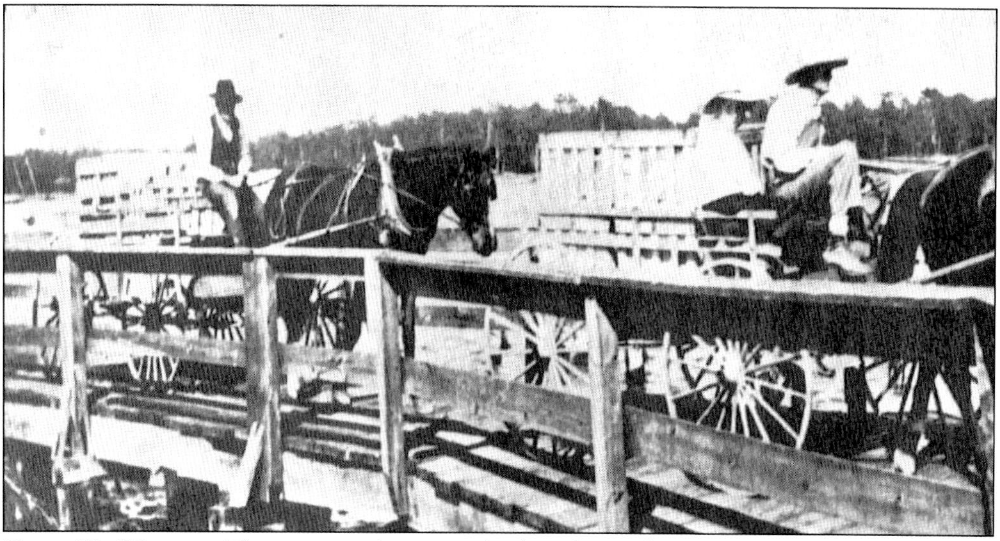

GUNG HO WAGONS. These wagon drivers are brokers for produce on the Eastern Shore—here, for the town of Nanticoke—to be shipped to Baltimore. Farmers from around the counties would bring their goods to the Nanticoke Wharf either to be delivered by wagons or by barges and ships, such as the *Virginia*. By the way the men are dressed and the need to use wagons instead of modern vehicles, this photograph is dated from around World War I. (Courtesy of Betty Webster.)

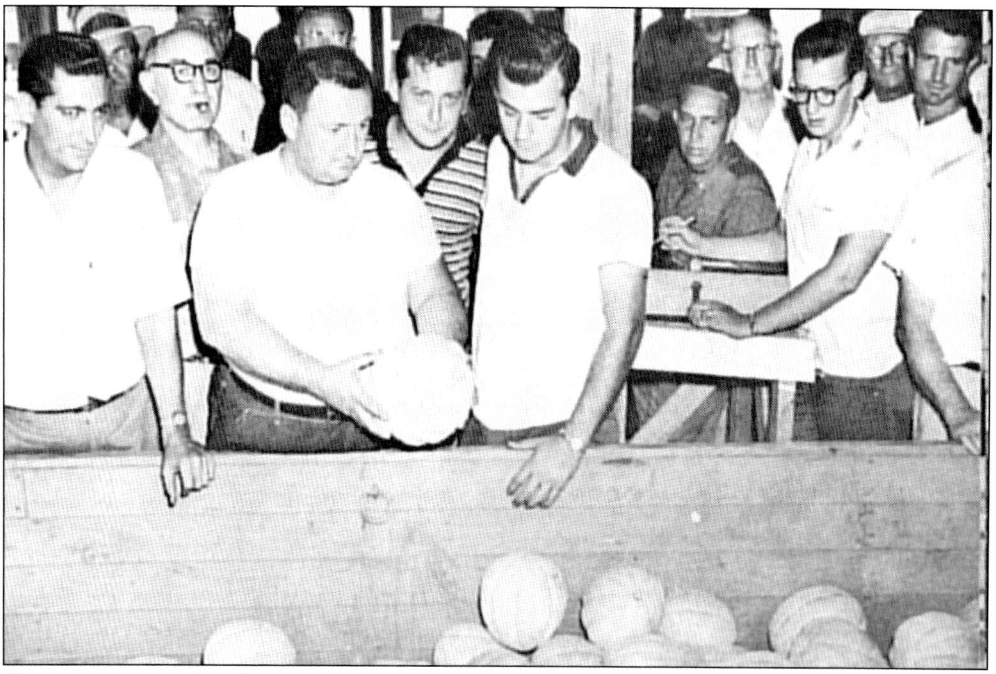

CANTALOUPES. Abundant crops in the county brought forth the canning industry, since not all commodities could be consumed immediately. At one time, there were canneries in every community. The most common crops were watermelons, cantaloupes, strawberries, blackberries, raspberries, tomatoes, corn, and peas. Many other industries depended on these crops to survive. Farming still exists today but in a limited capacity, as it has given way to other modern industries. (*Salisbury, Maryland: Central City of the Eastern Shore.*)

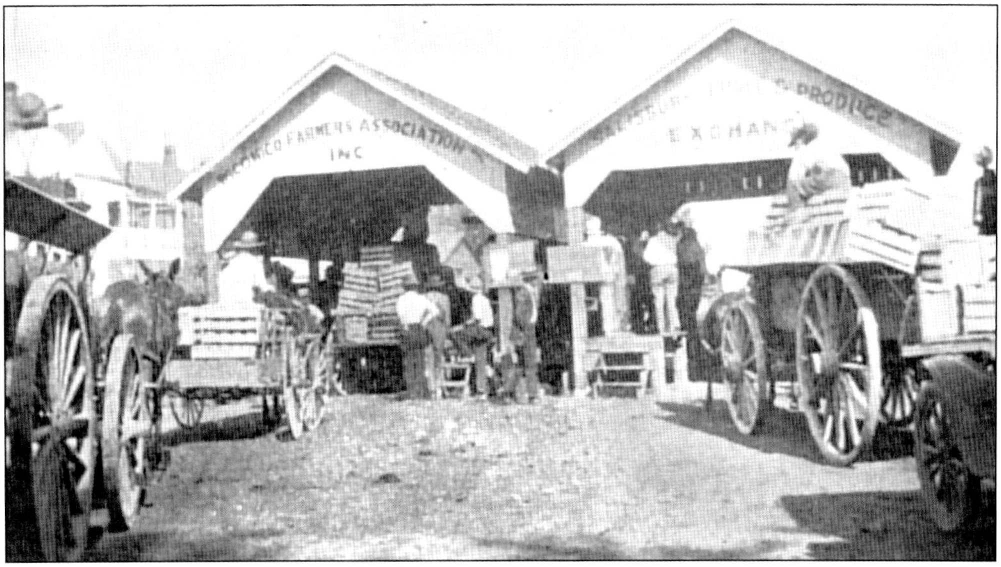

FARMERS' EXCHANGE. This pre-1926 photograph by G. R. Cobb demonstrates cooperative association among growers and shippers. Farmers bonded to improve quality for users while garnering larger profits for themselves. The lettering at the top of the building on the left reads, "Wicomico Farmers Association Inc," while at right reads, "Salisbury Fruit & Produce Exchange." Dairy farming was a minor enterprise compared to fruit and vegetable growing. (*Delmarva Eastern Shore Associations.*)

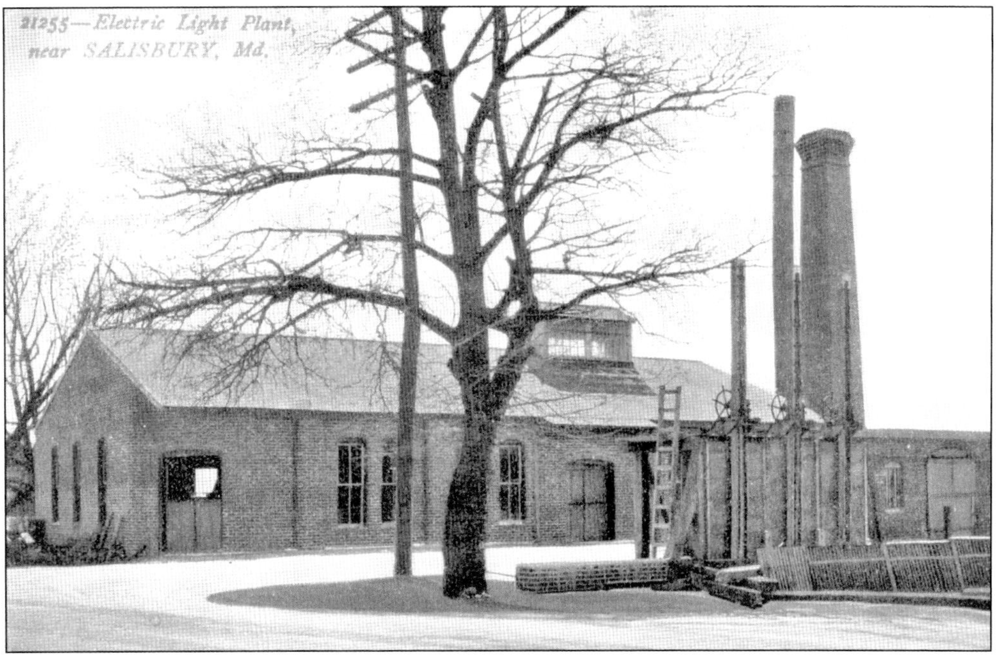

SPARK OF AN IDEA. The *c.* 1907 photograph of the Salisbury Power Company shows how small a facility was needed to supply the needs of the growing city. Salisbury Monument Company now sits on its riverside location. The dam that served it washed out in the torrential rains of 1926, and the flood destroyed the pivot bridge. It was replaced with a conventional dam. (Courtesy of George Chevallier.)

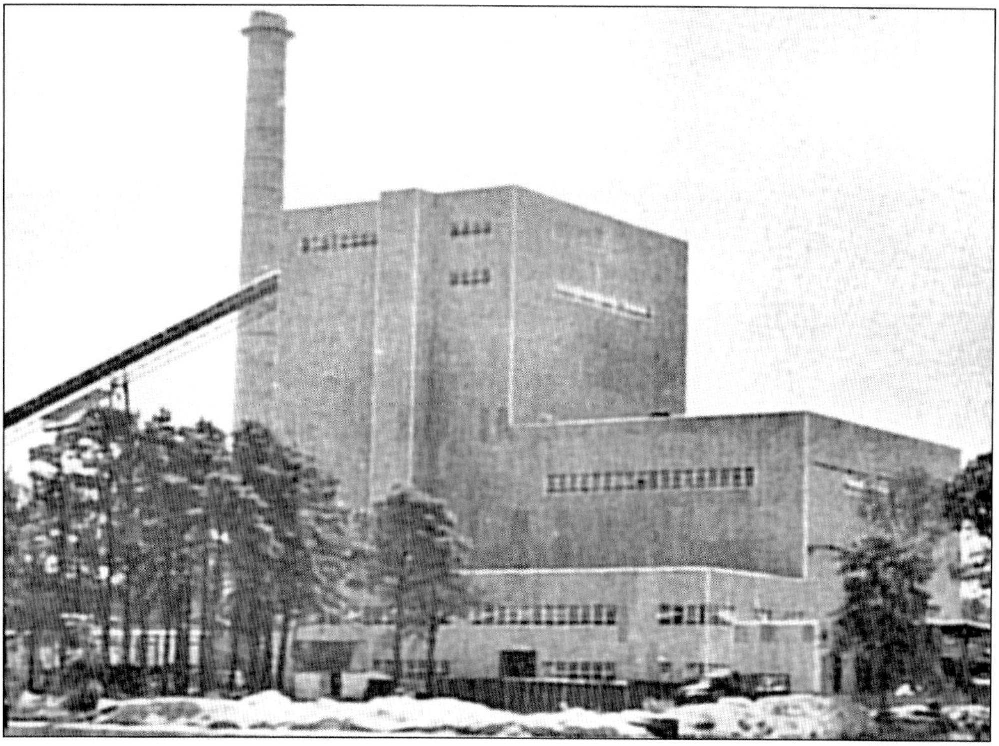

Lighting Up Our Lives. This 1950s updated power plant serviced Wicomico County and the surrounding area, which was interconnected with the Maryland, Pennsylvania, and New Jersey subsidiaries of the then–Delaware Power and Light Company. The two generating stations provided the area with 270,000 kilowatts and voltages ranging from 22,000 to 138,000. (*Salisbury, Maryland: Central City of the Eastern Shore.*)

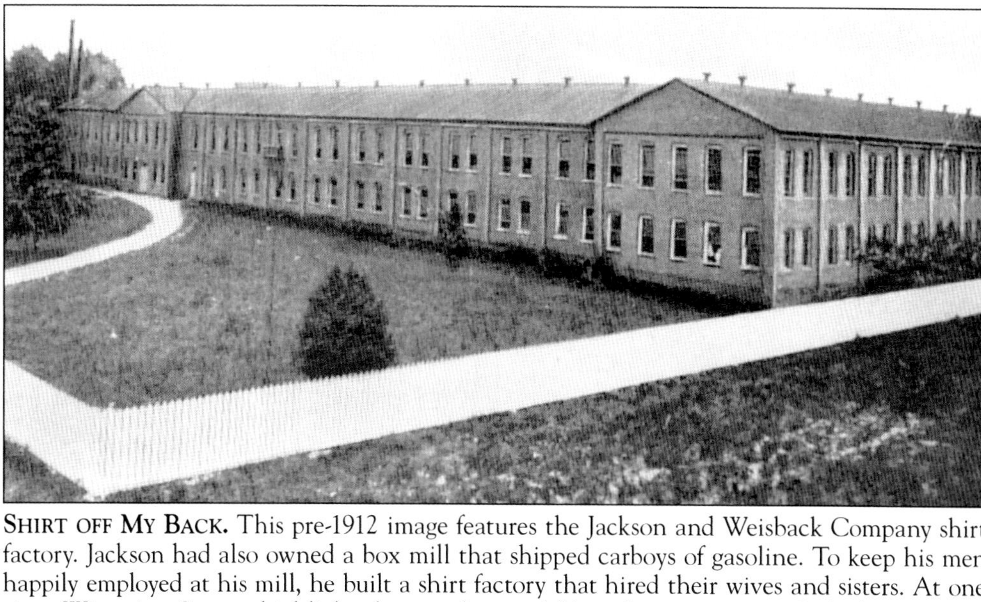

Shirt off My Back. This pre-1912 image features the Jackson and Weisback Company shirt factory. Jackson had also owned a box mill that shipped carboys of gasoline. To keep his men happily employed at his mill, he built a shirt factory that hired their wives and sisters. At one time, Wicomico County highlighted many shirt and fabric factories, none of which are extant now. (Courtesy of the John E. Jacob Collection.)

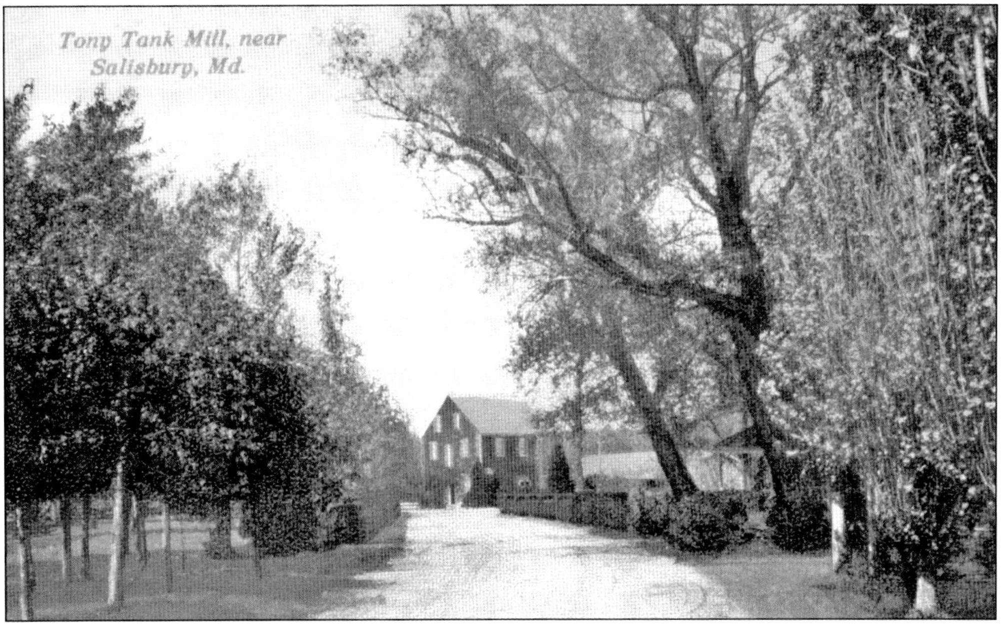

DASHIELL'S MILL. Bill Adams bought 61.25 acres in 1783 in the Tony Tank area of the county but then sold it to Capt. Robert Dashiell, who erected the Tony Tank gristmill in 1798. The gristmill processed wheat and corn and had a granary to store the processed grains, which aided in the increase of the demand for wheat in the 1800s. The mill burned to the ground in 1953. (Courtesy of the John E. Jacob Collection.)

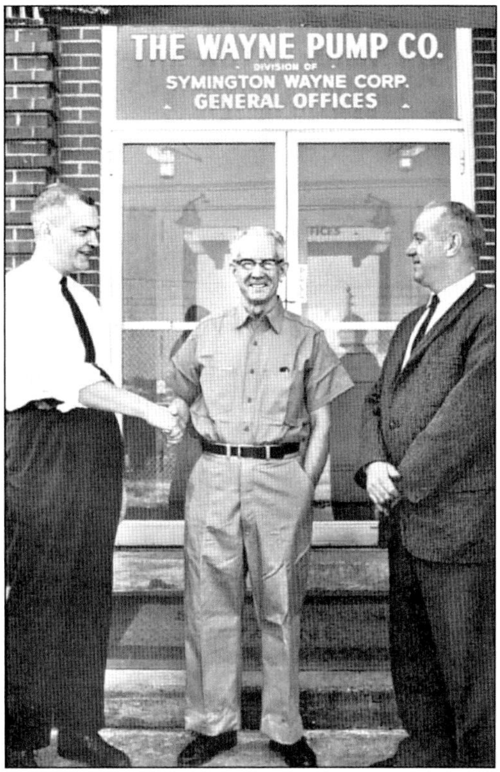

SIMPLY SYMINGTON, 1960S. William H. Bateman was president of Symington Wayne Corporation, based in Salisbury, which later became Wayne Dresser Industries. They manufactured gas station pumps. Their long history in Wicomico County ended in 2001 when they left Salisbury. The brochure featuring this image touted Salisbury's lifestyle to bring employees to the shore. (*Salisbury: Heart of the Maryland's Eastern Shore.*)

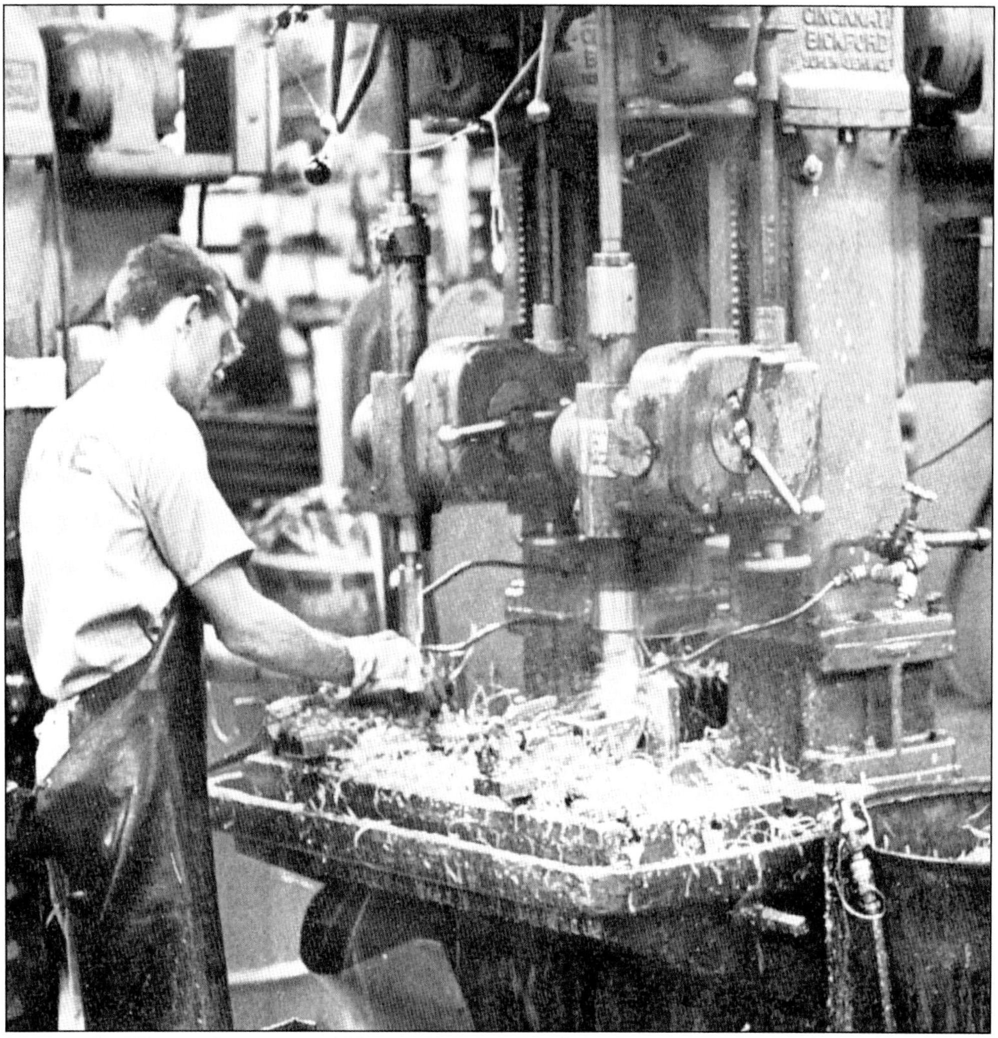

Dresser's Home. Symington Wayne Corporation became Dresser Wayne Industries; they manufactured gas station pumps. They've had a long history in Wicomico County, but about five years ago, they shut down the building and grounds. The chemicals used in making the pumps supposedly leached into the ground, making it difficult to get top dollar for the property. (*Salisbury: Heart of the Maryland's Eastern Shore.*)

Seven

CARRYING TO AND FROM

Early settlers to the county traveled by boat for long-term transportation needs and by horse otherwise. It wasn't until 1667 that a road system provided mobility from various plantations and landings to the towns for commercial purposes. From a number of these landings sprang villages, the most prominent being Handy's Landing, which later turned into Salisbury town, laid out in 1732. As commerce grew, a number of ferries were established to cross the Wicomico at various points for growing streams of wagons and carts to ply their way to market. Mills turned out lumber and flour that needed more and bigger methods of portage. Steamships carried passengers and goods to the bigger seaports. In 1860 came the railroad, which spelled the death of the steamship industry for all but the largest cargoes. At first, the tracks stretched from the Delaware line to Humphreys Lake, but its continuance was held up by the Civil War. Directly afterward, the rails plodded along to Pocomoke and Crisfield, tying them to Salisbury and the great metropolises of the north. Progress east and west began shortly after Wicomico became a county in its own right. The locomotive became familiar as bridges were built over rivers to accommodate its bulk.

As the railroad soon eclipsed the steamship, the automobile obscured both, and new, wider roads formed a network to every small community in the county. Salisbury lived up to its nickname as the Hub of Delmarva with the upgrading of Routes 13 and 50 in the mid-20th century. Travelers then bypassed Salisbury as they sped from Philadelphia to Norfolk or from Baltimore to coastal resorts such as Ocean City. The last to come was the airplane, but by World War II, small airfields such as Hebron emerged, and soon regular commuter service was established between Salisbury and the major air hubs of Baltimore and Philadelphia. Buses and shuttle services run to the airports, and the three counties of Worcester, Somerset, and Wicomico initiated ShoreTran, the mass-transit system. The Salisbury–Ocean City Airport is preparing to expand runways for jets and bring in another airline company.

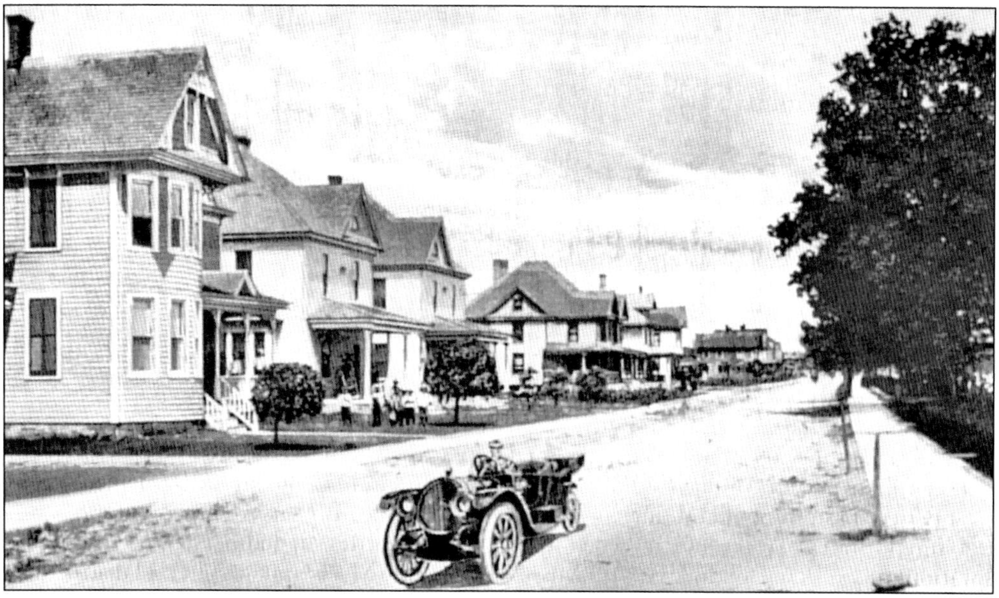

RIDING ALONG IN MY AUTOMOBILE. This roadster zipping along State Street in Delmar sets the tone for the times. A new breed was plying the avenues of the county, charging along the unpaved roads in horseless carriages. (Courtesy of the John E. Jacob Collection.)

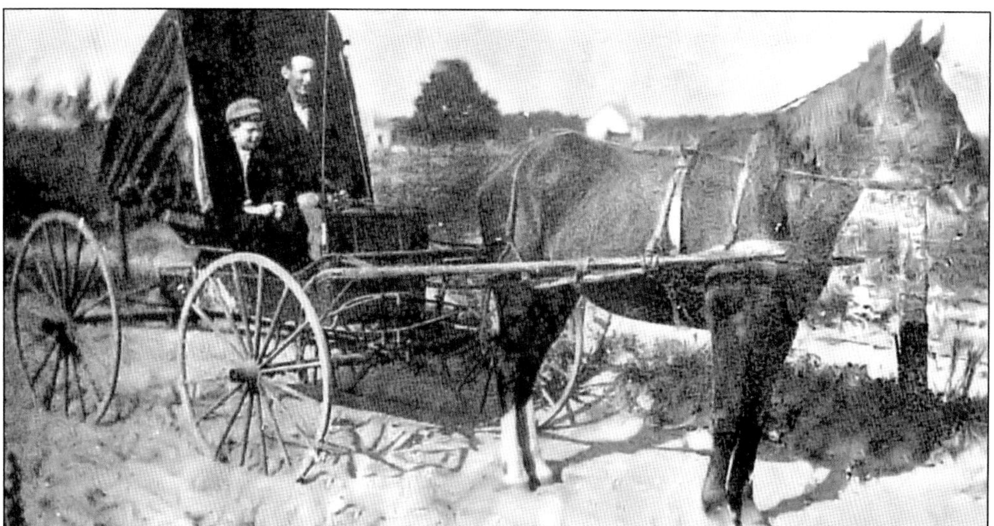

KLOP, KLOP, KLOP. This *c.* 1900 photograph appears to be a Mennonite-styled buggy with an accordion carriage, but the interesting points are the fellows' attire, the type of harness, and how deeply the wheels sink into the ground. The lower Eastern Shore is notorious for it sandy ground because it is so close to sea level. By the desolation of the area, it looks like this might be on the west side of town—an area that is now filled with homes and businesses. (Courtesy of Sylvia Taylor.)

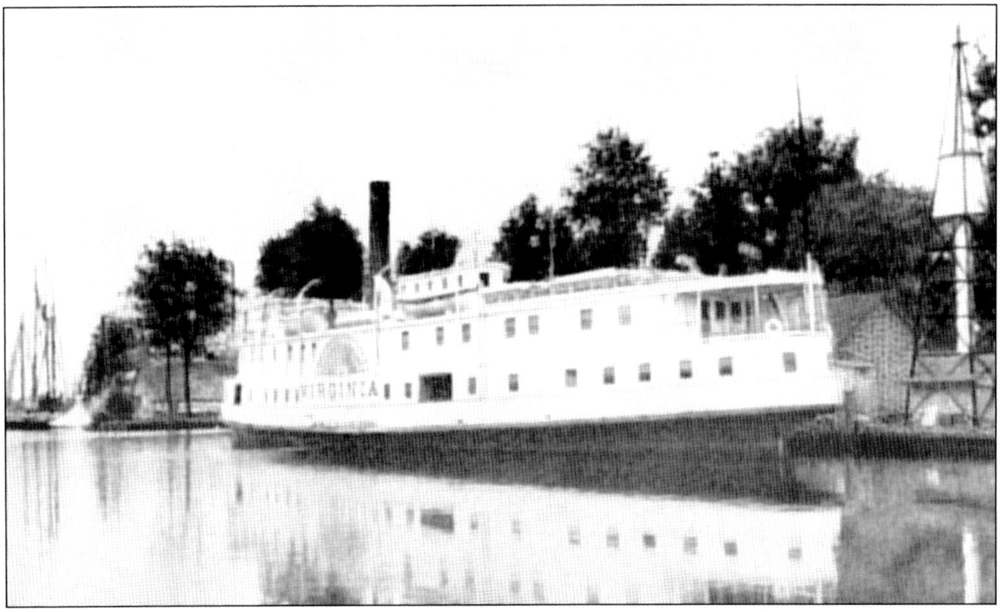

STEAMSHIP *VIRGINIA*. Seen around 1930, this section of town looked much different today. On the right is the H&P Wheat Market, but the buildings next to it are gone, allowing for a parking lot and the expansion of Mill Street. The Bridge Uniform Company building has the Port Exchange, and the building next to that is gone. The structure with the "Hardware" sign still remains as Parker Place. The *Virginia* played a vital role in loading up produce from farmers at wharves and shipping the goods. (Courtesy of the Palmer Gillis collection.)

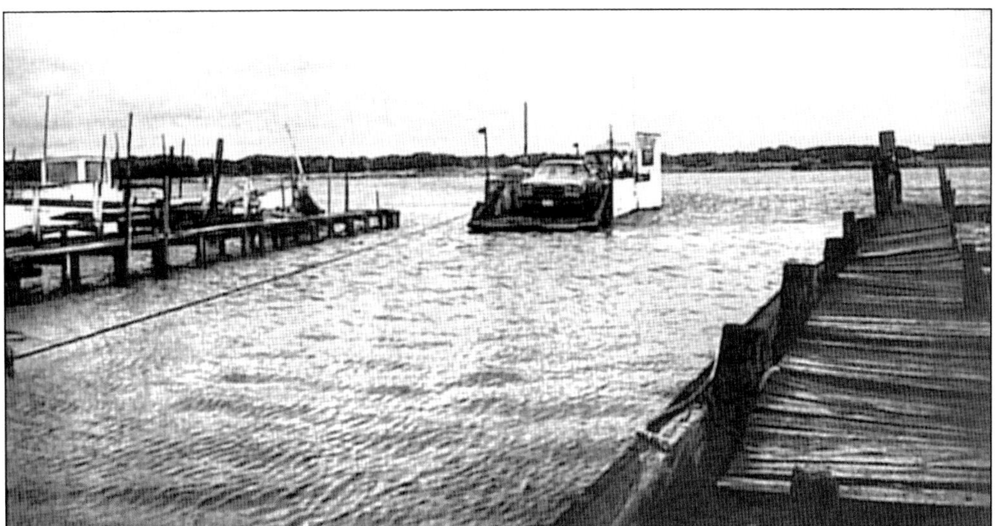

SHORTCUT ACROSS THE RIVER. This classic and well-known photograph of Whitehaven Ferry shows one of the two ferries in Wicomico County; the other is the Upper Ferry that crosses closer to the city of Salisbury; both carry three cars. The Upper Ferry makes about 200 crossing per day across the 5-mile river span. The Whitehaven Ferry is one of the oldest in the United States, and the town was a 19th-century steamboat stop. (*Salisbury, Maryland: Central City of the Eastern Shore.*)

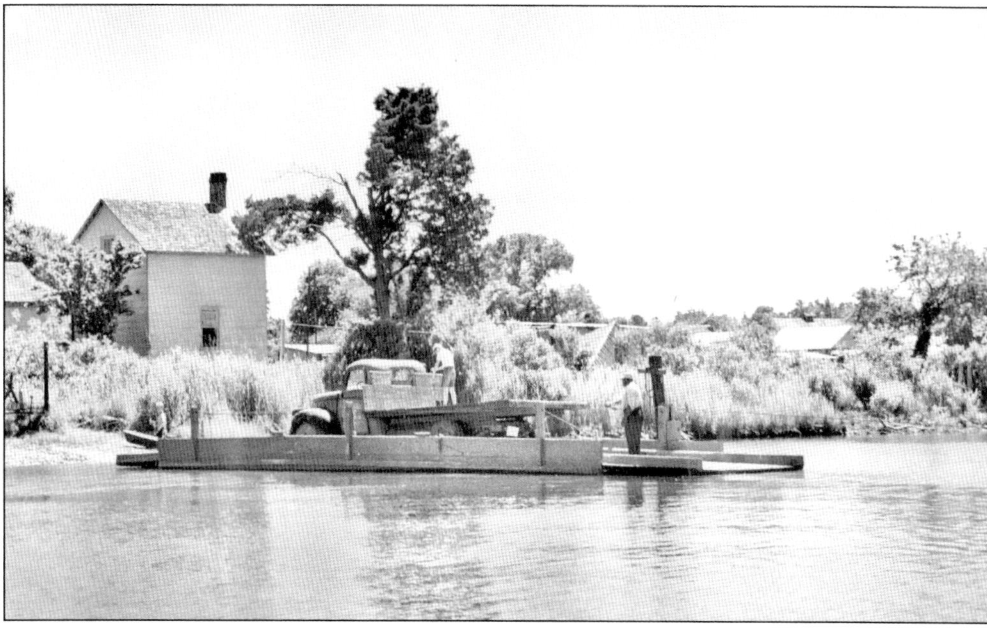

CONNECTING TO THE OTHER SIDE. Ferry traffic has been a part of life in Wicomico County for centuries, long before it became independent of Somerset County. Upper Ferry connects the fast-growing Pemberton Drive area with the sleepy communities of Siloam, Eden, and Allen to allow travelers heading south an alternative to a long journey down Nanticoke Road to Salisbury and around the Wicomico River. The county once boasted at least four ferries: Reading Ferry, Whitehaven Ferry, Upper Ferry, and Trap (now Allen). (Courtesy of Salisbury Chamber of Commerce.)

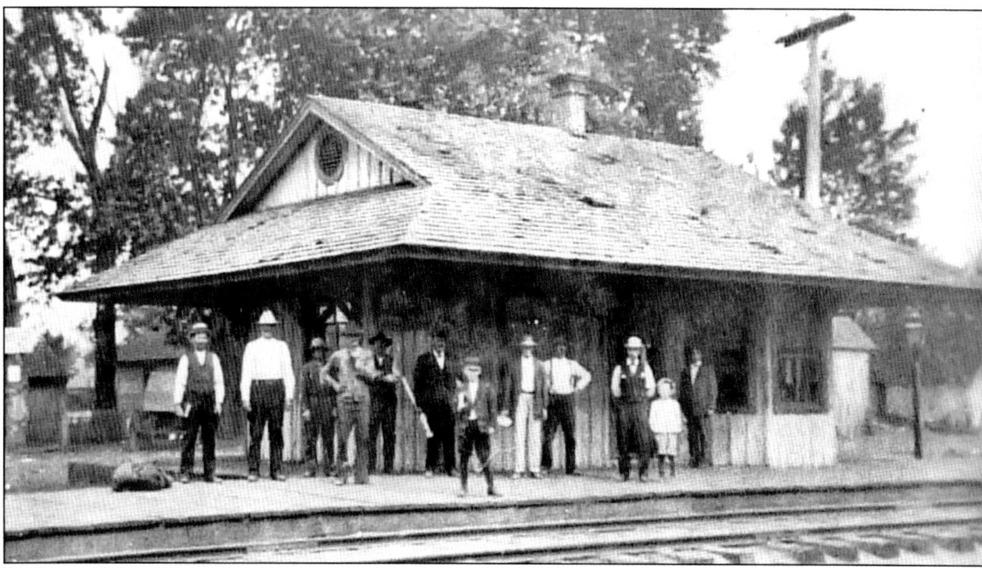

PITTSVILLE RAILROAD STATION. This 1906 photograph of the railroad station shows its considerable size, which was needed for crop transportation, especially the shipping of strawberries. Prior to the construction of this building, the Wicomico County station was the hub, but it proved too small and was moved to another location. The Pittsville Station went out of business when the railroad went into receivership. It's a professional office now. (Courtesy of the John E. Jacob Collection.)

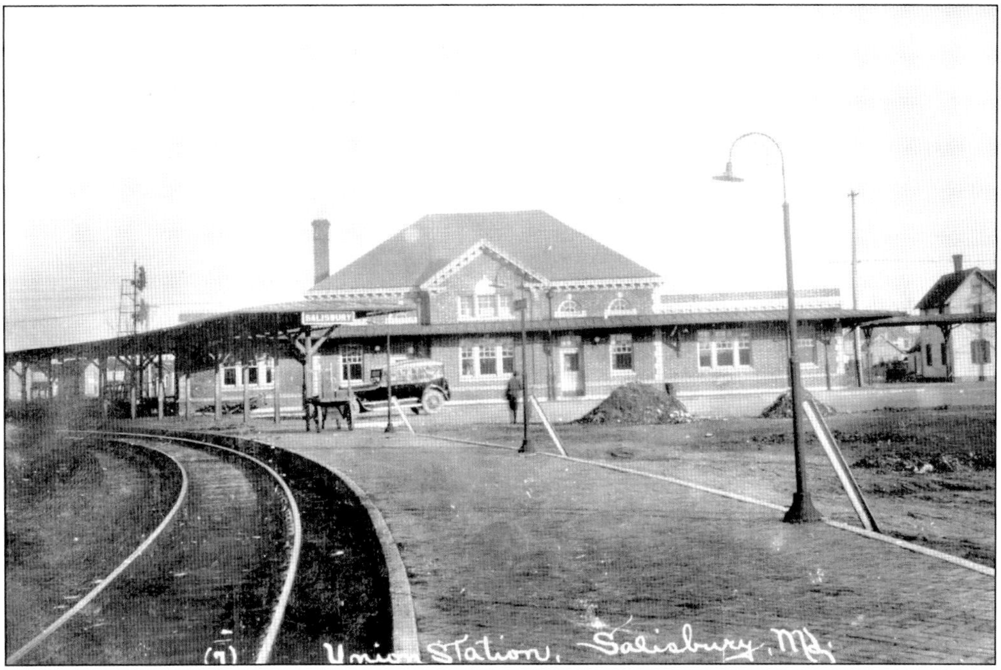

ALL ABOARD! Union Station, built in 1914, served both Pennsylvania and the B.C. & A. lines. It was eventually sold to a sign company and then passed into the hands of other entrepreneurs. Located in Salisbury, it served a wide area and was one of the larger rail terminals on the Eastern Shore, as the railroad was a major form of transportation for all of the peninsula and especially Wicomico County, where most residents were employed and much of the area's activities took place. (Courtesy of George Chevallier.)

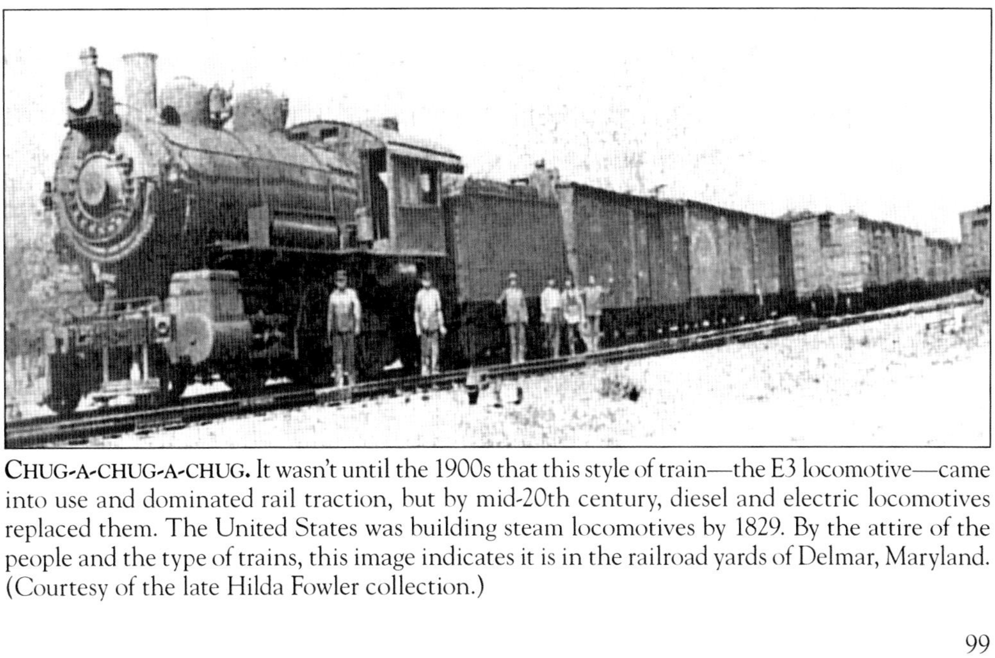

CHUG-A-CHUG-A-CHUG. It wasn't until the 1900s that this style of train—the E3 locomotive—came into use and dominated rail traction, but by mid-20th century, diesel and electric locomotives replaced them. The United States was building steam locomotives by 1829. By the attire of the people and the type of trains, this image indicates it is in the railroad yards of Delmar, Maryland. (Courtesy of the late Hilda Fowler collection.)

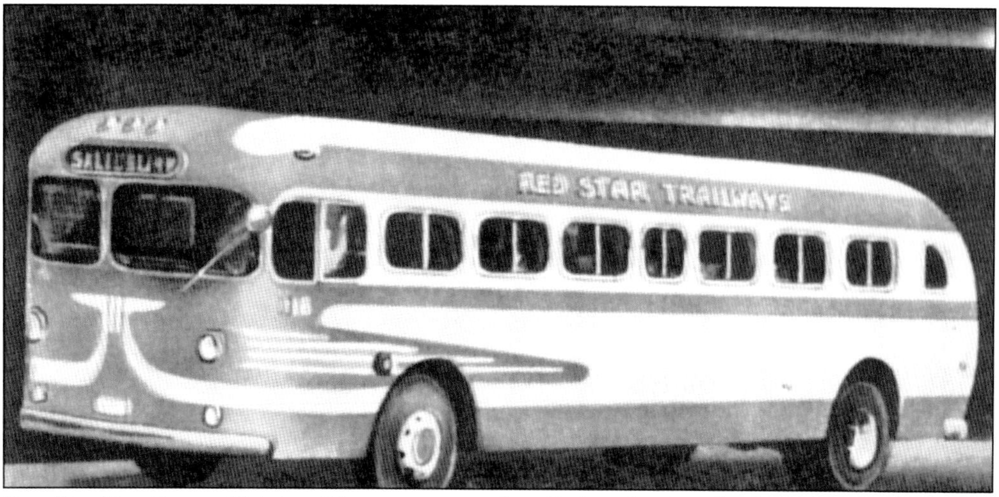

RED EYE RED STAR. This is a 27-seat passenger bus. Before this bus fleet went into receivership and was purchased by another company who sold it to Carolina Trailways, it was operated by Red Star Motor Coaches—a name that came about through a name-the-company contest in 1926. Bus service still operates to this day and serves as a major form of transportation along with the county's ShoreTransit metro system. (Courtesy of the John E. Jacob Collection.)

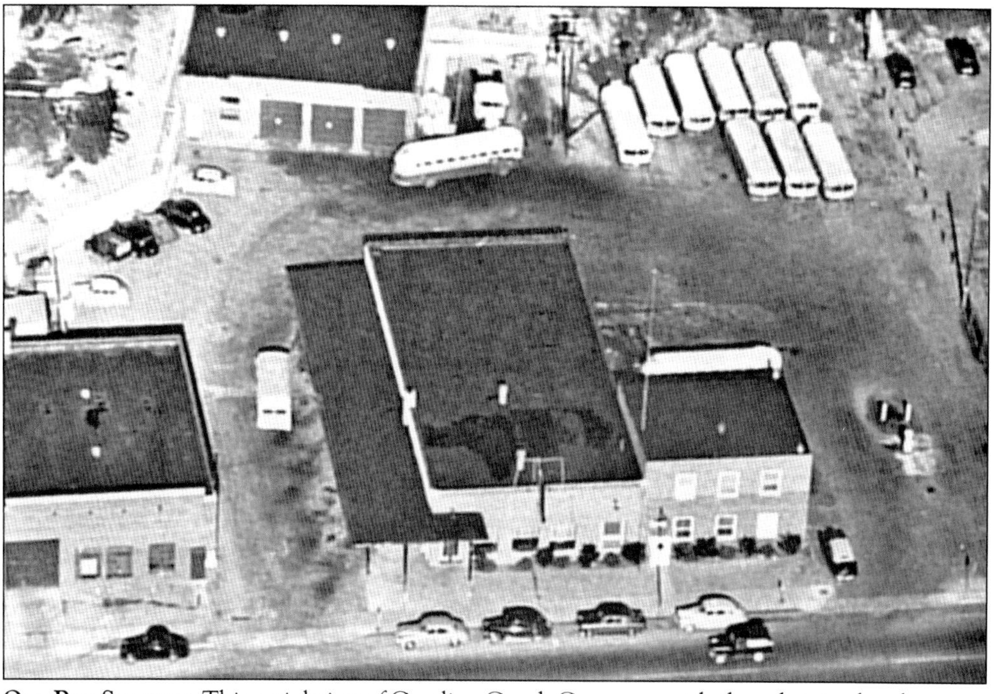

OLD BUS STATION. This aerial view of Carolina Coach Company, with their division headquarters in Wicomico, was taken around 1950. Because the shore is a peninsula, transportation to major cities was limited, so coach service was popular. The Greyhound Lines also ran from New York to Norfolk. Over 35 buses were scheduled out of Salisbury daily to Wilmington, Philadelphia, Baltimore, Washington, and Norfolk. This station moved from Main Street to Route 50 and Cypress Street. (*Salisbury, Maryland: The Central City of the Eastern Shore.*)

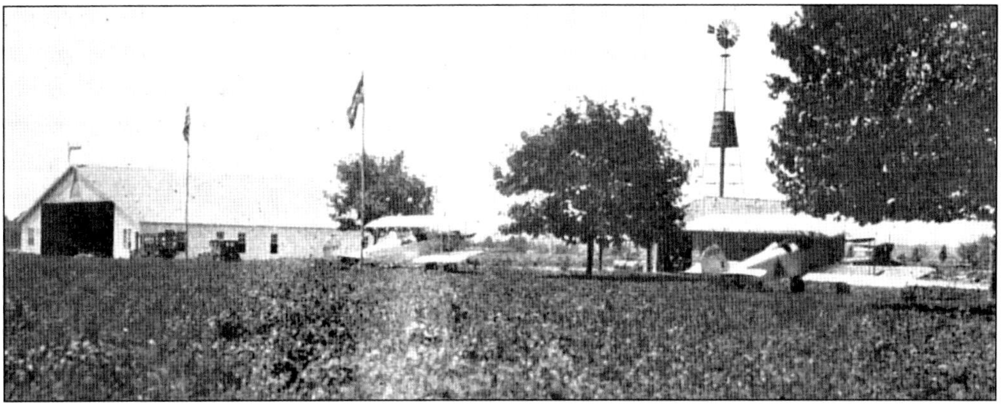

MORE THAN A FIELD. This 1928 photograph shows the field and hangars of Hebron Airport landing grounds with two Starlighter planes. This field was considered to have the longest runway at 1 3/8 miles long. This was believed to handle any "large planes in the future." Hebron airfield pales in comparison to today's Salisbury–Ocean City Airport—the second largest airport in the state. (*Del-Mar-Va Eastern Shore Airport Starlighters.*)

The Pride of Del-Mar-Va's

Eastern Shore

—THE—

Hebron Airport

Distributors for

American Eagle Aircraft and Monoid Propellers

Pennsylvania, Delaware, Maryland

Sightseeing Flights Over Eastern Shore

$3.50 per person Open Planes

$5.00 per person Cabin Planes

Night Advertising Illuminated Lettering

Aerial Surveys and Photography

General Advertising

Exhibition Aeroplane Agents

Crop Dusting Sightseeing

School of Aeronautics

PLEASURE OR BUSINESS FLIGHTS

—— Aviation ——

In All Its Branches

For Information Call

THE WICOMICO HOTEL TRAVEL BUREAU

OR PHONE 1849-F-12

THAT'S DEDICATION. This poster appeared in the 1928 "Del-Mar-Va Eastern Shore Airport Official Program" in honor of the new Hebron airport dedication. The program reads, "It was after a most thorough investigation that the present site was selected because there they found . . . a well located, fairly level, and a property which could be made into a model aviation field . . . [that] Del-Mar-Va described as . . . an 'Aviator's Paradise.' " (*Del-Mar-Va Eastern Shore Airport Starlighters.*)

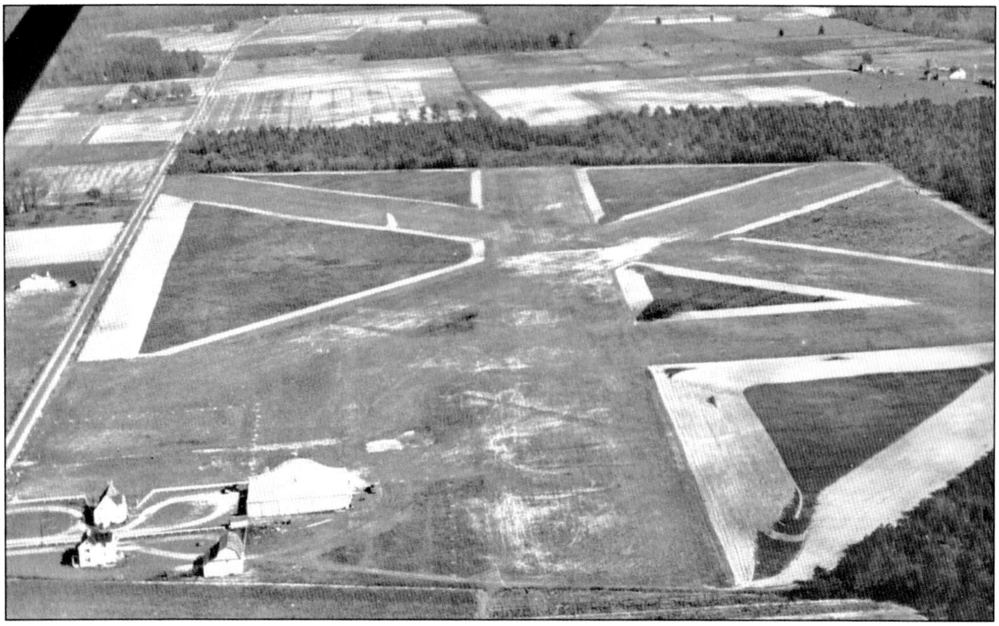

COME FLY WITH ME. Salisbury–Ocean City–Wicomico Regional Airport was created during World War II as a public works project, and navy pilots trained there during the war. After the war, it was acquired by the city and county and became home to a number of airlines over the decades until stabilizing in 1968, when Richard Henson brought his airline company to Wicomico County. It was sold to US Airways in 1992. (Photograph by James Perry; courtesy of Salisbury Chamber of Commerce.)

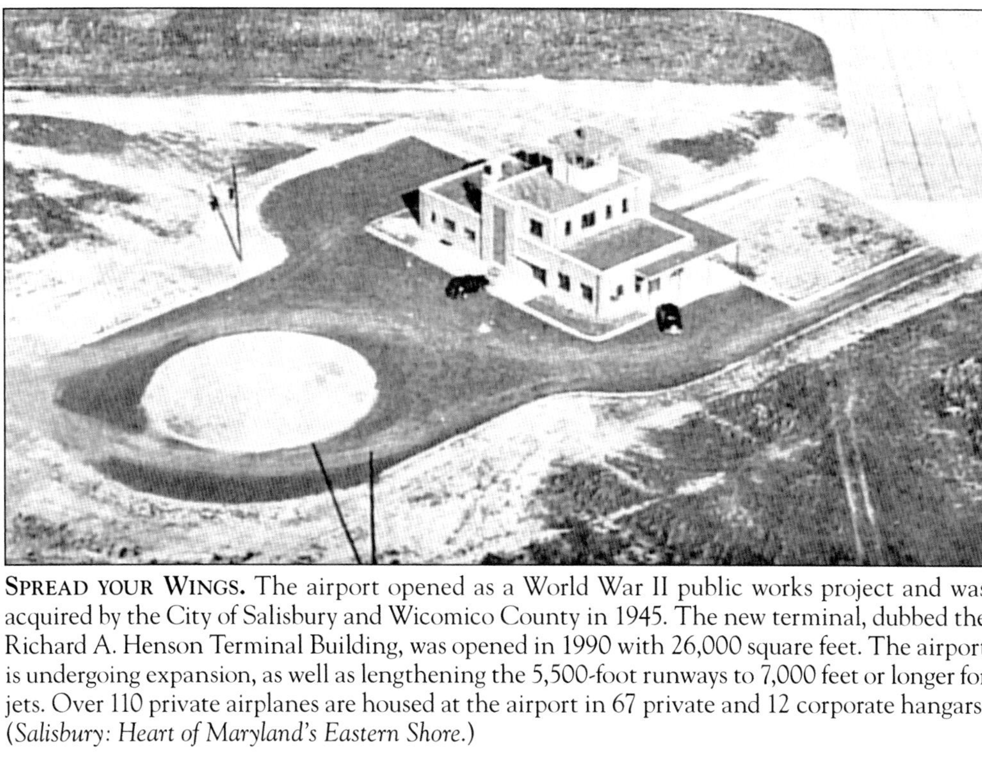

SPREAD YOUR WINGS. The airport opened as a World War II public works project and was acquired by the City of Salisbury and Wicomico County in 1945. The new terminal, dubbed the Richard A. Henson Terminal Building, was opened in 1990 with 26,000 square feet. The airport is undergoing expansion, as well as lengthening the 5,500-foot runways to 7,000 feet or longer for jets. Over 110 private airplanes are housed at the airport in 67 private and 12 corporate hangars. (*Salisbury: Heart of Maryland's Eastern Shore.*)

Eight

Playtime

The people of Wicomico County and its visitors have been blessed over the centuries with a multiplicity of things to do for fun and relaxation. Bounded by water, the county had numerous swimming beaches, notably along the Nanticoke, as well as the municipal park, where residents not only swam but also bathed many, many years ago. Several lakes also provided swimming areas, but these have all closed in recent years because of increasing levels of *E. coli* bacteria. Boating, fishing, and water sports continue to be popular around the county. Besides the water, a number of traditions have continued over the decades, starting with county fairs and spreading to communities on the West Side that hold firemen's carnivals. Diversity has spawned other festivals celebrating ethnic pride as well as various harvest and heritage events. Riverfest, the Salisbury Festival, and many other events provide family unity and the sharing of joy with others. Sports have always been a popular pastime, and the county boasts several great complexes and is home to the minor league Delmarva Shorebirds. Parks also dot the landscape, from the celebrated Salisbury Zoo to Bivalve. Campgrounds are available for the adventurous, and fishing piers allow communing with the water. There is something for everybody in Wicomico County.

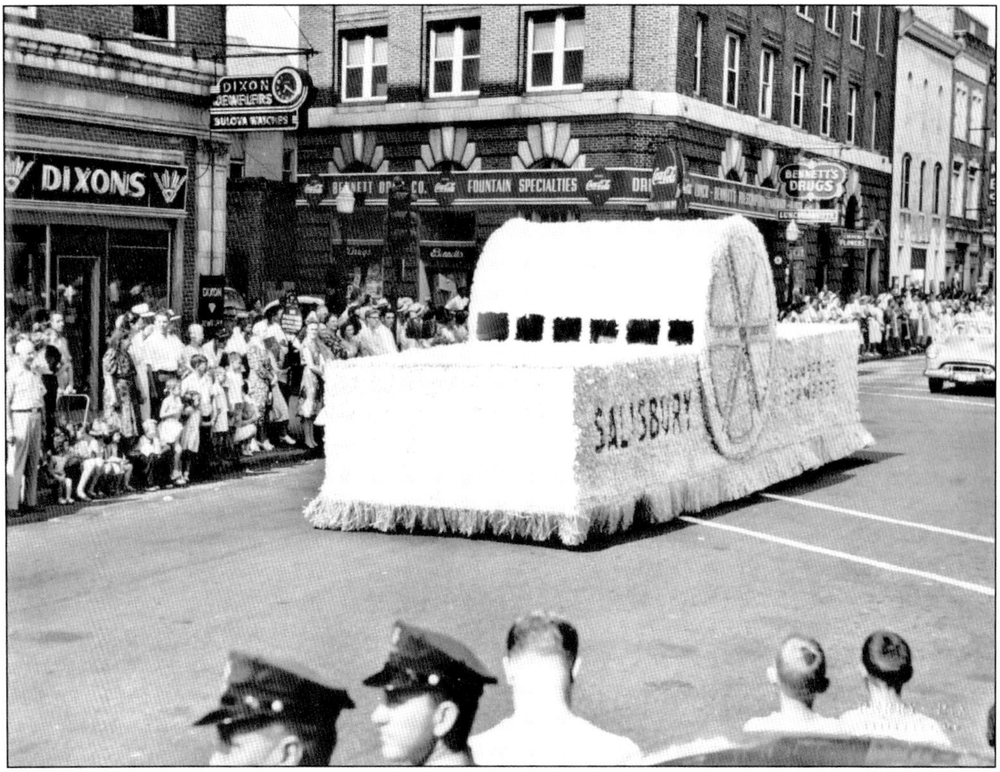

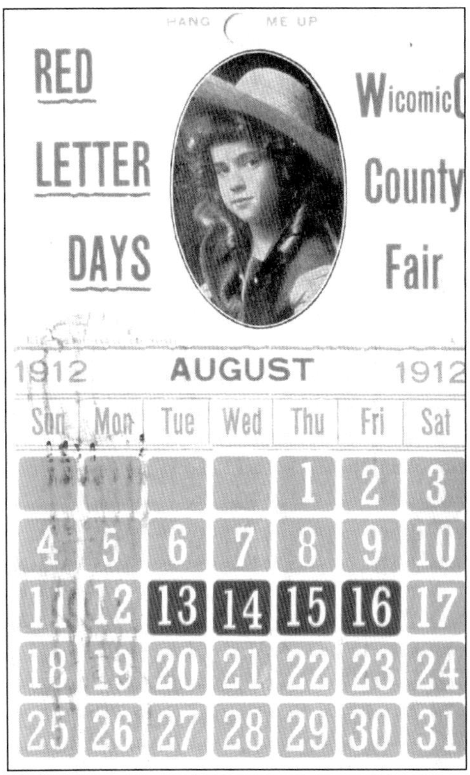

FLOAT ON BY. This undated photograph from the middle of the last century shows a chamber of commerce float heading down Main Street in one of the many parades held countywide, even today. With the closing of Main Street in the 1970s, new routes were found, and today the largest remaining parade is the Salisbury Christmas parade, which still draws a large crowd. (Photograph by Perry Pix; courtesy of Salisbury Chamber of Commerce.)

COUNTY FAIR-EST OF ALL. August 1909 featured the first county fair, with a built grandstand for 3,500 spectators; harness racing was a main event. The Depression closed it in 1933. The Jaycees tried a similar event about six years later. Fair buildings have long been torn down. It was located at Parsons Road and Pemberton Drive, which are now well developed with businesses, restaurants, school, and many subdivisions. (Courtesy of George Chevallier.)

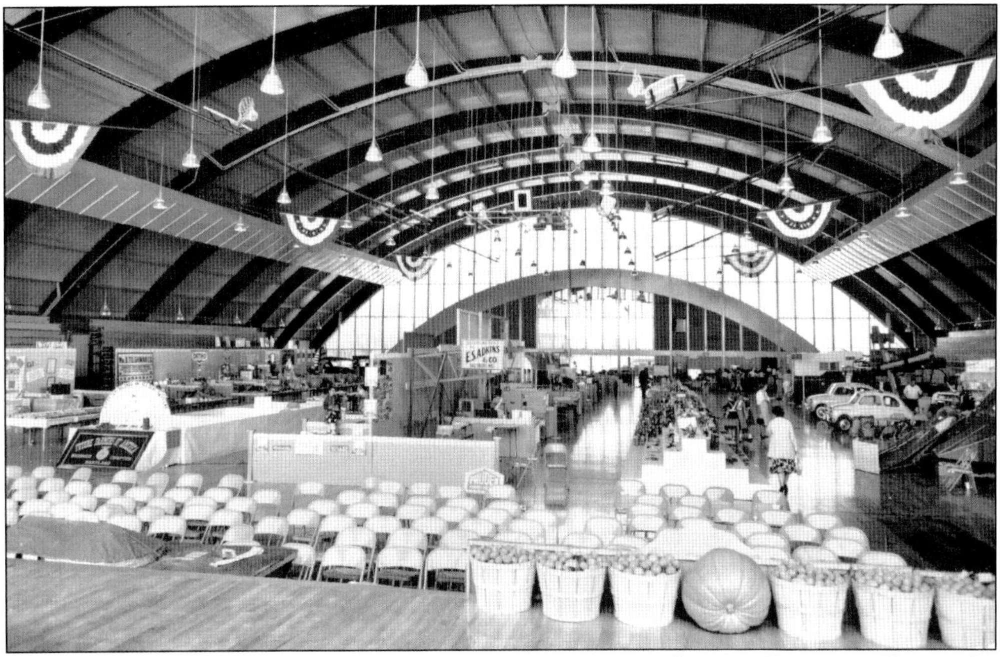

PRODUCE IT! This 1960 photograph of the Wicomico Farm and Home Show was taken at the old civic center. The show, not quite a county fair, was a popular event and drew crowds and politicians alike. (Courtesy of Salisbury Chamber of Commerce.)

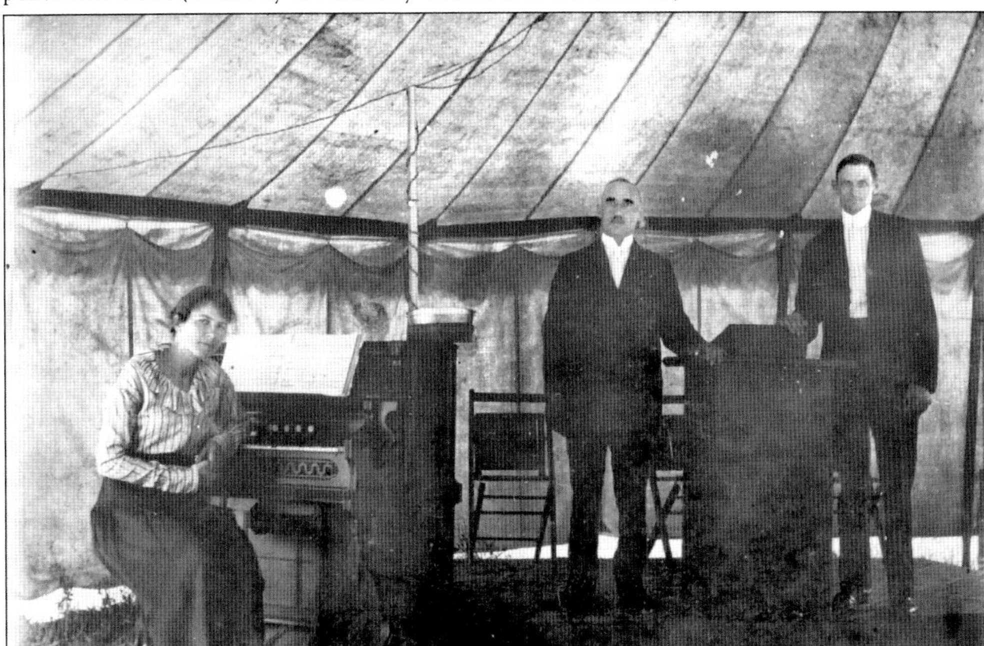

FAIR AMOUNT OF ENTERTAINMENT. This 1917 photograph shows a group of traveling singers during a performance at the county fair, which was a great place to show off talent, singing, acrobatics, political speeches, and magic. Rides, cotton candy, brass bands, and contests were all part of the fair, entertaining a society with no television and few radios. Nowadays you can't tear people away from the Internet. (Courtesy of George Chevallier.)

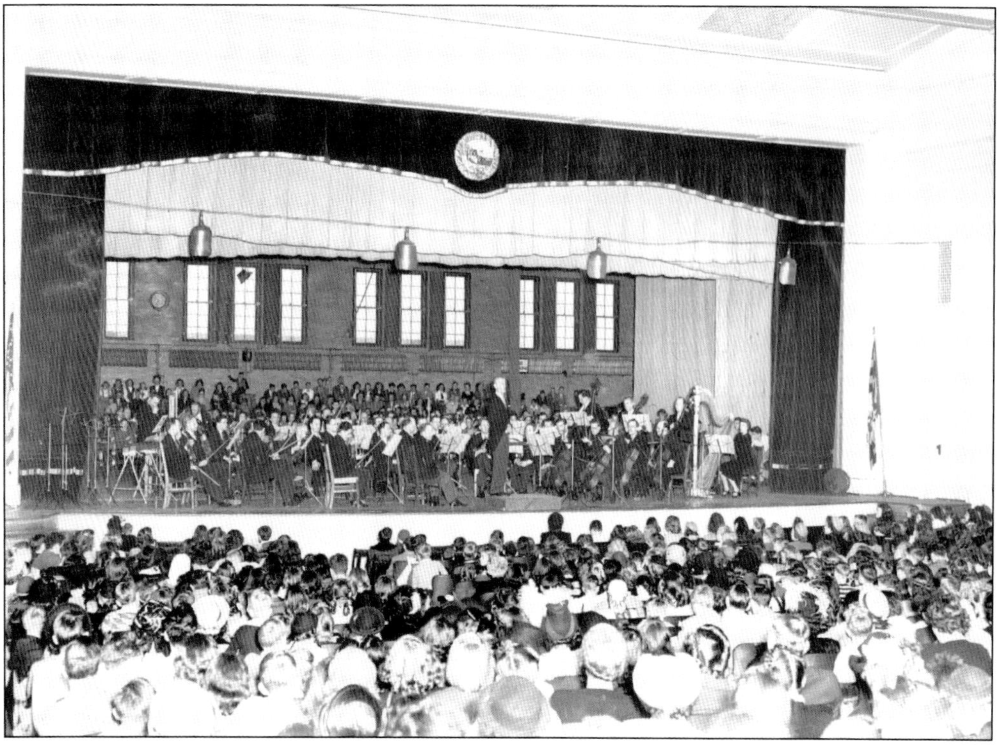

MUSIC HATH CHARMS TO SOOTHE THE SAVAGE BEAST. The Salisbury Symphony Orchestra has entertained county residents for generations, as shown in this undated photograph from the mid-1900s. It continues to operate from the campus of Salisbury University. (Courtesy of Salisbury Chamber of Commerce.)

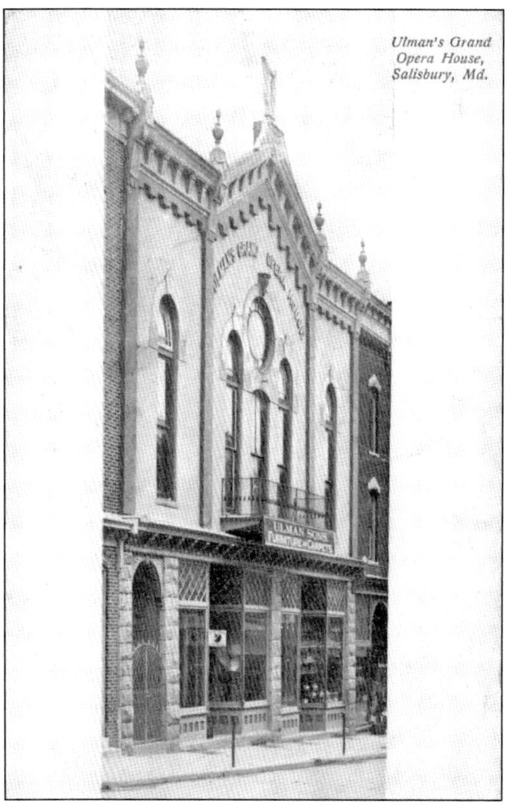

HIGH AND LOW DRAMA. The Ullman Opera House opened downtown in Salisbury on January 30, 1888, a 600-seat theater above a liquor store. It hosted a variety of stage shows, from the theatrical to the burlesque. It soon moved to movies until its destruction by fire. (Courtesy of George Chevallier.)

JUST A REMINDER. This postcard from May 1939 was meant to be hung in a handy location. The Arcade Theater opened in 1914 and burned some 30 years later and was refurbished as the Playhouse, where stage productions were performed. (Courtesy of George Chevallier.)

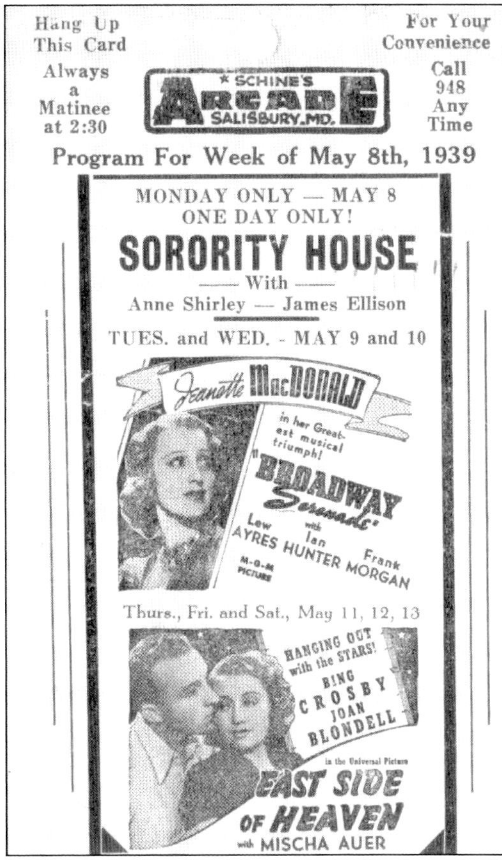

Hang Up This Card

For Your Convenience

Always a Matinee at 2:30

★ SCHINE'S ARCADE SALISBURY, MD.

Call 948 Any Time

Program For Week of May 8th, 1939

MONDAY ONLY — MAY 8
ONE DAY ONLY!

SORORITY HOUSE
— With —
Anne Shirley — James Ellison

TUES. and WED. - MAY 9 and 10

Thurs., Fri. and Sat., May 11, 12, 13

END OF AN ERA. One of the last of its breed, this movie theater was originally called the Boulevard. Furnished in art deco style, it opened in 1948 and remained popular even after theaters opened in the Salisbury Mall and the K-Mart shopping center. Regal Cinemas expanded the theater late in the last century, but it could not compete with Regal's Movies 10 at the Centre at Salisbury and was closed. The Salisbury-Wicomico Arts Council attempted to reopen it as a center for the performing arts, but funding was never found, and the building is now slated to be torn down. This recent photograph shows its faded glory. (Photograph by Andy Nunez.)

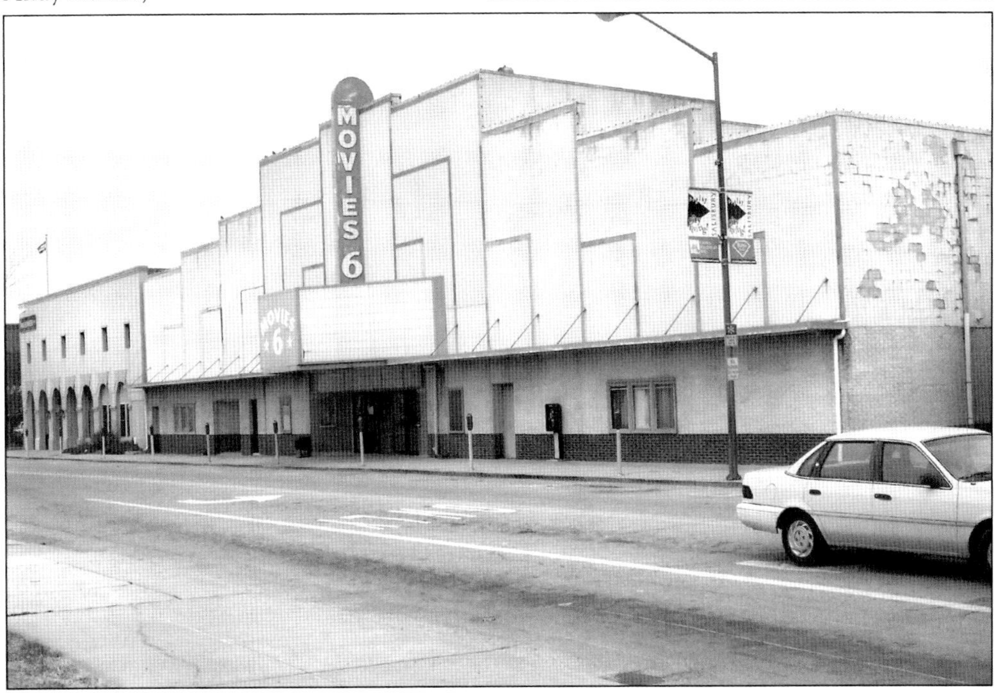

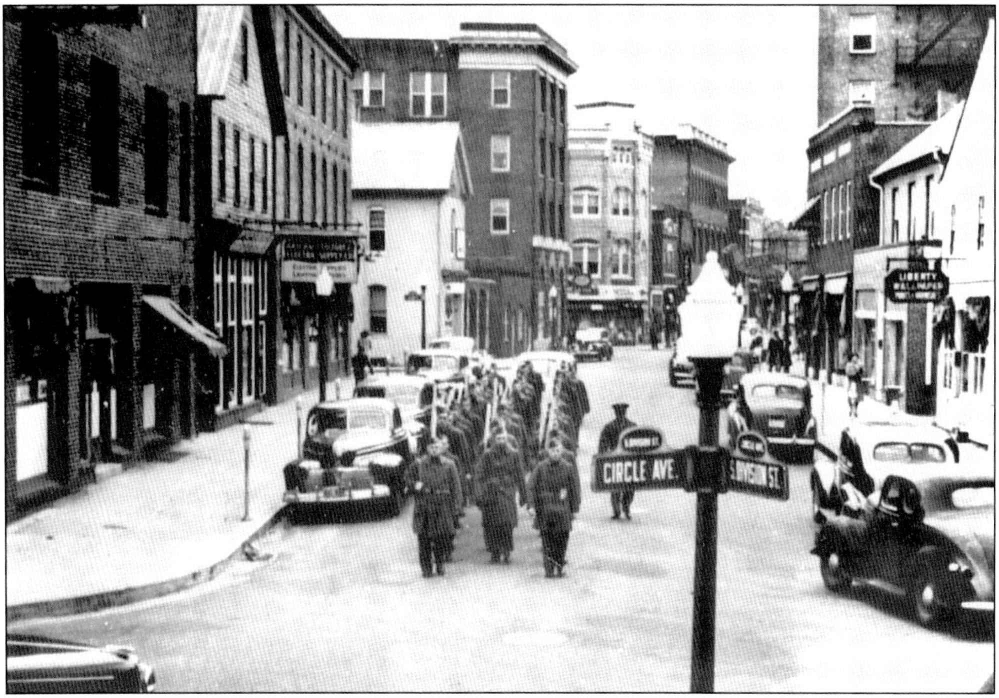

HUT TO! The Circle Avenue indicated on the lantern was likely renamed Camden Avenue, as it exists today. This mid-1940s photograph appears to be soldiers marching in memoriam or to their barracks for war. Most of the businesses on South Division Street have changed owners and names. The tall building to the right is the former Wicomico Hotel, which serves as an office building now. (Courtesy of the Palmer Gillis collection.)

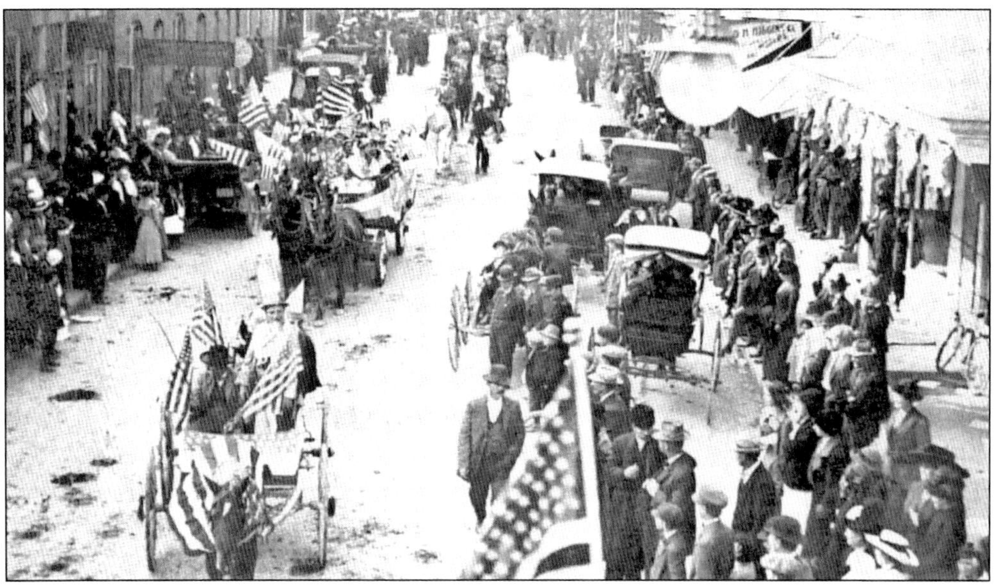

V FOR VICTORY. This is a 1912 photograph, as the celebration here in Salisbury is because of the presidential victory of Woodrow Wilson; this was the first parade for the Democratic winners since Pres. Grover Cleveland's second term. Notice the buggies and U.S. flags forming the parade. (Courtesy of Dr. Laurence Claggett.)

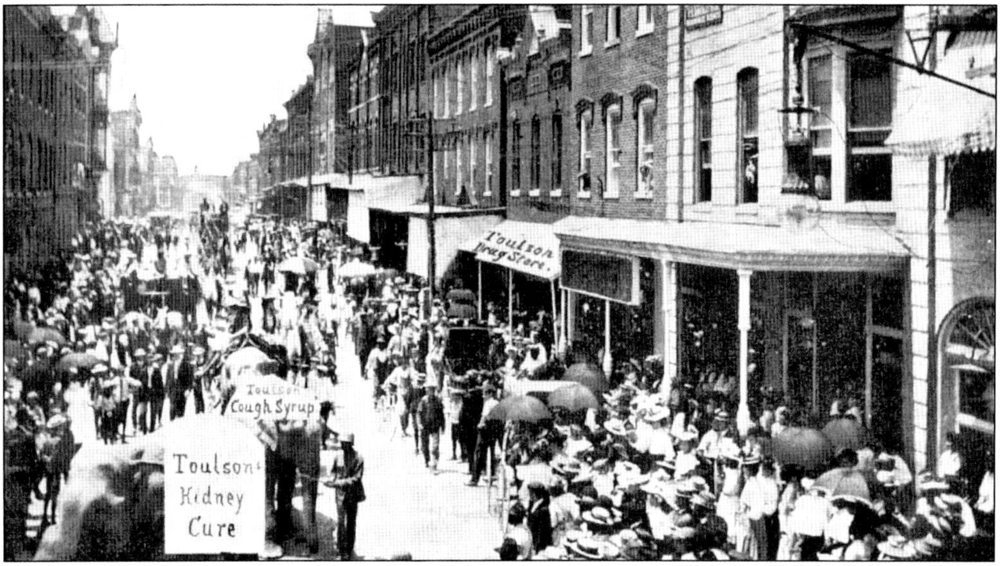

KIDNEY CURE, AROUND 1910. Fair Day was held in the summers and called "Whitsunday Fair." Toulson's Drug Store—which opened in 1907 and can be seen to the right in this *c.* 1910 photograph—was doing a fund-raiser for kidney disease. Notice the umbrellas and hats shielding the people from the sun and the vendors in the street selling their wares, such as cough syrup. (Courtesy of the John E. Jacob Collection.)

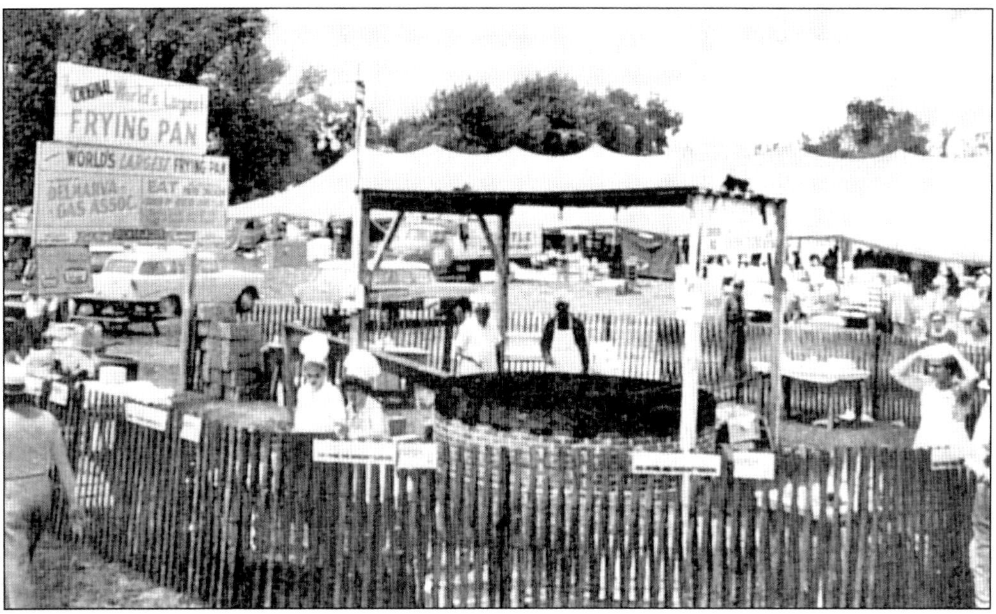

MAMA MIA. WHAT A FRYING PAN. A huge frying pan—10 feet in diameter—is one of the instruments for the Delmarva Chicken Festival. It's believed to hold over 100 gallons of oil and is able to cook about 10,000 pieces of chicken per day. Similar to this is the large rack used to barbecue chicken at the same festival. The year 2007 marked the 69th annual festival. (Courtesy of the John E. Jacob Collection.)

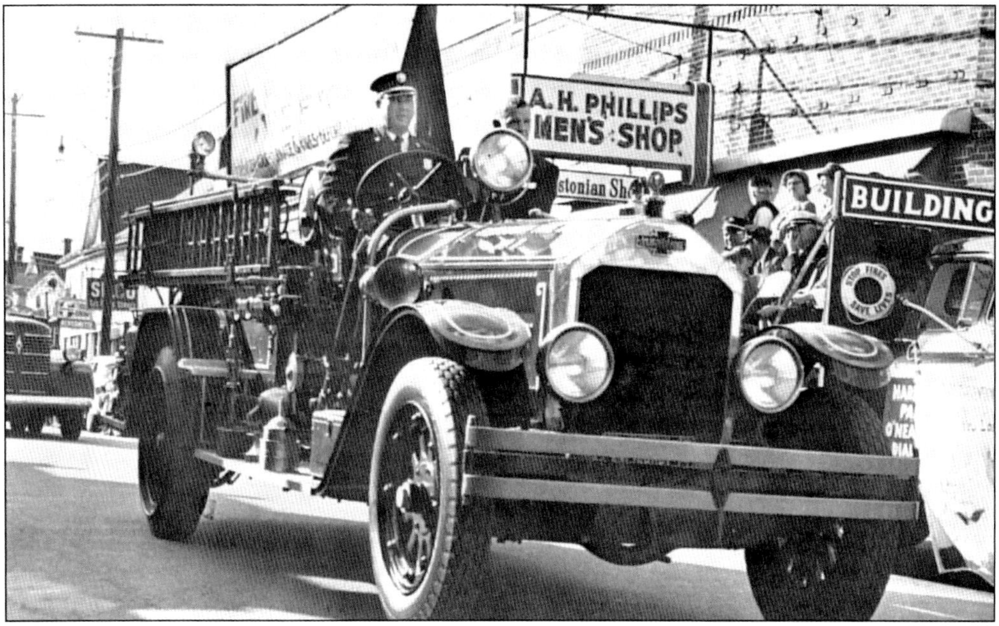

CHEERS FOR THE FIREMEN. This 1955 parade encouraged county residents to prevent fires. The small truck had a ladder, but it didn't extend far. In fact, today's buildings are not to be erected beyond seven floors because the county has no ladders long enough to meet those heights. The A. H. Phillips Men's Shop is still in business today but has moved to Civic Avenue. The sign above it reads "Fire Prevention Week." (*Our Anniversary: Salisbury Fire Department 1872–1972.*)

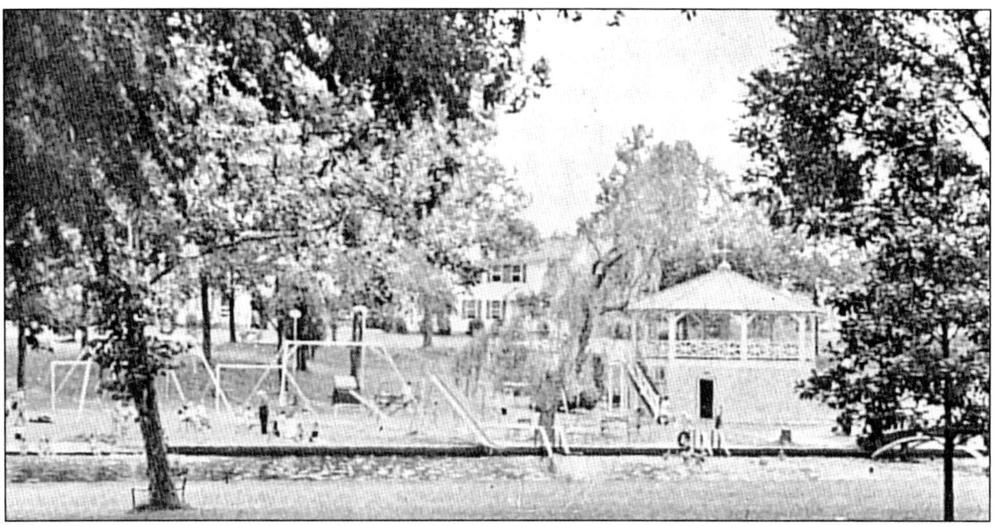

THE BAND PLAYED ON. The Municipal Park has always been a place for culture and recreation, where residents once swam (and bathed), played baseball, listened to music, and enjoyed paddle boating and the surrounding picnic and zoo facilities. Built around 1937, the bandstand had a concession stand underneath; on its top platform, a podium was erected for Vice Pres. Richard Nixon to speak to county residents. (Courtesy of the John E. Jacob Collection.)

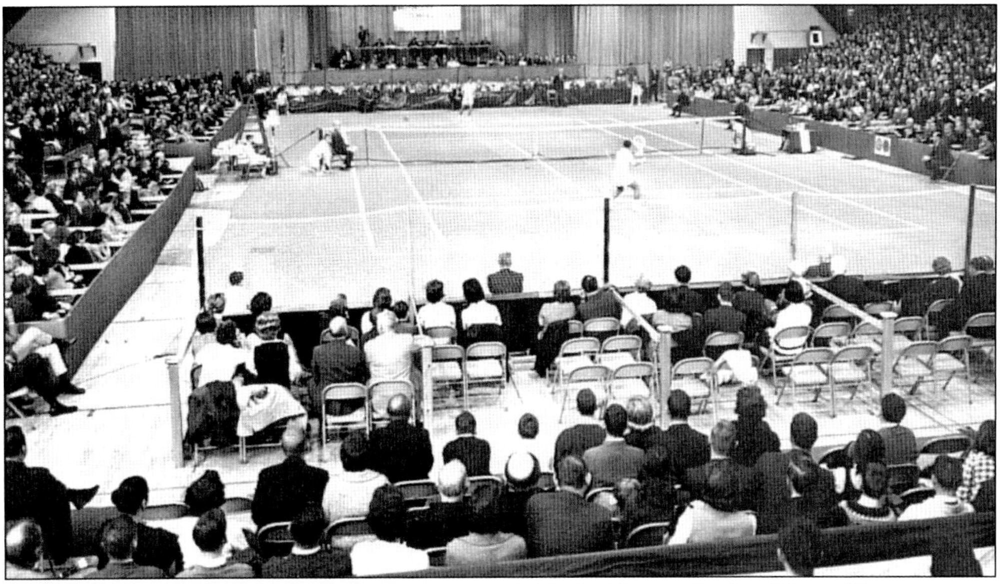

TENNIS ANYONE? This championship tennis—probably the National Indoor Tennis Tournament—was held at the Wicomico Civic Center sometime in the late 1960s or early 1970s. Natives remember well the day the civic center burned down. Today tennis remains a major recreational sport in the county, and many upscale home developments have their own private courts. (*Salisbury: Heart of the Maryland's Eastern Shore.*)

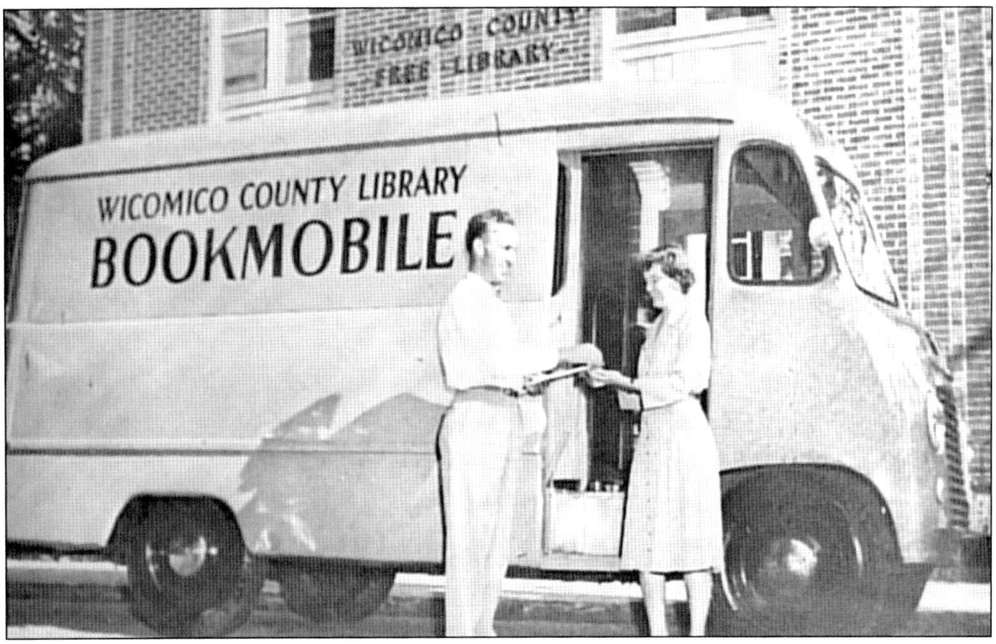

BOOKS ON THE MOVE. Wicomico County Library is the headquarters for nearly all area libraries. The bookmobile is part of its vast services for those unable to get to the libraries. This appears to be a 1955 version, while 2007 saw the purchase of yet another, larger bookmobile. Over the years, the county library has grown so much, it's currently looking at either enlarging or constructing an entirely new and larger library. Many community events take place at the library. (*Salisbury, Maryland: Central City of the Eastern Shore.*)

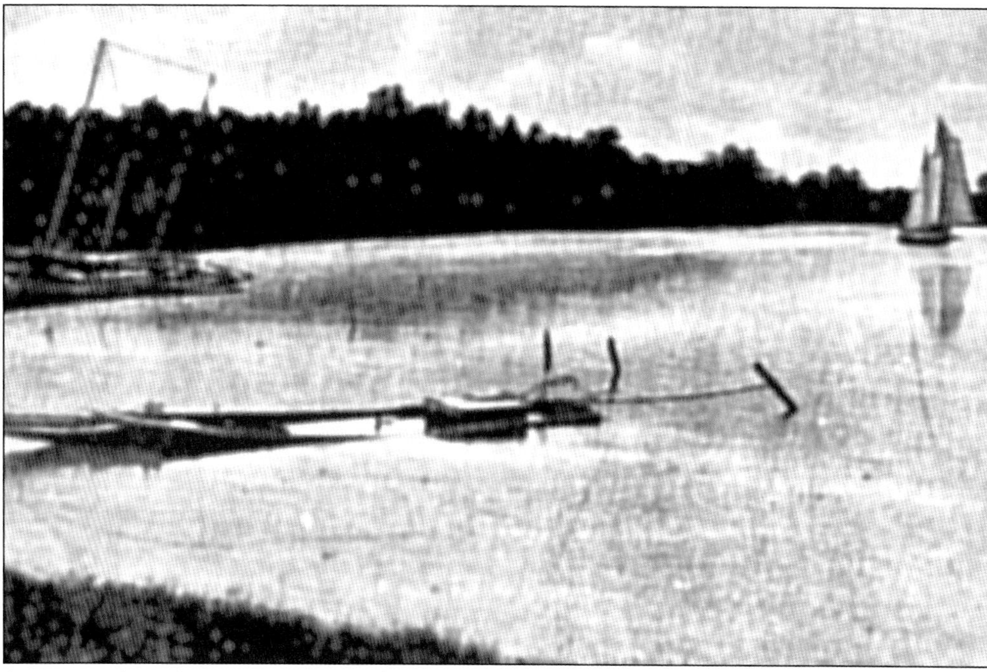

ANCHORS AWAY! Wicomico River offers a transportation seaway for ships and barges, fishing for a living, boating for fun, and beauty for everyone. A tributary of the Chesapeake Bay, it's about 33 miles long and is the second largest port in Maryland. The sailboat here appears to be sailing near Whitehaven in Wicomico County. (Courtesy of Salisbury Chamber of Commerce.)

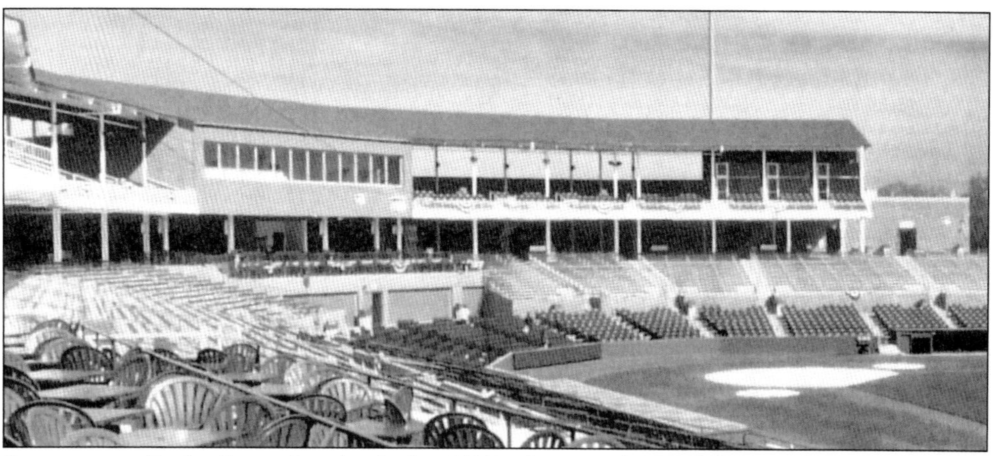

SHOREBIRDS. Perdue Farms founder Arthur W. Perdue was a baseball fan. His son Frank brought professional baseball back to the county and built a stadium in his father's name. It and the ball club—the Shorebirds—were sold to Comcast, which turned around and sold it to another investor. The club is a Baltimore Orioles Class A farm team and attracts a large spectatorship. The 12-year-old stadium houses a hall of fame, a playground, loges, and concessions. (Courtesy of Salisbury Chamber of Commerce.)

Nine

STORMS AND STARES

While the Chesapeake Bay and the Atlantic Ocean offer a playground for sunbathing, swimming, boating, and fishing, they also provide a sometimes unwanted twist and turn in the lives of county residents, as these two bodies of water can churn up some nasty weather. Nor'easters and hurricanes require residents to always be storm-prepared to move inland at the call of a warning. The storm of 1933 split Ocean City from Assateague/Chincoteague, and hurricanes make themselves known with downed wires, overturned trees, ripped-up roofs, and high river levels. Most homes in the area do not have basements because of the high water table: pounding in the footing for a swing set for the kids can cause a rush of water in one's backyard. So when storms hit, early warnings encourage "countians" to take shelter in schools or in the few underground buildings around. And while snow is limited to less than 10 inches over an entire winter, on occasion Mother Nature can kick up her heels and drop buckets of the white stuff, crippling everyone, since the cities and towns are not outfitted with heavy equipment, manpower, or abundant salt heaps to deal with the problem. More often than not, schools will close at the hint of a mild snowstorm. Until modern times, fire has been more of an issue than any storm, with the city of Salisbury having burned to the ground twice—once in 1860 and again in the Great Fire of 1886—not counting its other smaller infernos. Pair this with the hazard of overturned produce trucks accidentally releasing chicken to flap around on the roads and the occasional train mishap, and Wicomico County becomes one interesting place to live.

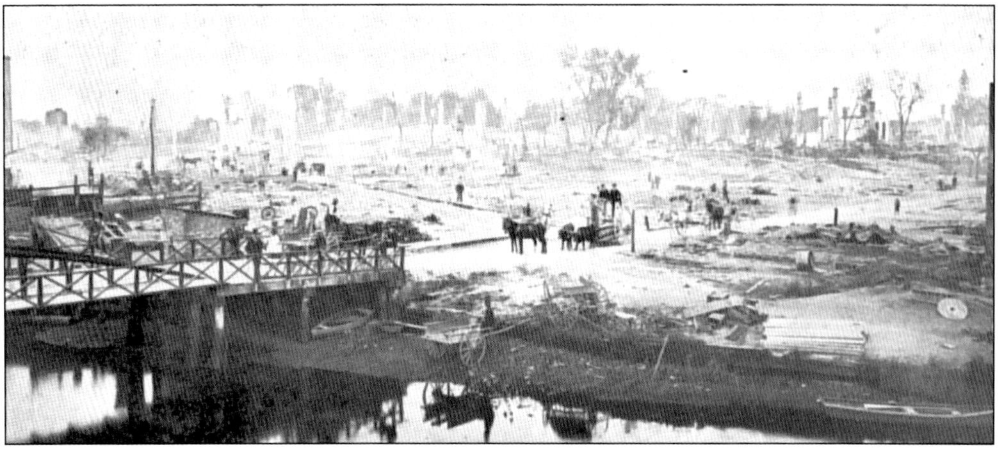

THE GREAT FIRE. The 1886 fire wiped out nearly the entire city. When the initial blaze first broke out at 7:00 p.m. at the livery, the fire was small enough to have been put out by the wooden hand-pumper, but the pumper couldn't be budged from a well only yards away, so the firemen relied on the bucket brigade. The hand-pumper had been the fire department's only equipment at the time. Ironically the fire started out 100 feet from the Wicomico River. (*Our Anniversary: Salisbury Fire Department 1872–1972.*)

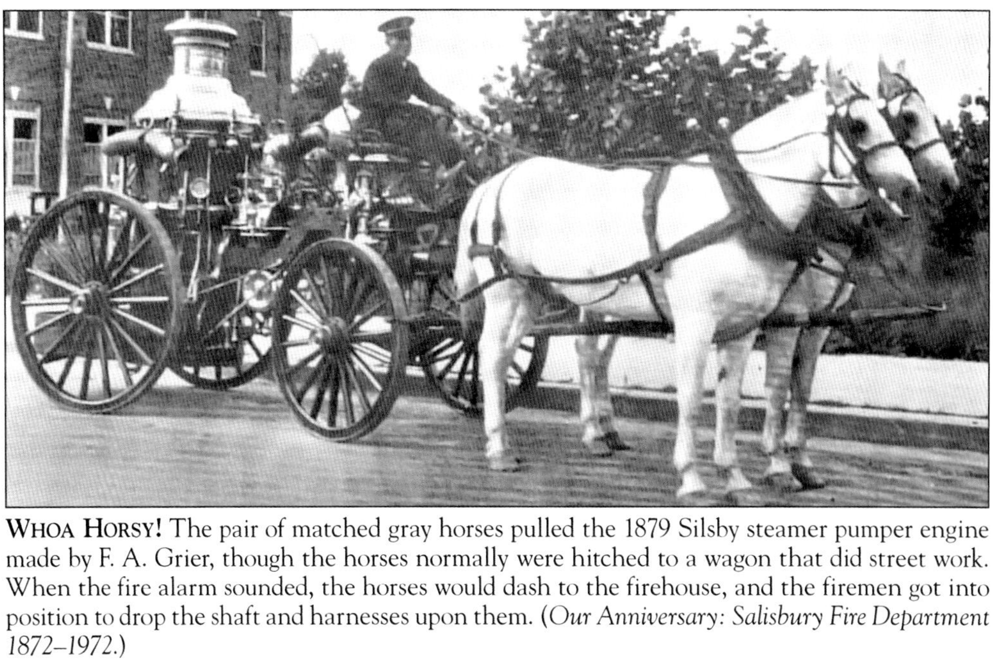

WHOA HORSY! The pair of matched gray horses pulled the 1879 Silsby steamer pumper engine made by F. A. Grier, though the horses normally were hitched to a wagon that did street work. When the fire alarm sounded, the horses would dash to the firehouse, and the firemen got into position to drop the shaft and harnesses upon them. (*Our Anniversary: Salisbury Fire Department 1872–1972.*)

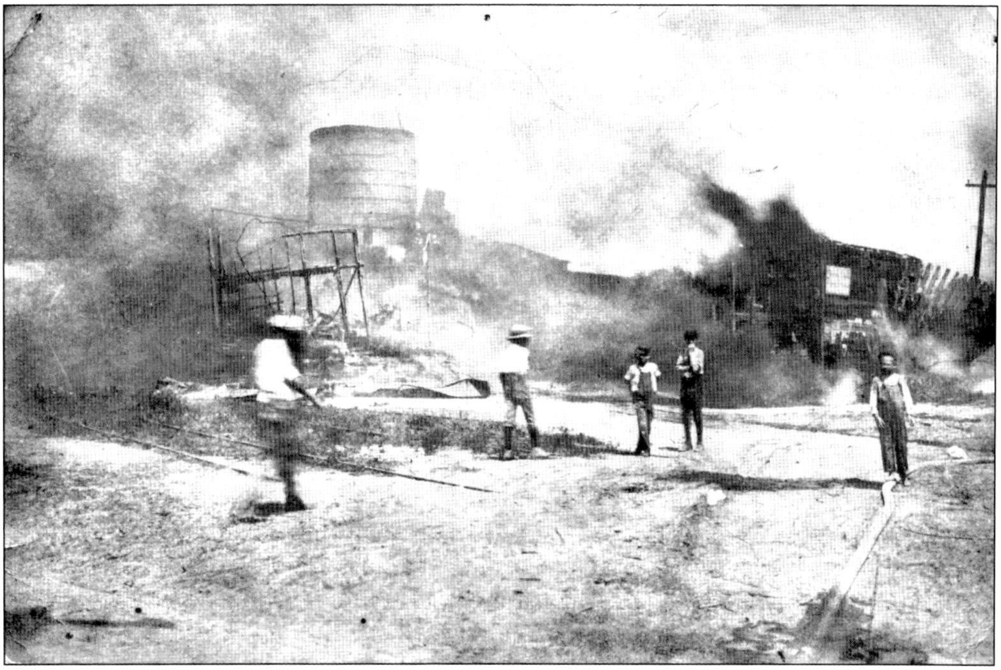

FIRE AND ICE. In 1907, the Jackson Ice Company suffered a devastating fire. It was located on the east side of Salisbury where currently an Arby's sits beside Route 50. (Courtesy of George Chevallier.)

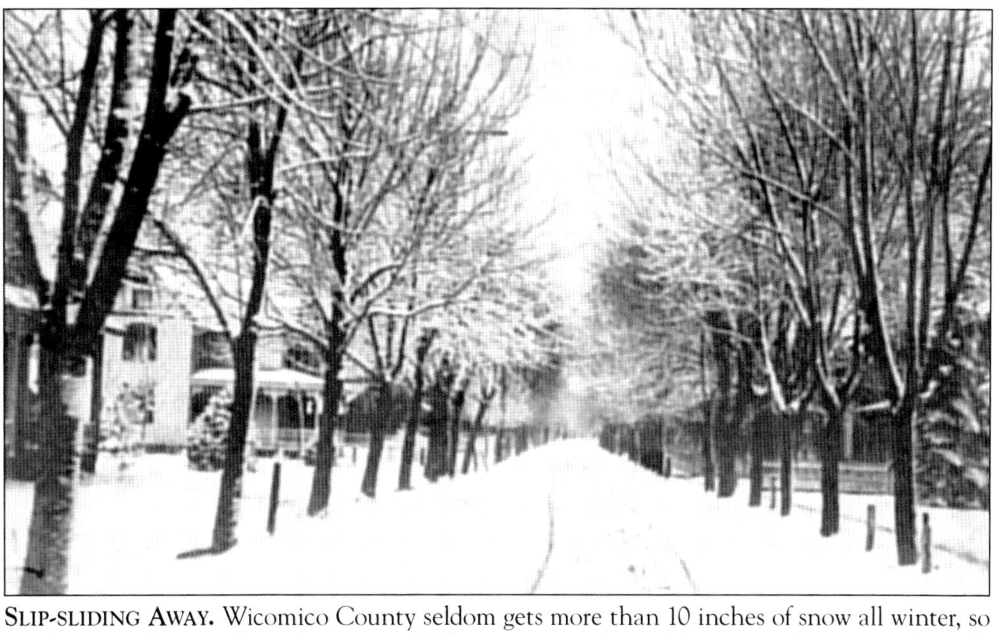

SLIP-SLIDING AWAY. Wicomico County seldom gets more than 10 inches of snow all winter, so anything similar to a blizzard is unusual. This appears to be a 1900s image showcasing how ill-prepared the town was to handle deep snow. The sign at the right reads "Southern Dairies Ice Cream." At the left is Wicomico Hotel. (Courtesy of the Palmer Gillis collection.)

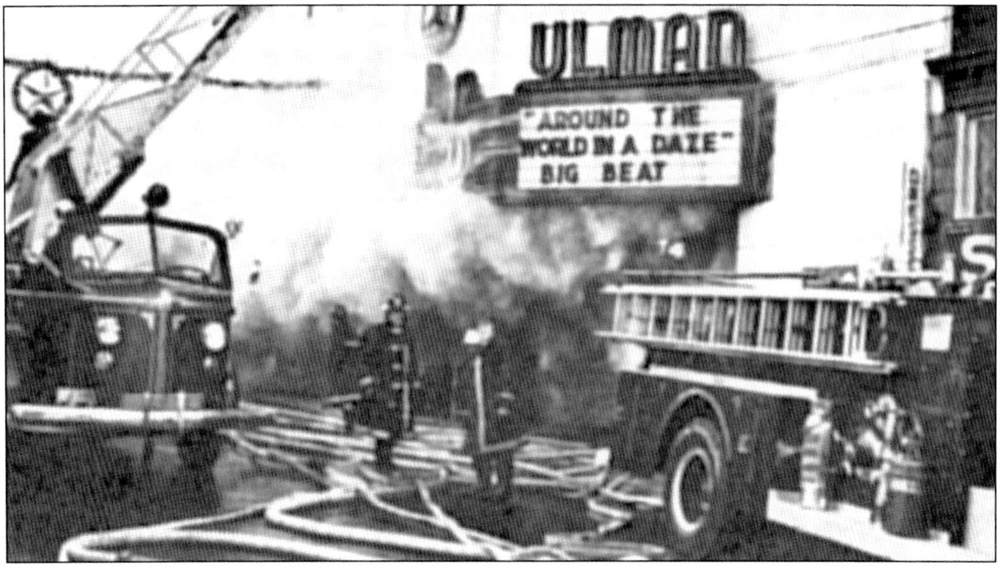

THE THREE STOOGES. Whatever the spark, the Ullman Theater burned to the ground in 1963 while the Three Stooges were going *Around the World in a Daze*. With competition from the Salisbury Mall, the old Wicomico Theater off North Division Street would barely last another decade before closing, leaving the Boulevard the single remaining theater after fire had taken out the Arcade and the Ullman. (*Our Anniversary: Salisbury Fire Department 1872–1972.*)

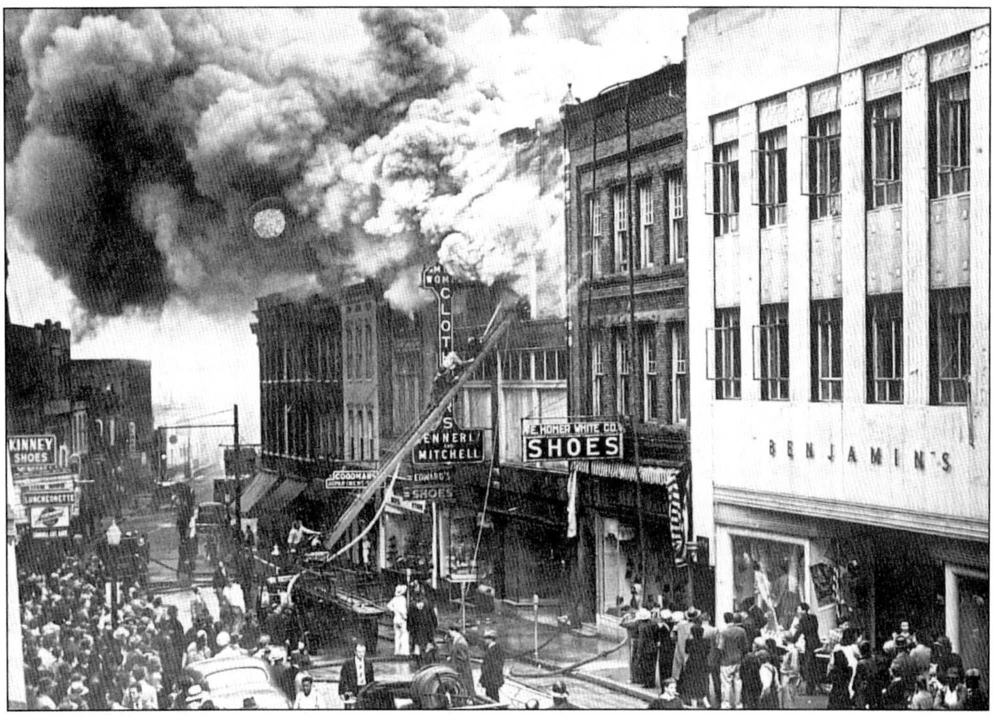

THE 1944 FIRE. This May 1944 fire took out the Kennerly building and was considered the second worst fire in the county's history. Here ladders and firemen are attempting to extinguish the fire at the top of a woman's clothing store. Next to it on the right is Homer's shoe store, and to the left is Goodman's department store. (*Salisbury, Maryland: Central City of the Eastern Shore.*)

Ten

Y'ALL COME BACK NOW

With all the growth and building going on in the county, workers need a place to stay. Couple this with visitors for popular events wanting to put their heads on nice pillows, and, voila, there is a budding hotel/motel/bed-and-breakfast business and restaurants. Wicomico County has experienced so much growth and expansion and an increase in events and recreational activities that the lodging entrepreneurs ogled the area to put their fingers in the pie. Besides the many already established motels, others are coming to the county and building faster than residents can pronounce their names. Within just the last few years alone, Marriott Inn, Ramada, Residence Inn, Microtel, Comfort Inn, and Hampton Inn have constructed large facilities, most located on Route 13. The zoning commission has recently approved even more well-known accommodations to be constructed within the year. While there are the old drive-in motels with maybe 6 to 20 rooms, new mammoth hotels are overshadowing them. Some favorites have closed to make room for more modern ones or sold out to big-box businesses such as Howard Johnson and the Lord Salisbury. The most famous hotel in the county was the Wicomico Hotel, built before 1928, charging lodgers $6 per night. When Route 50 was rerouted, the hotel hit hard times and was sold. Today it still stands with its stately look but serves as an office complex. People come to the county to visit and lodge for a variety of reasons. Ocean City, Maryland, is a major one, as hotels in Wicomico County charge less for a room than any in the resort during peak seasons. It's only about a 30-minute drive to the ocean. Drag races in nearby Delmar are another attraction, as are bike marathons, motorcycle shows, and more. People also need to eat. And Salisbury boasts some of the best restaurants on the Eastern Shore, a tradition picked up now by locally owned eateries such as Brew River, La Tolteca, the Sage Diner, Boonies, Waterman's Cove, and the Old West Steakhouse.

Our welcome mat is out. Y'all come and visit us.

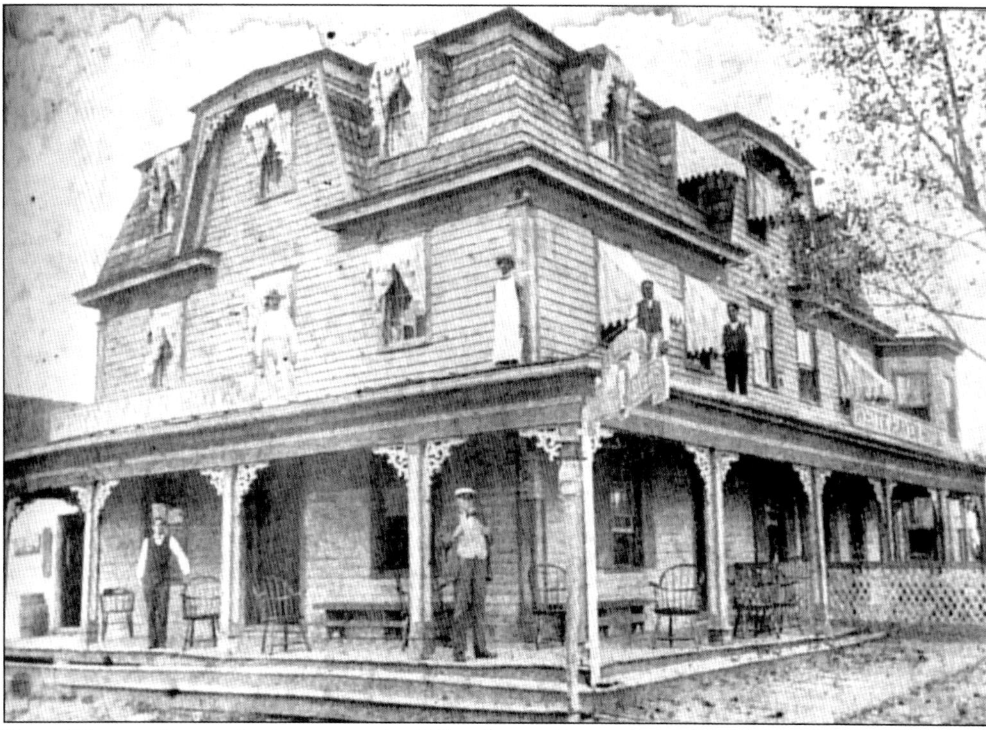

TRUE HAVEN. Situated adjacent to the Whitehaven Ferry, the Whitehaven Hotel was built in 1810 but was a private residence until 1877. As fortunes rose and declined in the Wicomico River town of Whitehaven, the hotel faced boom and bust until shipbuilding and steamboats dried up after World War II. Nearly torn down, this charming example of 19th-century architecture is now a bed and breakfast catering to a variety of upscale celebrations. (Courtesy of the John E. Jacob Collection.)

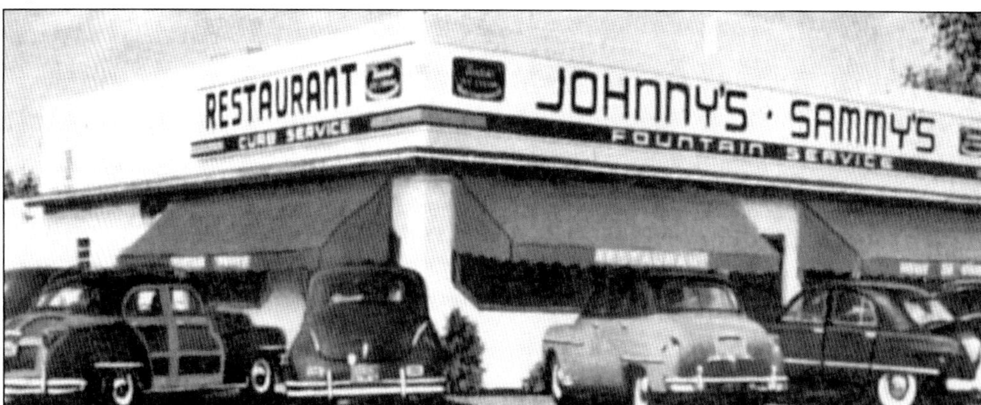

JOHNNY'S AND SAMMY'S. This restaurant was established in 1946 by Johnny Testa and Sammy Cerniglia as the premier dining spot in Salisbury. Situated on Route 13, it boasted the fashionable Alpine Room and featured live music. By 1960, it was at the peak of its popularity and even hosted then-Sen. John F. Kennedy as he drove through the city on his campaign for the White House. With the rise of fast food and trendy chain restaurants, the restaurant slowly declined and was out of business well before the end of the century. Today a WaWa convenience store stands on its site. (Courtesy of the John E. Jacob Collection.)

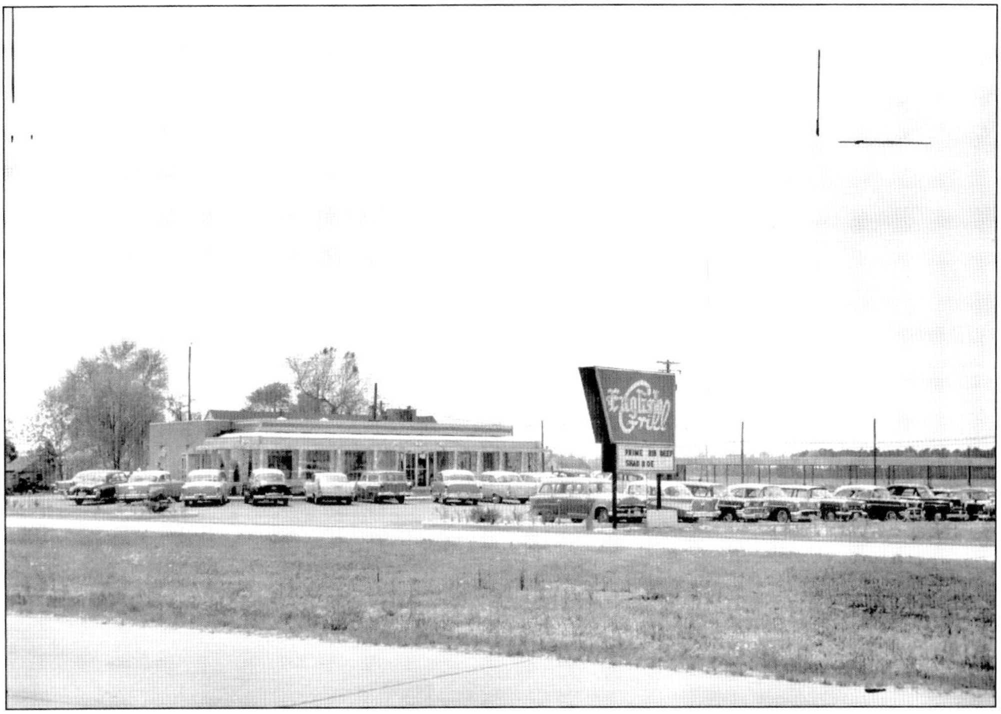

ENGLISH GRILL. In 1933, James English opened the first of many English Grills in Salisbury; originally it was a silver diner that looked like a railroad car, but in later days, the restaurants are distinctive brick buildings with diner-car window fronts. He parlayed his delightful fried chicken recipe's success into a chain of restaurants that spread in all directions before finally shrinking back to two Salisbury locations and finally closing its doors. A Walgreen's drugstore occupies the original spot. (Courtesy of Salisbury Chamber of Commerce.)

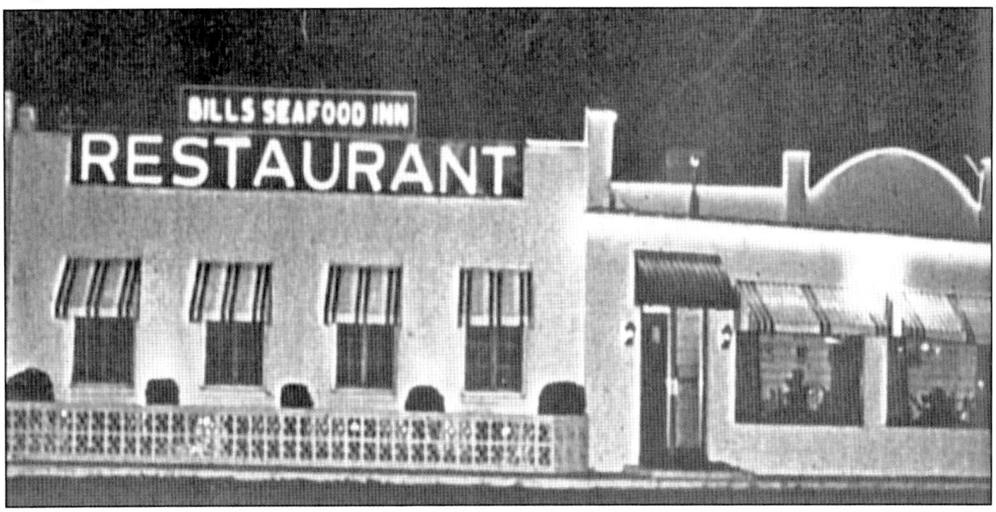

SAY "AAAAAHTES." Bill Ahtes's family, who owned Bill's Seafood Restaurant, was known for being in the restaurant business; their restaurant was widely populated by locals and then by travelers once they discovered the spot to go for good food and camaraderie. Bill Ahtes went on to own real estate and other businesses. One of his favorites was the high-end art gallery he founded named Objet D'art. (Courtesy of the John E. Jacob Collection.)

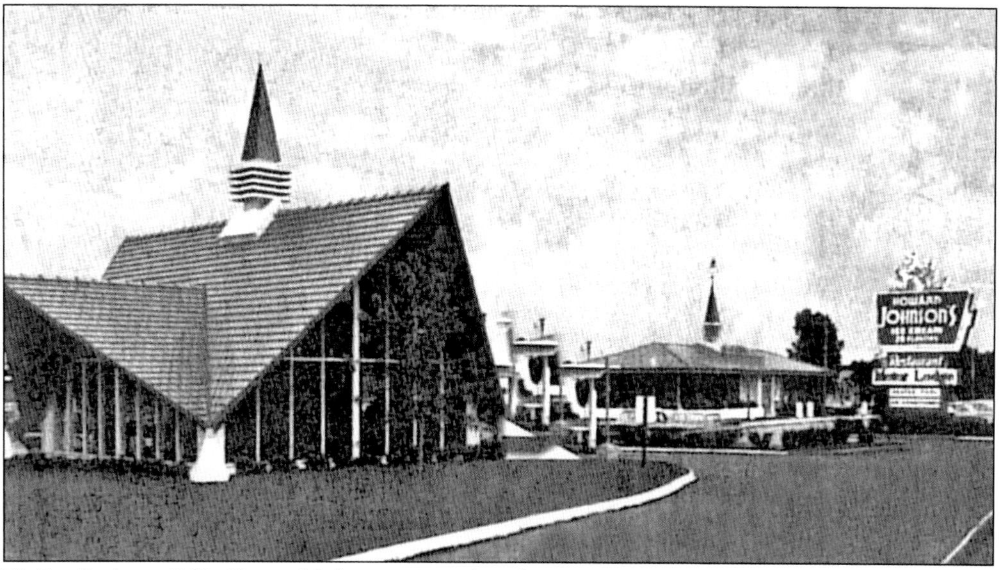

HoJo. Built in 1958, Howard Johnsons Motel and Restaurant was affectionately dubbed HoJos and was owned by a state senator, but it has come and gone. Local historian George Chevallier worked on its concrete awning, and his grandfather worked on the roof. The location on Route 13 North was on prime property, which through time has become even more expensive. Zias Restaurant, owned by the Bubbas brothers, sits in its location, and many businesses have sprung up around it. (Courtesy of Salisbury Chamber of Commerce.)

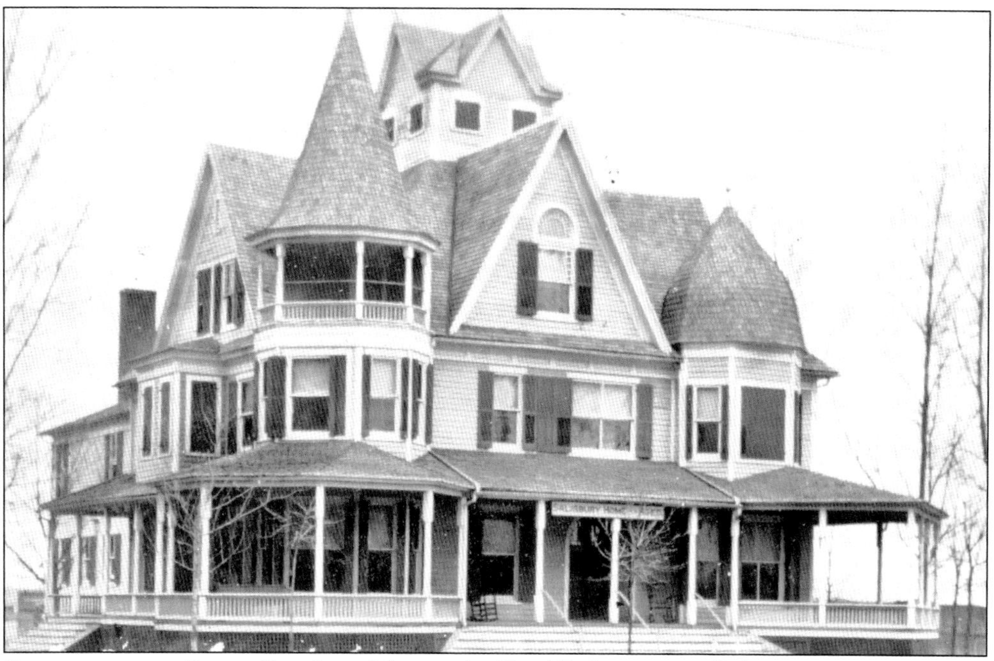

Old-time style. Originally a doctor's house, the Hotel Esther eventually became a rooming house and had a succession of owners and businesses. Situated on troubled Church Street, it is but a shadow of its more elegant days depicted in this old postcard. (Courtesy of George Chevallier.)

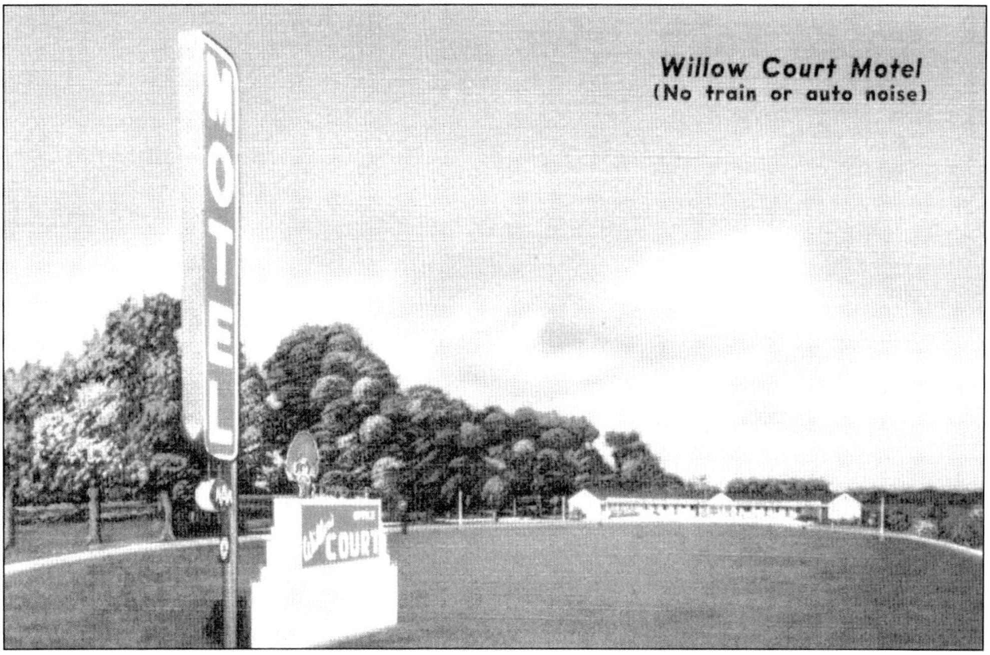

CALM AMONG THE WILLOWS. Willow Court Motel, built in 1946 by Ellsworth Sherman, was outside the main part of town, offered a quiet location, and boasted "No train or auto noise" in this postcard. (Courtesy of George Chevalier.)

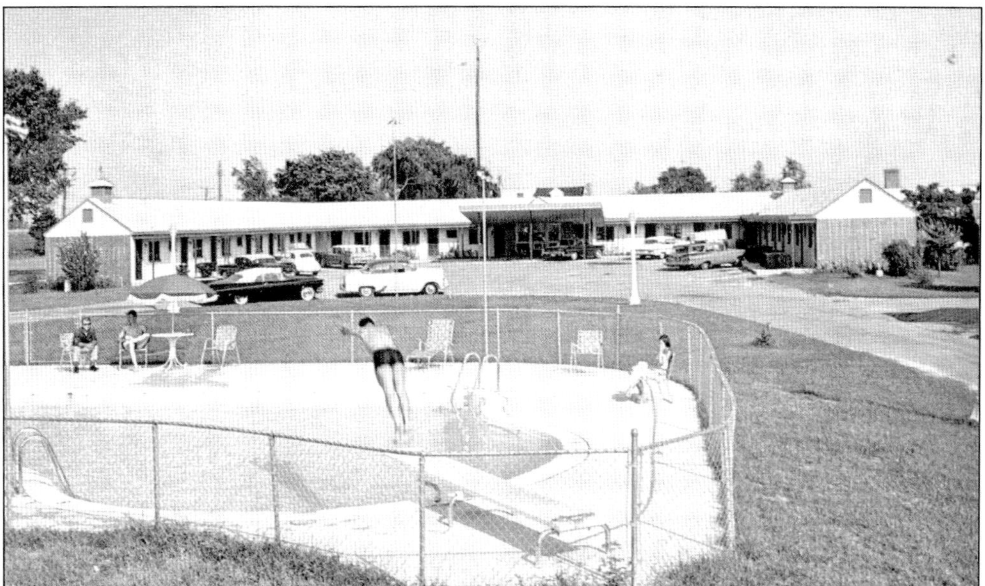

LORD SALISBURY. Sherman doubled the Willow Court's size and changed the name, but he sold it around 1973. It was still run as a hotel until about 2005, when it was razed and replaced with the Lord Salisbury Shopping center, holding Old Navy, Marshall's, Bed Bath and Beyond, and an additional plaza with Cold Stone Creamery, restaurants, and a health store. Here it is shown in its heyday around 1960. When it was torn down, graves of members of the Handy family, who helped found Salisbury, were uncovered. (Courtesy of George Chevallier.)

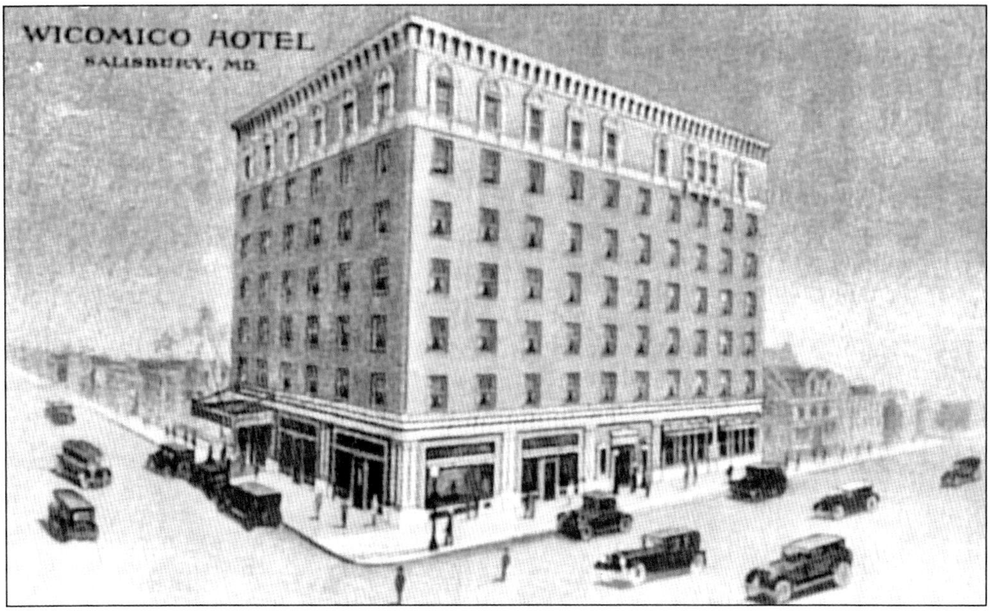

WICOMICO HOTEL. This was key and admired lodging prior to the late 1920s, when the main street was bypassed. Today much of it has been updated and is used as an office building. The postcard advertises that it's the "Eastern Shore's Finest and most modern hotel" and that it's "absolutely fireproof" and offers the European Plan—a type of meal service very popular for its period. (Courtesy of the Palmer Gillis collection.)

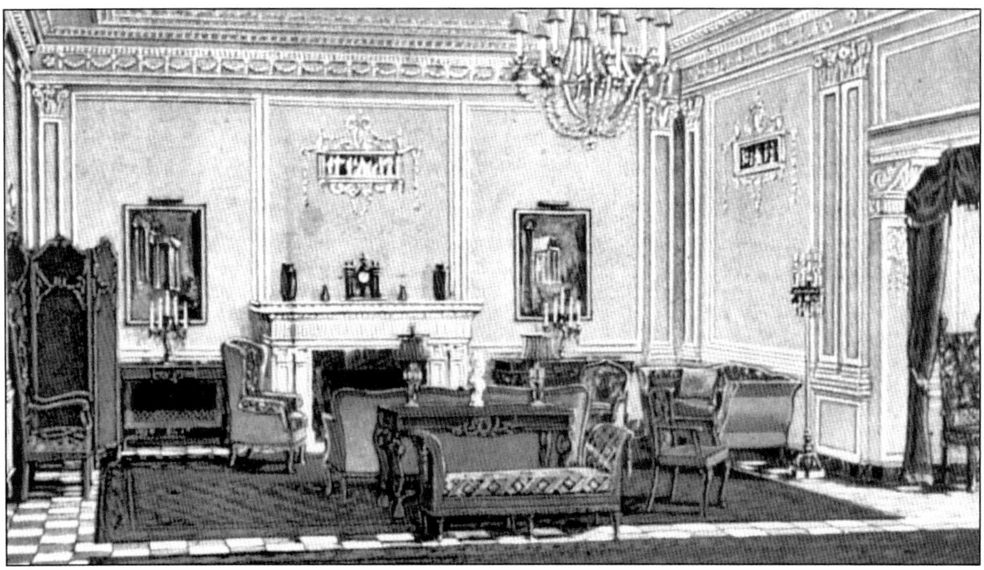

SWANKY LOBBY. The ritzy era is widely reflected in the fanciness of the Wicomico Hotel along with its solid construction of plaster and quality materials. This is the hotel where people went to be seen and socialize as well as to make use of the lodging. This old building is an office complex today. Talk abounds that part of it might be converted into condos. (Courtesy of the John E. Jacob Collection.)

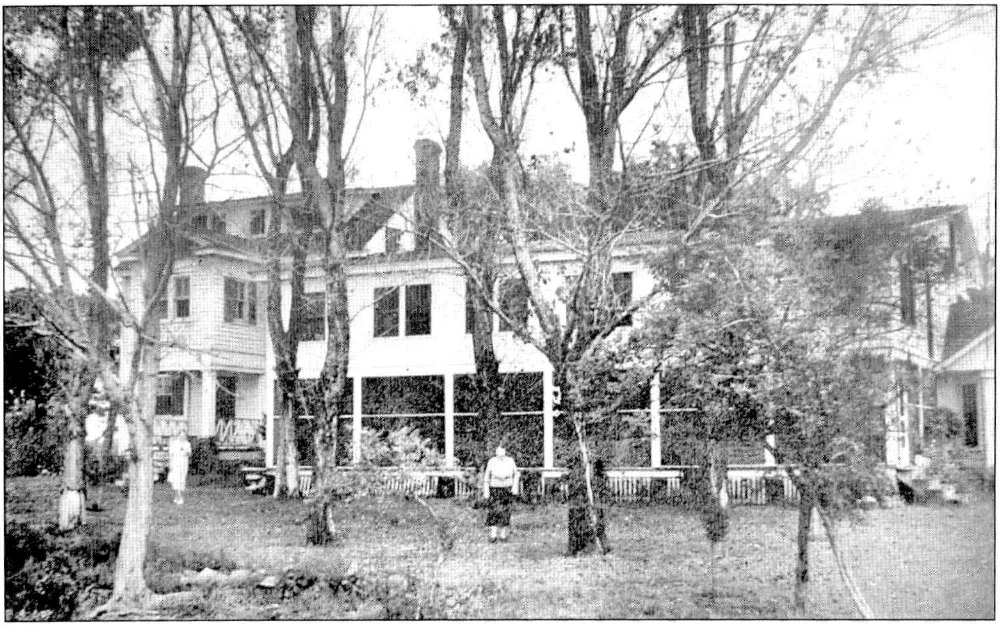

WATERVIEW. This picture, taken early in the last century, shows the venerable Waterview Hotel, once a popular resort along the Nanticoke River. Bill Evans opened this hotel around 1918, added on in 1929, and foreclosed in 1933 during the Depression. He even had the rocks in front of the inn hauled in. A graveyard is near the hotel with a 1792 tombstone. With the passing of the steamboat era, small resorts dried up in favor of larger summer meccas like Ocean City in nearby Worcester County. However, the hotel again gained some notoriety in 1967, when the building was leased to a number of Soviet embassy employees and their families for the summer. (Courtesy of Brice Stump.)

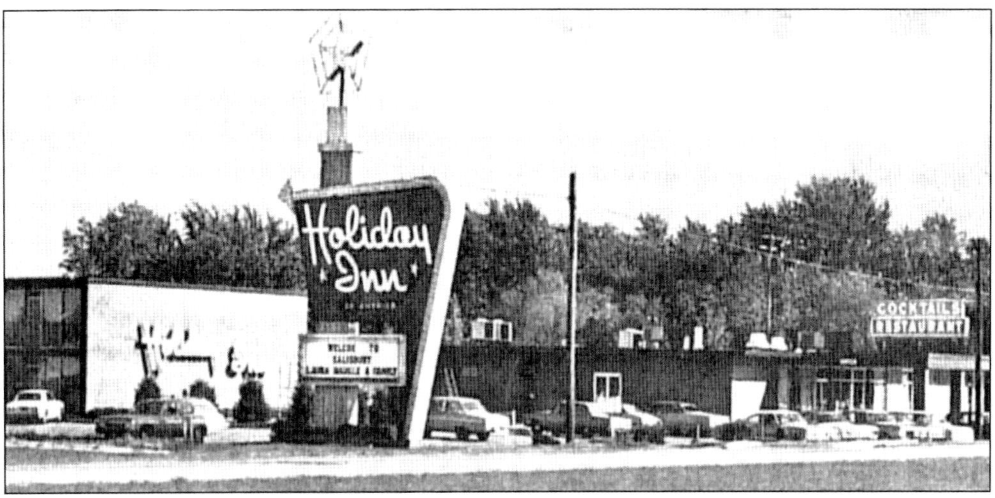

HOLIDAY ALL YEAR LONG. Holiday Inn was constructed in 1964 on Route 13. It moved to the other side of the street and was sold again to another hotel company. A new Holiday Inn Express was to be built less than a mile from its former site, but construction has not been underway, probably because of the flood of hotels desiring to meet the growing population. (Courtesy of the John E. Jacob Collection.)

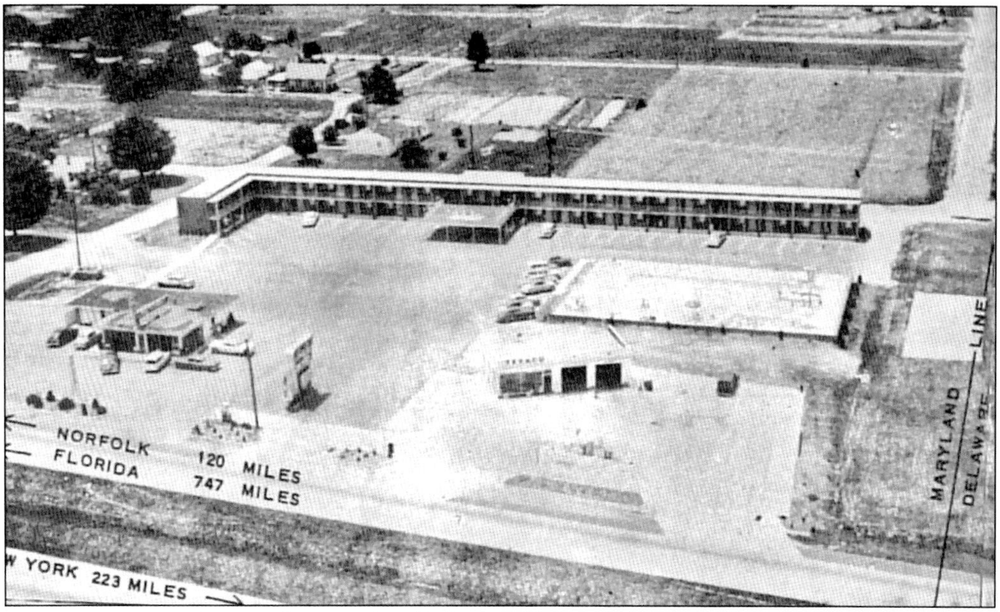

SLEEPING ON THE LINE. This motel in Delmar, which no longer exists except for a remnant of rooms, started out as a restaurant, but hard times foreclosed it, at which time the Wainwright family bought it. On that site, a gas station was erected that expanded into a motel in 1959. Five years later, Ed Wainwright built another addition to the hotel followed by a convention center in 1970. The motel has since been razed. (Courtesy of the John E. Jacob Collection.)

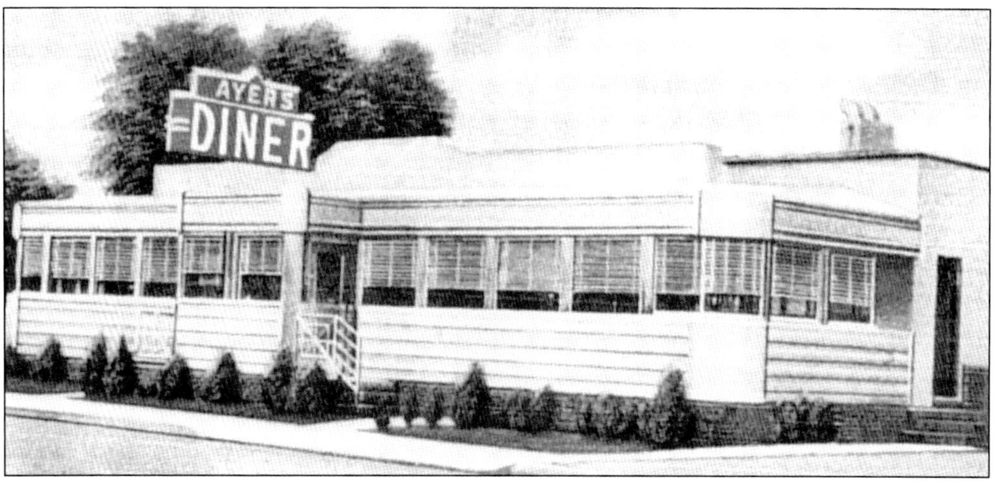

DINNER BELL. Having opened in 1952, Ayers Diner billed itself as "Shore's Finest." It was questionable if the business would succeed because the owners had no experience in the food service industry, but succeed it did. It was located on Route 13 North (then referred to as Ocean Highway) at a time when that area had virtually nothing there. Now it's almost shoulder-to-shoulder businesses. (Courtesy of the late Thomas Irvin collection.)

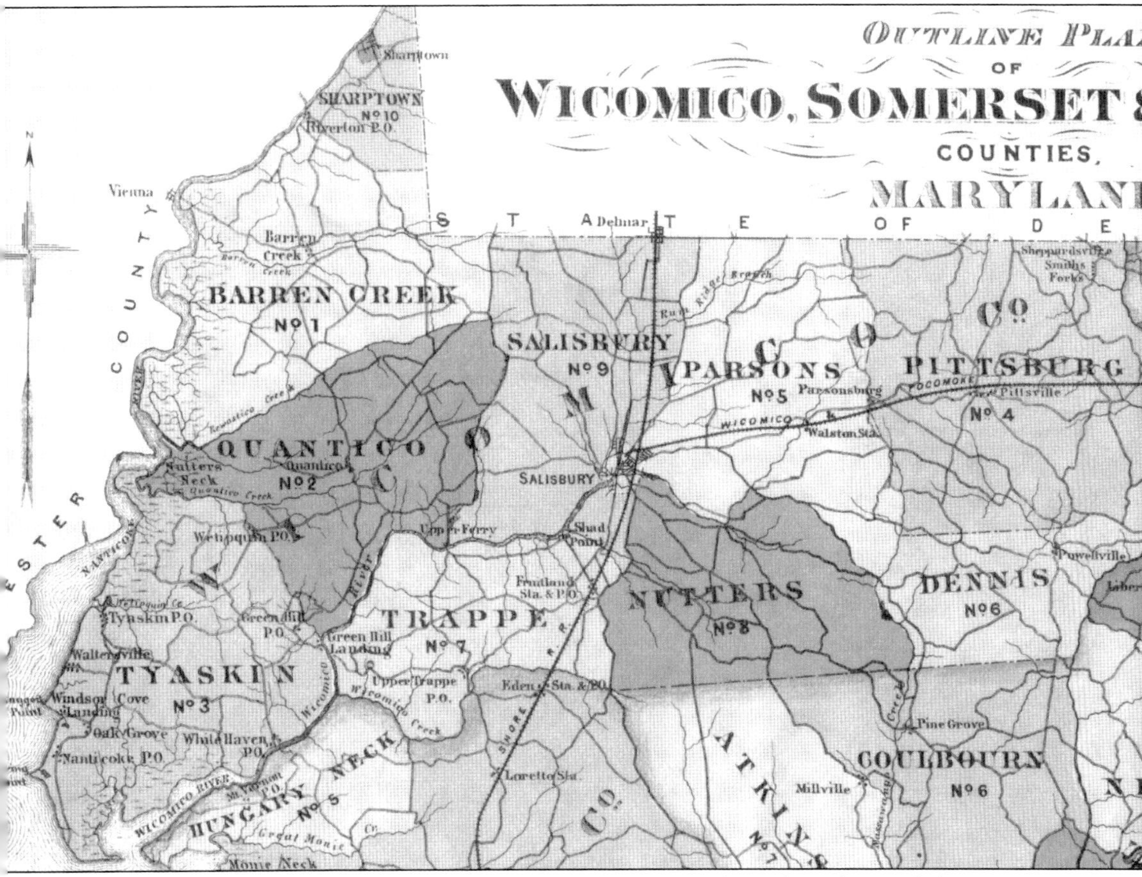

THAT WAS THEN. This facsimile of an 1877 map of the Eastern Shore shows how Salisbury was an important nexus for travel and trade. Only a county for 10 years, Wicomico quickly overshadowed the two counties (Somerset and Worcester) that it was carved from. Its population grew by leaps and bounds; the county remains the centerpiece of growth and commerce on Maryland's Eastern Shore. (Reproduction courtesy of the Wicomico County Historical Society.)

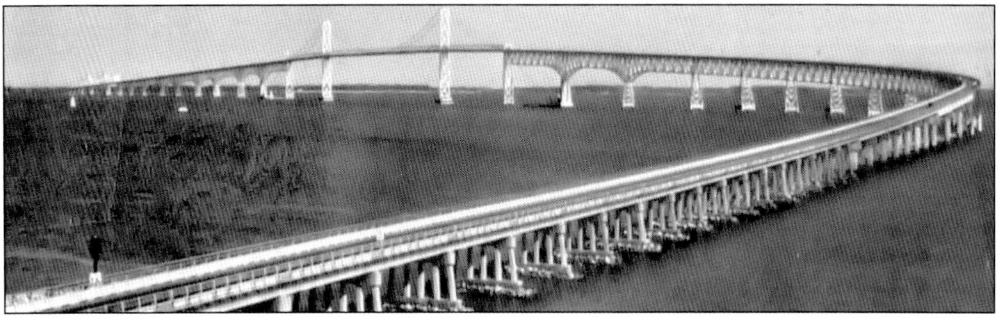

Chesapeake Bay Bridge. The unofficially named Chesapeake Bay Bridge joins Maryland's western shore to Delmarva Peninsula. The 4.3-mile long span is a modern engineering wonder. The original two lanes opened in 1952, replacing two ferries, while its three-lane parallel structure opened in 1973. It is 186 feet high. Nearly 30 million vehicles cross it annually. In May, it is opened (since 1975) for the Bridge Walk, where about 60,000 people traverse it. (Courtesy of the Maryland Department of Transportation.)

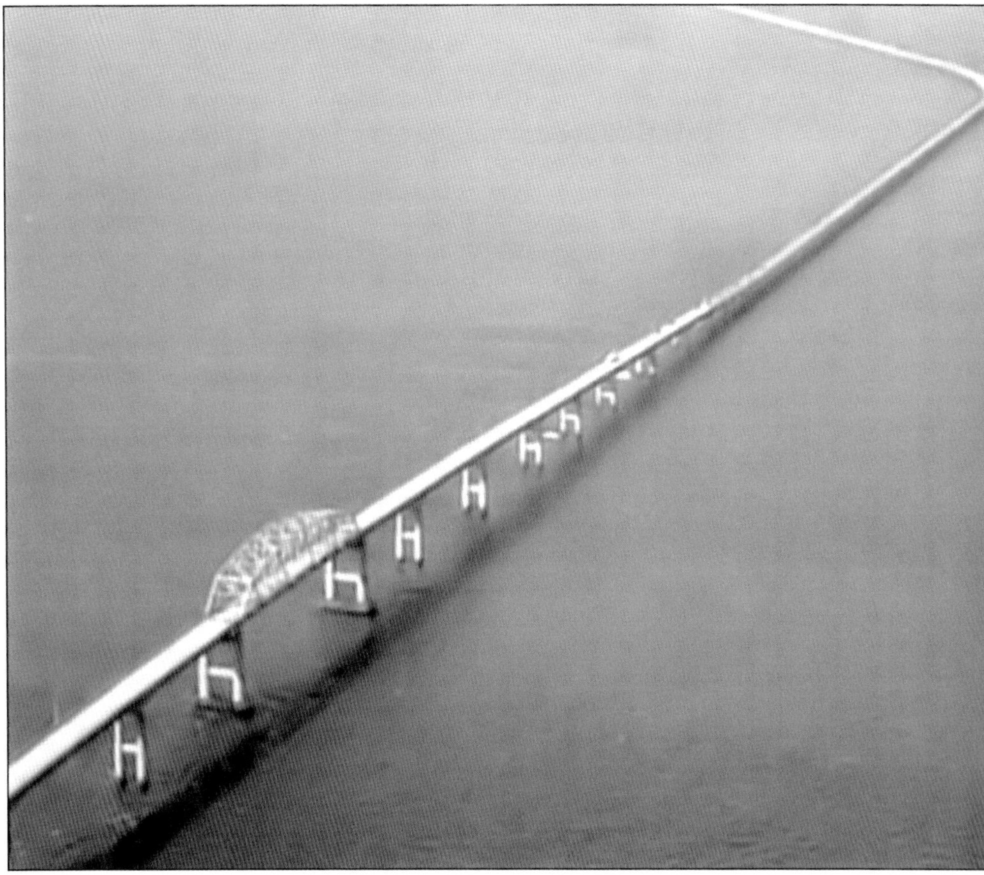

Virginia Bay Bridge. Officially named the Lucius J. Kellam Jr. Bridge-Tunnel, the commonly called Chesapeake Bay Bridge-Tunnel is a four-lane, 20-mile-long span, with two 1-mile tunnels connecting the Eastern Shore to Norfolk. It sports manmade islands about 5 acres in size. The northbound side opened in 1964; the southbound side opened in 1999, with each costing about $230 million. It's considered to be one of the modern wonders of the world. (Courtesy of Chesapeake Bay Bridge-Tunnel Authority.)

BIBLIOGRAPHY

100th Anniversary Committee. *Our Anniversary: Salisbury Fire Department 1872–1972*. Salisbury, MD: no publisher, no date.

A Heritage of Caring. Peninsula Regional Medical Center 1897–1997. Salisbury, MD: Community Relations Department's Records from the Archives of the Peninsula Regional Medical Center, 1997.

Chesapeake Bay Bridge. Pamphlet by Maryland Transportation Authority, no date.

Chesapeake Bay Bridge-Tunnel. Pamphlet by Chesapeake Bay Bridge-Tunnel Authority, Cape Charles, VA, no date.

Corddry, George H. *Wicomico County History*. Salisbury, MD: Wicomico Historical Society, 1981.

Delmarva Eastern Shore Association Executive Offices. *Reprints of Unsolicited Articles Published in the* Pennsylvania Farmer *(May 15, 1926) and* Economic Geography *(April 1926) Concerning the Del-Mar-Va Eastern Shore, the Peninsula of Plenty*. Salisbury, MD: Del-Mar-Va Eastern Shore Association, 1926.

Historic Sites Inventory, Vol. 2. Annapolis, MD: Maryland Historical Trust, 1976.

Jefferson School of Business. *The Independent*. Salisbury, MD: Jefferson School of Business, 1964.

Nabb Research Center at Salisbury University and Preservation Online and the John E. Jacob Photo and Postcard Collection.

Nunez, Andy. *Treasures of the Eastern Shore*. Cambridge, MD: Cambridge Books, 2005.

Official Program, Opening Del-Mar-Va Eastern Shore Airport; Hebron Airport. Labor Day, September 3rd, 1928. Hebron, MD: American Eagle, American Distributors, Starlighters, Inc., 1928.

The personal archives of Susan Purnell.

The personal collection of Palmer Gillis.

Salisbury Chamber of Commerce Archives.

Salisbury Chamber of Commerce. *A Survey of Salisbury, Maryland*. Salisbury, MD: Salisbury Chamber of Commerce, Mayor and Council of Salisbury and County Commisssioners of Wicomico County, 1952.

———. *Salisbury Maryland, the Central City of the Eastern Shore*. Salisbury, MD: Salisbury Chamber of Commerce, no date.

Symington Wayne Corporation. *Salisbury: Heart of the Maryland's Eastern Shore*. Salisbury, MD: Divisions of Dresser Industries, Inc., no date.

Truitt, Charles J. *Historic Salisbury Maryland*. Garden City, NJ: Country Life Press, 1932.

Wicomico Bicentennial Commission. *The 1877 Atlases and Other Early Maps of the Eastern Shore of Maryland*. Salisbury, MD: Wicomico Bicentennial Commission, Salisbury, 1976.

Wicomico Senior High School. *The Tom Tom*. Salisbury, MD: Wicomico Senior High School, 1969.

www.rootsweb.com/~mdwicomi/photos.htm